BASEBALL

Acknowledgements

Chronicling baseball history can be a daunting task. When you consider there have been millions of pitches, thousands of games and, now, a hundred seasons in its modern era, it's difficult to capture all the highlights.

But when you have passion for the game, baseball history is a privilege to chronicle. Since 1886, it has been The Sporting News' privilege, week-in and week-out, during peace time and war, during depressions and recessions.

It also has been our privilege to have an accomplished student of the game, TSN senior editor Joe Hoppel, editing and compiling this book. Joe's passion for the game is fervent, his knowledge deep. Combine that with his care and attention to detail; there is no one else we would trust to tell the story of The Sporting News and baseball.

Ron Smith, another senior editor at The Sporting News, provided invaluable assistance with his vision for this book, the essays he wrote to introduce each chapter and his photo editing. Associate editor Dave Sloan was there to proofread and catch any mistakes that might have slipped through.

The design of this book was a team effort, necessitated by the thousands of TSN volumes that had to be scanned and processed. Led by TSN Prepress Director Bob Parajon and Creative Director Bill Wilson, that team included Michael Behrens, Chris Callan, Russ Carr, Matt Kindt, Jack Kruyne, Chad Painter and Christen Sager. Let's not wait another 100 years to do it again!

Our thanks go, also, to a talented team of people who make bad images good and good images great. Led by Steve Romer, that team included Chris Barnes-Amaro, Dave Brickey and Vern Kasal.

In our daily jobs, Steve Gietschier and Jim Meier, who preside over The Sporting News Archives, also known as our Research Center, provide invaluable insight and assistance. Thank you not only for your work in digging back through the century, but for what you do for us every day.

A final thanks must go out to everyone who works at The Sporting News and all those who have ever worked here. They were the ones who have made TSN's place in history—who wrote, edited and photographed baseball history each and every week. It's our privilege to continue that work today.

ISBN: 0-89204-649-X

FROM THE ARCHIVES OF

The Sporting News

BASEBALL

100 Years of The Modern Era: 1901-2000

Edited by
Joe Hoppel

Contents

Introduction

I can't say for sure the first time a manager was second-guessed in print or a player ripped for demanding too much money. But my hunch is that it was done in The Sporting News. The weekly publication, created in 1886 by a love of sports and the theater, stands alone as baseball's historian. Regardless of who might lay claim to the "official" history of the game, let there be no doubt that The Sporting News writes the complete history of the sport.

From the time Al and Charles Spink brought The Sporting News to life, baseball was a special part of its content. Likewise, TSN played a special part in the development of the game. Long before cable television, commercial TV or even radio brought games into homes across the country, The Sporting News was there. Before the American League was founded and a World Series contemplated, The Sporting News was there.

For 48 years, Taylor Spink was the reigning personality that drove The Sporting News, and many people swore he drove baseball nearly as relentlessly as his own business. Yes, Judge Kenesaw Mountain Landis was the first commissioner of baseball, but if you wanted to measure the feelings of the people who ran the game, you needed only to read the pages of The Sporting News.

So, for the first time, we offer you a unique view of the history of the sport we love—through the eyes and pages of

Ty Cobb had a distinctive batting style—and his letters were unusual, too, with their green-ink trademark. Cobb and TSN publisher J.G. Taylor Spink corresponded over a long period.

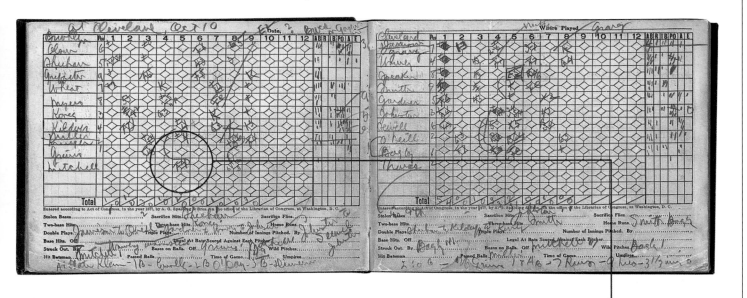

The Sporting News itself. We are reminded daily, in our building, of our role in the game's history, in big ways and small. We can linger over the page in the official scorebook that documents the only unassisted triple play in World Series history. We can imagine the conversations as they unfolded between Taylor Spink and Ty Cobb after reading some of the correspondence they exchanged, with Cobb's notes written in his trademark green ink. We see the wonderful picture of Cal Ripken, who was TSN's Sportsman of the Year in 1995, and our emotions are still close to the surface when we view the pictures of his triumphant lap around the field at Camden Yards on the night he broke Lou Gehrig's consecutive-games record.

From the birth of the American League—which does not happen without Charles Spink's fervor—through the heroics of Mark McGwire's remarkable assault on the most prestigious of all sports records, the stories are here. Some will startle you—rumors of a Stan Musial-to-the-Yankees trade, for example—some will chill you and some simply will make you smile.

Baseball is truly the game of the people, and TSN is its chronicler.

JOHN D. RAWLINGS
Senior Vice President, Editorial Director

J.G. Taylor Spink's scorekeeping for Game 5 of the 1920 World Series is on display at The Sporting News' headquarters. That's the game in which Brooklyn pitcher Clarence Mitchell hit a fifth-inning line drive that Cleveland second baseman Bill Wambsganss turned into an unassisted triple play.

About the TSN Archives

The landscape of baseball is hallowed by its special places. Travel the length and breadth of North America and you will find them, the stuff of history and myth, fact and legend, the twine that binds past to present and present to future. Visit them and listen to the generations whisper of their love for the game. Ebbets Field. Camden Yards. The House That Ruth Built. Wrigley. Pac Bell. Rosenblatt. Durham. Vero Beach. Ho-Ho-Kam. Williamsport. Dyersville. Wahoo. Factoryville. Brandon Mills. Lonaconing. Van Meter. Donora. Cairo. Alvin. Cooperstown.

But do not, in your haste, bypass St. Louis. For the Mound City, the Gateway to the West, has its own baseball story to tell. Host to Cardinals, Stars, Terriers, Maroons and several varieties of Browns, birthplace of Yogi, stomping grounds of Rajah, Dizzy, Ducky, the Man, Ozzie and Big Mac and final resting place for Cool Papa, St. Louis has, since 1886, been home to The Sporting News.

This book celebrates our coverage of baseball over the past 100 years, but it should be noted that when Byron Bancroft Johnson opened the 20th century by playing midwife to the American League, the journalistic enterprise started by his friends, Al and Charles Spink, was already more than a decade old. The Sporting News had missed the start of the National League by a mere 10 years, but Charles Spink enthusiastically gave editorial aid and comfort to its upstart competitor. Moreover, when Johnson and the senior circuit made peace in 1903, Spink's editor, Alonzo Joseph Flanner, helped write the treaty and his typographers set its type. A few years later, Charles' son, Taylor, badgered his father's friend to be named the American League's official scorer for the World Series. The boon

J.G. Taylor Spink (above, and left, with Ban Johnson) might not recognize today's "Research Center" at The Sporting News. Yet the longtime TSN publisher oversaw the compilation of much of the archival material still on hand at the St. Louis office.

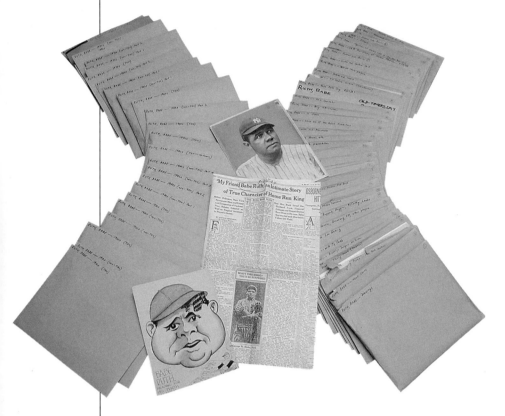

**The Sporting News'
clipping files
(above) are
crammed with
stories out of TSN
itself, daily
newspapers,
magazines and
various other
publications. There
are 25 envelopes on
Babe Ruth alone.
The clips are
invaluable as a
reference source.**

was granted, and when Taylor and his wife had
their only son, they named him Charles Claude
Johnson Spink to honor both grandfather and
family friend.

Sometime after, an unknown-but-enterprising
employee must have decided that The Sporting
News was itself a part of baseball history and
that its past needed to be preserved. He—or
perhaps she—started clipping and filing stories
from each weekly issue. Someone else perhaps
commenced a daunting project to record on index
cards the contract history of everyone who
signed to play professional baseball. When
precisely these things happened we do not
know, but clearly they mark the beginning of The
Sporting News Archives. And now, in our 116th

year, the odyssey continues. And the ties still bind.

Over the years, thousands of baseball fans, finding themselves in St. Louis, took
advantage of a standing invitation to tour our offices. At one time, there was much to see:
secretaries huddled over typewriters, bookkeepers fingering adding machines, writers
digging for the latest dope, editors fussing over copy, typesetters preparing pages, presses
churning out next week's issue and maybe a glimpse of Taylor Spink himself, publisher for
48 years. Even the wallpaper honored the past, reproducing pages from Volume 1, Number
1. Now, thanks to the microchip, we are reduced to a casually clad work force sitting in

**Questionnaires first went out to gather
data for a new TSN publication, the
Baseball Register, which made its
debut in 1940. Hobbies, nicknames
(and their derivation) and outstanding
baseball feats were among the facts
gleaned from players' responses.**

The Sporting News

Baseball Questionnaire

Date *Dec 18, 1947*

Name *Jack* (First) *Roosevelt* (Middle) *Robinson* (Last)

Born in *Cairo, Ga.* City, Town or Township State *Ga*

on *Jan 31 1919* Month, Day, Year Present Height *6 ft* Weight *195*

Playing Position *1st base* Bat—R or L *R* Throw—R or L *R*

Date of Marriage and to Whom *Feb 10 1946 Rachel Isum*

Children (Name and Ages) *Jack R. Robinson Jr.*

Player's Nickname *Jackie* How did you acquire the nickname *from football*

Nationality *American Negro* Color of Eyes *Brown* Color of Hair *Black*

Hobby or Hobbies *Golf* Name Pronounced

If a graduate of preparatory school, junior college or college, list name of institution, the years attended or when graduated and degree received *Muir Tech High School*

Address during off-season *1283 W. 35th St* Street *Los Angeles* City *Calif* State

Position during winter months *—*

Baseball Experience (List Clubs and Years)

Kansas City Monarchs 1945
Montreal Royals 1946
Brooklyn Dodgers 1947

If in U. S. Service—Date Joined *April 1942* Date Discharged *Nov 1944 Inactive status*

Present Rank *2nd Lt* Branch of Service *Cavalry*

Organization and Station *attached Fort Riley Kansas*

What do you consider your outstanding performance in baseball *—*

—

The undersigned grants to the publishers of THE SPORTING NEWS the right to consent to the use of his autograph and above information for publicity purposes as may in its judgment seem desirable, with stipulation that same may in no instance be used as an endorsement for any product, nor carry any advertising matter.

TSN prizes its collection of Charles Conlon photos, some of which were made into cards (below). Conlon's portraits were posed shots that conveyed a natural look. TSN has 8,000 negatives of the photographer's work— 5,000 of them glass negatives. Conlon took baseball photos from 1904 to 1942.

pods and staring at screens. Not much for tourists to see except for the Archives, where the magic yet abides.

Come to The Sporting News today and you will note that the Archives is now called the Research Center. But much that was, still is. The clipping file occupies more than 180 drawers each three feet deep, and the player contract cards, if packed one behind the other, would stretch from home plate to short center field. Add to this a fantastic sports library of over 8,000 volumes and our photo collection containing more than 600,000 images, and we are still a joy to see.

The modern world of sports information demands established technologies like microfilm, photocopying and faxing plus fancier ones like movable shelving, temperature and humidity controls, online searching and digitized photographs. But at the heart of the Research Center is the same stuff of sports history that has helped us produce The Sporting News so successfully for so long.

Visitors come to our offices for a multitude of purposes. Some are vendors trying to

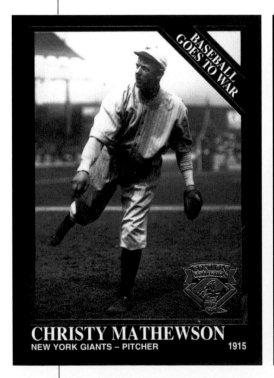

CHRISTY MATHEWSON
NEW YORK GIANTS – PITCHER   1915

BAN JOHNSON
AMERICAN LEAGUE – PRESIDENT   1914

BABE RUTH
NEW YORK YANKEES – OUTFIELD   1927

establish a business relationship with our company. Others are students, teachers, artists, researchers, writers, filmmakers and collectors. Each comes in eager expectation, and most leave more than fulfilled. Some, too, are just fans, hoping to see one of the special places in the baseball landscape. For them, a personal visit can be quite emotional.

Readers of this book can now visit our home without leaving theirs. Our editors have done an extraordinary amount of research, scrolling through reels of microfilm, sifting through mountains of clips and poring over thousands of images to tell the story of baseball over the past century as we told it at the time. Our designers have contributed mightily, too, making this book a pleasure to hold and a joy to read and ponder. Novelist William Faulkner once wrote, "The past is never dead. It's not even past." That's our belief, too. . . . .

STEVE GIETSCHIER
Senior Managing Editor/Research

The Sporting News' massive card file traces a player's contractual assignments from team to team during his pro career (even if the player never got out of the minors). The card for Kevin "Chuck" Connors— future star of TV's *The Rifleman*—shows Connors made stops with the Dodgers and Cubs.

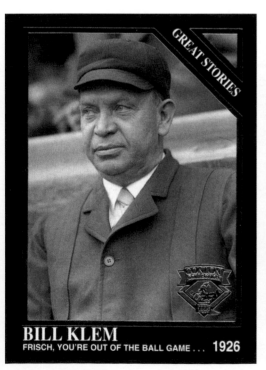

BILL KLEM
FRISCH, YOU'RE OUT OF THE BALL GAME . . . 1926

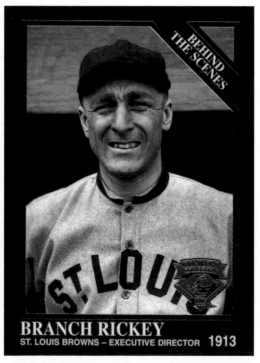

BRANCH RICKEY
ST. LOUIS BROWNS – EXECUTIVE DIRECTOR 1913

1901
THE EXPANDING

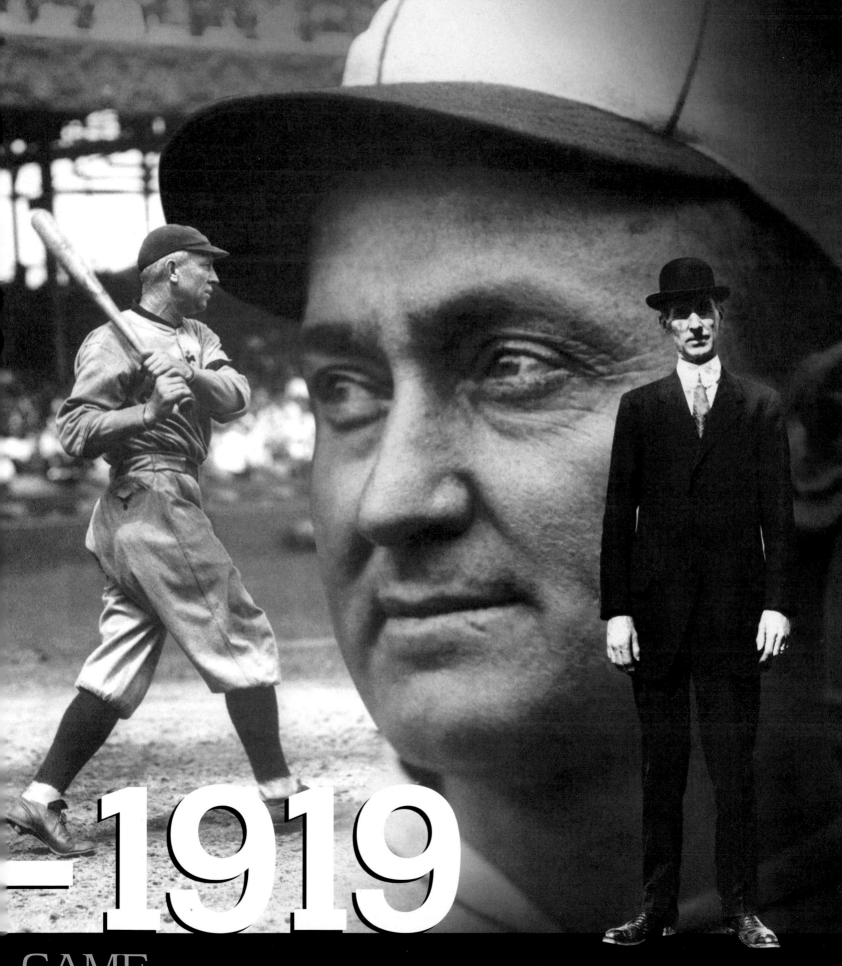

=1919

GAME

**L**ike airplanes, radios, movies, computers, antibiotics and the income tax, you weren't even around in 1900 when Americans stumbled into a new millennium, optimistic but unprepared for the industrial and technological revolution that would sweep them to such unlikely destinations as the North Pole, the ocean floor, the moon and cyberspace.

This was three years before the Wright brothers took a flyer at Kitty Hawk, less than two years after Theodore Roosevelt's legendary charge up San Juan Hill. There were 8,000 horseless carriages ("devil wagons" to most of the rural population) operating over 144 miles of paved roads in the 45 states, limited in most cities to a maximum speed of 10 mph. Only 14 percent of American homes had a bathtub, 8 percent had a telephone—and 95 percent of all babies were delivered at home. The average wage of 22 cents per hour was adequate, but far from affluent.

Columbus, Ind., was the geographic center of United States population in 1900 when Byron Bancroft Johnson, perhaps inspired by the daring and enterprising Roosevelt, plotted

Napoleon Lajoie

the final stage of his grandiose plan to introduce an expanded version of baseball to the 20th century. The former Cincinnati sportswriter, an eloquent baseball evangelist, wanted to broaden the game's horizons, make the emerging national pastime attractive to the growing urban masses and tie it closely to the social revolution sweeping the nation.

Physically daunting, sociable, complicated and sometimes abrasive, Johnson was the perfect man for such an ambitious undertaking. He was bursting with energy and ideas, obsessively dedicated to his convictions and a brilliant strategist—a mover and shaker with attitude. He had observed and learned from previous unsuccessful challenges to the "major league" monopoly of the National League, which had operated with minimal competition since 1876.

Johnson, who had directed the Western League since 1894, laid a new foundation for baseball in 1900 when he renamed his circuit the American League and lined up a deep-pocket ownership base that could meet the challenge of survival. Johnson claimed major league status in 1901—the same year Roosevelt became president of the United States after the assassination of William McKinley—and declared war on the N.L., which he waged with ruthless determination.

With franchises located in Chicago, Boston and Phil-

1901

President William McKinley is assassinated in Buffalo, N.Y.; Theodore Roosevelt assumes office.

The Victor Talking Machine Co. is formed. Its phonographs will be called Victrolas.

1902

The National Biscuit Co. begins selling animal crackers.

The first Cadillac is manufactured.

1903

Orville and Wilbur Wright make historic flights near Kitty Hawk, N.C.

1904

Helen Keller graduates with honors from Radcliffe.

The Teddy Bear makes its debut.

adelphia (all National League strongholds) as well as Detroit, Baltimore, Washington, Cleveland and Milwaukee, the American League opened play in 1901 with an all-star managerial lineup (Connie Mack, Clark Griffith, Jimmy Collins, Hugh Duffy, John McGraw, George Stallings) and such high-profile players as Cy Young, Napoleon Lajoie, Joe McGinnity and Wilbert Robinson, all N.L. refugees.

National League owners, restricted by the reserve clause in player contracts and a $2,400 yearly salary ceiling, did not take the challenge seriously at first. But alarm set in as Johnson methodically stole their marquee players, lured fans away in key markets and outwitted them at every turn. One of the N.L.'s brightest stars, Lajoie, jumped crosstown from the Philadelphia Phillies to Mack's Athletics and won a Triple Crown in the A.L.'s inaugural season. When the Pennsylvania Supreme Court upheld the legality of the reserve clause and ordered him to return to the Phillies in

1902, Johnson orchestrated a deal that transferred the player's contract to Cleveland. Out of the court's jurisdiction, Lajoie then had to bypass only games being played in Philadelphia. And one by one, the courts in other states upheld the legality of A.L. contracts.

Johnson needed only two seasons to bully his rivals into submission. More and more players jumped ship and the new league even won the 1902 attendance battle, forcing the

Grover Cleveland Alexander

Christy Mathewson

N.L. to press for peace. Johnson dominated the 1903 peace talks and dictated terms, resulting in two separate leagues under one governing umbrella—a three-man national commission featuring A.L. president Johnson, the acting N.L. president and Garry Herrmann, owner of the Cincinnati Reds. By sheer force of personality, Ban Johnson would rule baseball for the next two decades.

THE LORD OF DISCIPLINE

By 1903, Johnson's improved American League featured a team in New York (the former Baltimore Orioles) bucking heads with the N.L. Giants and Brooklyn Dodgers and a St. Louis team (the former Milwaukee Brewers) battling head-to-head with the Cardinals. The 1903 A.L. and N.L. team and city alignments would not change for the next half-century.

With stability guaranteed, Johnson turned his attention inward. Baseball had entered the century in a period of stagnation, the result of its growing reputation as a rowdy, pugilistic sport played by unsavory characters and watched by rough-around-the-edges fans who some-

Walter Johnson

1906

An earthquake and fire lay waste to San Francisco, kill more than 500 people.

1908

The Model-T Ford is produced. The price tag: $850.

1909

Admiral Robert E. Peary reaches the North Pole.

The NAACP is founded.

19

times behaved violently. Early- 1900s cities were expanding urban islands in a frontier society that had accepted and enjoyed that brand of baseball, but its uncivilized aura repulsed the gentility that might ordinarily have been attracted to the sport. That would have to change.

Johnson took immediate steps to ensure that it did. He started with the players, demanding that they play and comport them-

selves with decorum and dignity. Woe to transgressors, who were brought into compliance with stiff fines and suspensions. Johnson ordered owners to provide better ballpark security, and he brought respect to the umpiring profession. Arbiters no longer had to deal with the threat of violence from irate players or fans.

While retaining a rugged, take-no-prisoners style of play, baseball promoted its softer, fuzzier personality —and prospered. By the end of the decade, owners were working together for the common good and uniform rules were in place. The game's popularity was enhanced by an annual playoff in which the A.L. and N.L. pennant winners battled to become undisputed champions of the baseball world.

The A.L.'s Boston Red Sox shocked Pittsburgh in an eight-game 1903 World Series inaugural that played to rave reviews. No World Series was played in 1904 because Giants owner John T. Brush and manager McGraw, a former Johnson ally who defected to the National League, refused to pit their pennant winner against an "inferior American League team," but the fall classic resumed in 1905 and continued uninterrupted for the next nine decades.

IF YOU BUILD IT ...

While the game groped for an identity, it did not lack for gate attractions.

Such greats as McGraw, Young, Lajoie, McGinnity, Willie Keeler, Christy Mathewson, Mordecai "Three Finger" Brown, Honus Wagner, Jimmy Collins and Kid Nichols helped usher in the new decade. Coming attractions like Walter Johnson, Tris Speaker, Eddie Collins, Joe Jackson and Grover Alexander soon exploded into prominence. But no one epitomized the rough-and-tumble spirit of dead-ball-era baseball more than Detroit Tigers outfielder Ty Cobb, a snarling Georgia wildcat who cut a swath through the record books with his 12 A.L. batting titles and 4,191 career hits and a bloody path to immortality with his razor-sharp spikes.

Fueled by such star power and surrounded by a healthier, wealthier and more mobile society that was interested in expanding its entertainment horizons, baseball owners looked to establish more permanent ties to their communities. The result was an explosion

Mordecai "Three Finger" Brown

1910	1912	1913	1914
The Boy Scouts of America organization is formed.	The Titanic hits an iceberg in the North Atlantic. Death total exceeds 1,500.	The Federal Reserve System is authorized. *Billboard* magazine publishes its first chart showing song popularity.	The Panama Canal is opened. The first movie appearance of Charlie Chaplin's "The Little Tramp."

of large steel-and-concrete stadiums that would help fuel the popularity of the game while promoting a regional identity for the teams and their ever-increasing legions of fans.

Philadelphia's Shibe Park, the stately creation of Athletics owner Ben Shibe and manager Mack, opened the floodgates in 1909 and spelled the end of the wooden, single-decked fire hazards that had served as ballparks since the beginning of baseball time. Pittsburgh's Forbes Field opened 2½ months later, and seven more large, attractive and functional new

facilities were unveiled by 1916. Fans poured through the turnstiles and cash flowed into the pockets of suddenly prosperous owners.

But prosperity did not come without obstacles. In 1914, baseball peace was shattered by the arrival of another "major league." The eight-team Federal League conducted player raids, competed in big cities for the sports dollar and generally raised the price of doing business. But the A.L. and N.L. survived the challenge intact, and the Feds ended their war after two seasons— a signal of just how deep baseball's roots had grown.

But not even deep roots could ensure survival when a different kind of war cast a dark shroud over the nation in 1918. More than half of the players listed on major league rosters heeded a call to duty in World War I, and cost-cutting measures were taken to keep the game afloat. Baseball, battling against the man-

Ty Cobb and Kenesaw Mountain Landis (above); Babe Ruth as a pitcher in 1918.

power drain, reduced its 1918 schedule drastically, completing its World Series in early September. Many stars were missing from their teams' lineups during this difficult season, and several prominent players lost their lives fighting overseas.

This was a period of innocence and discovery, of transition and survival. The dead-ball era showcased the marvelous talents of Cobb and Wagner, the team success of the Red Sox (five World Series winners) and Athletics (three Series champions). Not lost in the shuffle were the incredible 1908 and 1914 pennant races—the first decided by a special season-ending makeup game dictated by an untimely, misguided play by Giants first baseman Fred Merkle, and the other featuring the amazing late-season charge of Boston's Miracle Braves.

But the century's second decade would close on a more ominous note. With rumors circulating about a 1919 World Series fix and the stench of scandal hovering menacingly over the baseball world, the game's survival instincts were put to another, more insidious test.

Little did anybody know that a savior was already on the scene. Ready to usher in the first "Golden Age of Sports" was an offensive powderkeg cleverly disguised as a stocky, lefthanded pitcher.

1915
The first transcontinental telephone call—from New York to San Francisco—is made.

The excursion steamer Eastland capsizes in the Chicago River; 812 die.

1916

Montanan Jeannette Rankin is the first female ever elected to the U.S. House.

1917
The United States is thrust into World War I.

1918
An influenza epidemic kills millions worldwide; U.S. death toll surpasses 500,000.

Daylight Savings Time is introduced.

1919
Prohibition amendment is ratified.

The American Legion organization is founded.

21

The birth of the American League

Former sportswriter Ban Johnson, believing baseball had the capacity for enormous growth, renamed his minor league entity the American League in 1900, conferred major league status upon it in 1901 and waged war on the National League. With three of his teams (Boston, Chicago, Philadelphia) located in N.L. strongholds, Johnson was fearless—thanks, in part, to a well-heeled ownership base that built solid franchises and lured N.L. stars.

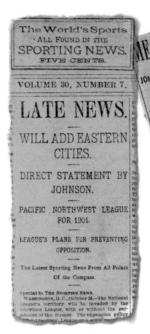

AMERICAN LEAGUE.

NEW NAME ADOPTED BY THE WESTERN MAGNATES.

National League Will Be Asked to Double Drafting Price and Allow Two Years Service.

CHICAGO, Ill., October 11.—SPECIAL CORRESPONDENCE:—The Western Base Ball League is now of the past and in its place is the American Base Ball League, organized at the annual meeting of the Western Base Ball League, held today at the Great Northern Hotel. The change of the name of the league occasioned much discussion, but was finally settled by a unanimous vote in the affirmative. The meeting of the league was long, and when the magnates adjourned they had not completed all they had laid out in their programme, and will convene again tomorrow at 10 a. m., to complete their work.

President Ban Johnson called a meeting of the Board of Directors of the League this morning, which awarded the pennant in the Western League, which went to Indianapolis. The other clubs finished in the following order: Minneapolis, Detroit, Grand Rapids, St. Paul, Milwaukee, and Kansas City and Buffalo tied for seventh and eighth places.

MAGNATES IN ATTENDANCE.

The board also heard the report of the treasurer, Ban Johnson, and adopted it. The following representatives of the Western League clubs were at the meeting:

President Ban Johnson, Chicago; C. A. Comiskey, St. Paul; M. R. Killilea, Milwaukee; James Franklin, Buffalo; J. H. Manning, Kansas City; C. H. Salspaugh, Minneapolis; F. C. Cross and Connie Mack, Milwaukee; W. F. C. Golt, Indianapolis; G. A. Van Derbeck, Detroit, and Robert Allen, Indianapolis.

The World's Sports
'ALL FOUND IN THE
SPORTING NEWS.
FIVE CENTS.

VOLUME 30, NUMBER 7.

LATE NEWS.

WILL ADD EASTERN CITIES.

DIRECT STATEMENT BY JOHNSON.

PACIFIC NORTHWEST LEAGUE FOR 1901.

LEAGUE'S PLANS FOR PREVENTING OPPOSITION.

The Latest Sporting News From All Points Of the Compass.

Special to THE SPORTING NEWS.
WASHINGTON, D. C., October 24.—The National League's territory will be invaded by the American League, with or without the permission of the former. The expansion policy of the American League on a scale and...

MEANS BUSINESS.

JOHNSON WILL CARRY OUT HIS EXPANSION POLICY.

American League Prefers Peace, But Is Fully Prepared for a Fight to a Finish.

BAN JOHNSON IS HUSTLING.

SELECTING SITES FOR PARKS.

NATIONAL LOSING PLAYERS.

STARS GO TO AMERICAN LEAGUE.

POOR PATRONAGE.

BAD START MADE BY NATIONAL LEAGUE CLUBS.

American League Will Depend for Its Success upon Good, Clean Ball and Honest Methods.

BALTIMORE, Md.

BASE BALL CRAZY.

EASTERN CITIES ENTHUSE OVER AMERICAN LEAGUE.

Baltimore and Washington Abandoned by National Are Strongholds of Johnson's Organization.

"

Last month these (National League) 'magnates' were 'ignoring' Ban Johnson and the American League. ... (Now) they are all hard at work trying to fight back this formidable new rival, that bids fair sooner or later to put them all out of business. They are badly frightened, that is plain—and well may they be so. The methods the National Leaguers have adopted are so characteristic of them—the same old underhanded attempts at trying to promote treachery by bribery, the same old misrepresentation, the same old game of bluff—the methods that have been in vogue in the National League for years—they are all doing duty in this fight.

—*January 26, 1901*

"

GAMES OF APRIL 24.—AT CHICAGO.									
CHICAGO.	AB.	R.	P.	A.	E.	CLEVELAND.	AB.	R.	P. A. E.
Hoy, cf	5	1	3	0	0	Pickering, rf	4	1	0 0 0
Jones, rf	2	1	4	0	0	McCarthy, lf	4	2	4 0 0
Mertes, lf	3	1	4	0	0	Genins, cf	4	0	1 0 0
Shugart, ss	2	0	4	4	0	Lachance, 1b	4	1	13 0 1
Isbell, 1b	3	1	8	0	0	Bradley, 3b	4	0	3 5 0
Hartman, 3b	4	1	0	5	1	Beck, 2b	3	2	9 4 0
Brain, 2b	4	0	3	3	0	Hallman, ss	3	0	1 3 1
Sullivan, c	4	2	0	0	0	Wood, c	4	1	2 2 0
Patterson, p	4	0	1	1	0	Hoffer, p	4	0	1 1 0
Totals	31	7	27	13	1	Totals	34	7	24 15 2

Chicago ....2 5 0 0 0 0 1 0 †—8
Cleveland ....0 0 0 1 0 0 1 0 0—2

Left on bases—Chicago 5, Cleveland 3. Two-base hit—Beck. Double plays—Brain, Shugart and Isbell; Hoffer, Hallman and Lachance. Struck out—By Hoffer 1. Bases on balls—Off Patterson 2, off Hoffer 6. Umpire—Connolly.

Note—All other games postponed on account of wet grounds and rain.

GAMES OF APRIL 25.—AT DETROIT.

Boxscore of the first American League game, April 24, 1901, at Chicago.

SLAVERY REVIVED.

—

BAN JOHNSON'S VIEWS ON THE LAJOIE DECISION.

A shaker and mover with attitude, American League founder Ban Johnson (above, right, with baseball executive Garry Herrmann) wanted to broaden baseball's horizons by making the game highly appealing to the growing urban masses. He had a plan—and the conviction to carry it through.

Johnson wasn't pleased when Napoleon Lajoie (left), who had jumped to the American League and won the Triple Crown in 1901, was ordered back to the N.L. by the courts. But he worked out a deal that kept Lajoie in the A.L.

A star National League infielder for nearly a decade, John McGraw (right, as Giants manager) was a pivotal figure in the N.L.-A.L. war. He jolted the senior league in 1901 by jumping to Baltimore of the A.L., then angered the fledgling league in July 1902 by bolting to the N.L.'s New York franchise.

Winner of two N.L. batting titles (the first achieved with a .432 mark), Wee Willie Keeler (above) took his considerable skills to the A.L. in 1903 when he signed with the New York Highlanders.

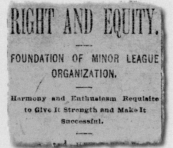

NATIONAL CRAVING PEACE.

SPEEDY SETTLEMENT PROBABLE.

SCHEDULE FOR NEXT SEASON ADOPTED.

GREEMENT REACHED BETWEEN

JOHNSON FOR TWO LEAGUES.

CONSOLIDATION IS NOT POPULAR.

ASSOCIATION WILL ABANDON ST. PAUL.

RFUS WILL BE WITH THE 100

The National League, under siege from player defections and attendance slippage, got the peace it wanted in 1903 with a new National Agreement, under which the N.L. and A.L. would be governed by one body, the National Commission.

The formation of the National Association in 1901 gave unity and structure to the minor leagues. It set up league classifications, salary and roster limits and a player-draft system.

RIGHT AND EQUITY.

FOUNDATION OF MINOR LEAGUE ORGANIZATION,

Harmony and Enthusiasm Requisite to Give It Strength and Make It Successful.

WILL INVADE NEW YORK.

GROUNDS SECURED BY AMERICAN.

Moving the Baltimore club to New York in 1903 was a masterstroke for the A.L., giving it key exposure and a landmark base.

Early baseball wasn't always family fare, with umpires targeted for all manner of abuse. Future Giants standout Joe McGinnity (right), for one, was fined for spitting at an umpire while pitching for Baltimore in 1901.

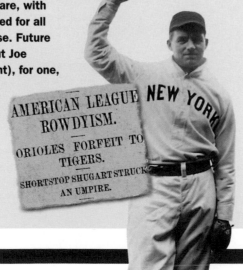

AMERICAN LEAGUE ROWDYISM.

ORIOLES FORFEIT TO TIGERS.

SHORTSTOP SHUGART STRUCK AN UMPIRE.

Baseball was stunned in '03 by the mysterious in-season death of Washington batting star Ed Delahanty. A career .346 hitter who twice batted .400 and had a four-homer game, he died in a plunge off a bridge.

LATE NEWS.

FELL THROUGH A BRIDGE.

SEARCH FOR BODY OF DELAHANTY.

The first World Series

The National League had been around for more than a quarter-century—since the year of the Custer Massacre, in fact—so it saw little danger in agreeing to play the upstart American League in a "world championship" in 1903. Hostilities between the leagues having cooled after player raids and territorial wars,

the N.L. got its comeuppance when Honus Wagner and the Pirates were upended by the Red Sox (also known as the Pilgrims, Puritans and Americans), five games to three. Bill Dinneen and veteran Cy Young pitched Boston to the first Fall Classic title, working 69 of their staff's 71 innings.

The emergence of Ty Cobb

"

Outfielder Cobb is the center attraction in this league at the present time. He is playing phenomenal ball and has done so all the season and is considered by all the old heads in the league to be the fastest youngster that ever broke into professional ball.
—*September 2, 1905*

(Dick) Cooley's place in center field has been assigned to a youth of 19 summers who bears the Georgia name of Tyrus C. Cobb. His home is near Augusta and when Armour recalled Cicotte, Cobb's release from the Augustas was purchased. ... He has speed in plenty and just at present he is a bit too fast for the good of the team. He is not content to catch the flys that go to his territory, but wants to get those that go to left and right.
—*September 23, 1905*

"

Former National League standout Cy Young won 33 games in the American League's first season, 1901, and threw a perfect game in 1904. He wound up posting a record 511 career wins — and having baseball's premier pitching award named in his honor.

PERFECT PITCHING.

CY YOUNG HAD ATHLETICS AT HIS MERCY.

Not One of Mack's Men Reached First on a Hit, Error or Base on Balls.

BOSTON, Mass., May 8.—SPECIAL CORRESPONDENCE:—It will be remembered that I remarked last week that the fans of this greatest of all base ball cities were in for some good base ball. But when I made that statement I, nor no one else, had an idea that we

Cobb after being called up.

The 1904 N.L. titlist Giants said no to a World Series against the pennant-winning Red Sox. Giants owner John T. Brush and manager John McGraw, at odds with American League President Ban Johnson, dismissed the A.L. as an inferior league.

WORLD SERIES 1905: Having devised rules under which world championships would be played, Brush quickly evolved from postseason critic to advocate. His Giants, under the direction of McGraw (top, with A's manager Connie Mack; above, with pitcher Christy Mathewson), defeated Philadelphia in five games as Mathewson (right) tossed three shutouts. Mathewson also pitched for McGraw's club in 1911, 1912 and 1913 Series play.

1901–1919

ST. LOUIS, AUGUST 12, 1905.

ROOT FOR YANKEES.

The winningest

Competing in a rough-and-tumble era in which rowdyism and other vices still plagued baseball, Pirates shortstop Honus Wagner always was above the fray. A man of integrity and talent, he captured eight batting crowns.

ROASTED WAGNER.

CHEAP GAMBLERS GET AFTER PIRATES' STAR PLAYER.

Often Bet on the Champions and Always Cause Trouble When They Do Not Win.

PITTSBURG, Pa., May 3.—Special Correspondence :—The week just closed has been one of the most remarkable in the history of any base ball season. The Pirates were scheduled to play six games here, but five of them

WORLD SERIES 1906: The Cubs, boasting a gifted pitching staff headed by Three Finger Brown and sparked by a legendary infield combination, were coming off a record 116-victory regular season when they took on their intracity rivals, the White Sox, for baseball's top prize. As wondrous as those Cubs were, they were upset in the Fall Classic by the opportunistic "Hitless Wonder" Sox, who batted a collective .228 during the season and only .198 in the Series.

The American League's New York franchise was known officially as the Highlanders through the 1912 season, but as early as 1905 the press was referring to the club by a name that appeared certain to catch on.

WORLD SERIES 1907: Stunned in the Series the year before, the Cubs became champions when, after a tie against the Tigers in Game 1, they won the next four games. Jack Pfiester, Ed Reulbach, Orval Overall and Three Finger Brown held Detroit and young star Ty Cobb to three runs over the final 40 innings.

team ever

Shortstop Joe Tinker, second baseman Johnny Evers and first baseman Frank Chance (left to right) made a habit of turning double plays and winning games. From 1906 through 1910, they helped the Cubs to four pennants and two World Series titles.

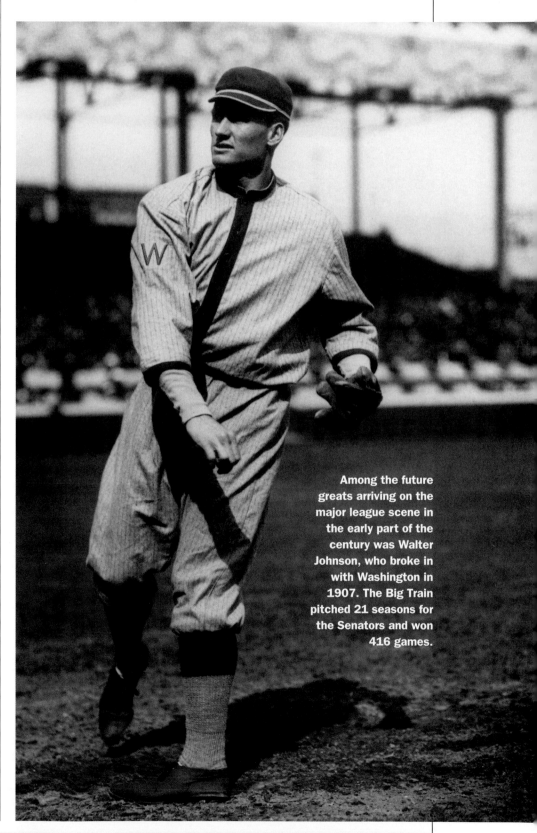

Among the future greats arriving on the major league scene in the early part of the century was Walter Johnson, who broke in with Washington in 1907. The Big Train pitched 21 seasons for the Senators and won 416 games.

PULLING FOR SOX

CHICAGO FANS SURE THAT CUBS WILL WIN.

Walsh's Poor Work in Final Inning Stopped Long Winning Spurt of Comiskey's Whirlwinds.

CHICAGO, August 27.— SPECIAL CORRESPONDENCE:—Base ball interest in this huge...

SOX HUMBLE CUBS.

WON BY BETTER PITCHING AND BATTING.

Comiskey Presents His Players with Purse of $15,000 for Winning World's Series.

COMISKEY'S White Sox, to whom championship caliber was not conceded by rivals...

'An enormous crowd of hopeful fans turned out—probably 28,000—and were almost killed.'

—October 1, 1908

Merkle's boner

"

The mob came back on Wednesday and before the sun set there was an old time riot ... It was caused by the stupidity of (the Giants') Fred Merkle. It was in the last half of the ninth with two men out and runners on third and first bases (Merkle on the latter bag), when Bridwell drove the ball past (the Cubs') Evers to center field. The man on third hiked for the plate with what looked like the winning run, but Mr. Merkle, losing his head, never went near second base, but made a bee line for the clubhouse, thinking the game had been won. Evers called to Hoffman to throw the ball to second base for a force-out, but McGinnity, who wasn't in the game at all, rushed out on the field and intercepted the throw. Mathewson, meanwhile, hustled after Merkle and told him to run to second base. ...

The ball, by this time, had been thrown to Evers while Merkle was fighting his way through another mob to his bag. Half a dozen fist fights were soon going on and it looked as if somebody would be seriously injured. The cops took the umpires under the grandstand where O'Day declared that the run did not count and that the game was a tie—1 to 1.

"

DISPUTED GAME A DRAW.

WILL BE PLAYED OFF THURSDAY.

TIGERS FINISH IN FIRST PLACE.

CENTRAL LEAGUE TO BAR FARMED PLAYERS.

Latest Base Ball News From All Points of Compass.

WORLD SERIES 1908: The late-season Giants-Cubs tie (which ended on the blunder by New York's Fred Merkle, above) had to be replayed when the teams finished the season tied for first. The Cubs won the makeup game—and their third consecutive pennant. They again beat Ty Cobb and the Tigers in the Series, becoming the first team to repeat. The class of the majors, the Cubs seemed capable of winning many Series titles. But through 2000, '08 marked their last.

ENEMIES OF CLEAN BALL.

LATE NEWS.
ASSAULTED AFTER GAME.
—
UMPIRE KERIN'S NOSE BROKEN.

The Sporting News recognized that the game's reckless—and occasionally injurious—style of play created a major image problem that needed to be addressed. Razor-sharp spikes were singled out as a particularly dangerous element.

Having endured too many jarring foul tips and menacing cleats, Giants catcher Roger Bresnahan said "enough" and introduced shinguards to the profession in 1907.

ROGER BRESNAHAN,

"

The dedication of Shibe Park, the $500,000 home of the Athletics inaugurated an era in professional base ball. The attendance at games in major league cities has outgrown the capacity of the one-story structures.

—*April 15, 1909*

"

The debut in Philadelphia of the Athletics' Shibe Park (left, below) in 1909 signaled baseball's move away from wooden, fire-hazard ballparks and toward upscale steel-and-concrete structures. Later in the 1909 season, another fan-friendly stadium, the Pirates' Forbes Field, opened for business in Pittsburgh.

WORLD SERIES 1909: Pittsburgh posted 110 N.L. wins to dethrone the Cubs, then edged Detroit in the Fall Classic (the first to go the limit). Pirates rookie Babe Adams won three times in the Series, which pitted Ty Cobb against Honus Wagner (right).

1901-1919

The tradition of a President attending Washington's season opener began with William Howard Taft in 1910.

When the Chalmers Motor Co. got around to presenting an automobile to the major leagues' leading hitter of 1910, Napoleon Lajoie (below, left) and Ty Cobb both went along for the ride. Detroit's Cobb edged Cleveland's Lajoie, .385 to .384, in a highly contested and notably contentious battle that led to Chalmers' decision to give new cars to both players.

WORLD SERIES 1910:
A's second baseman Eddie Collins (left) and Cubs catcher Johnny Kling were at opposite ends of the Fall Classic spectrum, with Collins hitting a robust .429 for the champion A's and Kling a sickly .077 for the losing Chicagoans.

WELL! WELL! LOOK WHO'S HERE

A lot of questions needed answering when Cubs stalwart Johnny Kling returned to his catching duties in the spring of 1910 after sitting out a year because of a contract dispute.

After Cleveland pitching great Addie Joss died in 1911, an all-star team led by Ty Cobb (first row, in a borrowed uniform) staged a benefit game.

PLACE IN HALL OF FAME AWAITS

—Jim Nasium in Philadelphia Inquirer

WORLD SERIES 1911:

After a cartoonist wondered who would be the next player to make a name for himself in postseason play, the Athletics' Frank Baker (left) hit two key homers in a six-game conquest of the Giants and John McGraw (above, hand on shoulder). The exploits turned the A's star into *Home Run* Baker.

WORLD SERIES 1912:

Fans on the streets of New York kept up with the Giants-Red Sox Series via a message board. Ultimately, the news was bad for New Yorkers: A muffed fly ball by Giants center fielder Fred Snodgrass (far right) in the 10th inning of Game 8 helped Boston to a 3-2 victory and the Fall Classic championship.

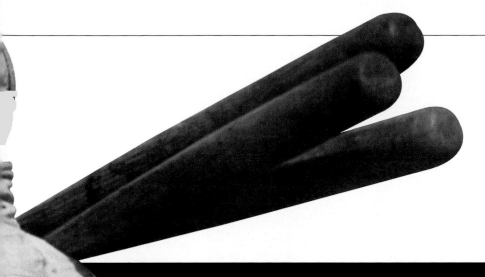

Ty Cobb was a fierce—even mean—competitor who arrived in the majors in 1905 and won the first of his nine consecutive batting titles two years later. Hitting above .400 three times in his career, Cobb captured 12 batting crowns overall. He also had 892 steals, flashing an unrelenting intensity on the bases (as the Athletics' Home Run Baker, below, could attest).

The Georgia Peach

'Connie Mack gave out bitter interviews...
He described Cobb as a man who
was undesirable in baseball, a man who
stopped at nothing to gain his ends.'

—1909, concerning Cobb's controversial spiking of Home Run Baker

Known for his hands-apart style at the plate, Cobb had an unequaled grip on the art of hitting a baseball. And when he wasn't instilling fear in pitchers' hearts, he was creating uneasy moments for infielders (such as New York's Jimmy Austin, below) and catchers (the Browns' Paul Krichell, left) with his barreling, spikes-high slides.

THE STANCE ALL PITCHERS FEARED

When Brooklyn Dodgers president Charles H. Ebbets (third from left among the dignitaries) opened Ebbets Field in 1913 amid flag-raising hoopla, he introduced a park that became the site of more than its share of zany goings-on.

BRANCH RICKEY, AS HE APPEARS ON BENCH

Branch Rickey's genius as a baseball man was apparent in his early 30s, when he took over as manager of the struggling St. Louis Browns. Still about a decade away from introducing the farm system and more than 30 years away from integrating the modern big leagues, Rickey already was winning attention as a thinker.

WORLD SERIES 1913: The Athletics took the measure of the Giants' Rube Marquard (left) in Game 1 and went on to vanquish the N.L. titlists in five games. Home Run Baker batted .450 with one homer and seven RBIs for Philadelphia, which got solid pitching from Chief Bender, Bullet Joe Bush and Eddie Plank.

THIS LAYOUT WILL HELP SOME

Connie Mack's $100,000 Infield

'Tendency of opinion favors the Athletics to win World Title, but the Braves have made record for upsetting dope and they may continue doing it.'

—*October 8, 1914*

Fenway Park, October 1914

The Miracle Braves

WORLD SERIES 1914: Boston's National League club rose from last-place tenants in mid-July to Series champions, rightfully earning the label of Miracle Braves. Manager George Stallings' team wound up winning the pennant by 10½ games, then swept Connie Mack's Philadelphia Athletics juggernaut in a stunning turn of events in the Fall Classic. The Braves' miracle men included (left to right) catcher Hank Gowdy, 26-game winner Dick Rudolph, pitcher George "Lefty" Tyler and outfielder Joe Connolly. Rudolph won twice against the A's, whose embarrassing loss led to their dismantling. A's second baseman Eddie Collins was traded over the winter, pitchers Eddie Plank and Chief Bender fled to the Federal League and third baseman Home Run Baker sat out the 1915 season before being sold to the Yankees. By the middle of 1915, shortstop Jack Barry, outfielder Eddie Murphy and pitcher Bob Shawkey also had been traded or sold.

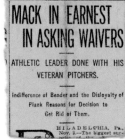

MACK IN EARNEST IN ASKING WAIVERS

ATHLETIC LEADER DONE WITH HIS VETERAN PITCHERS.

Indifference of Bender and the Disloyalty of Plank Reasons for Decision to Get Rid of Them.

PHILADELPHIA, Pa., Nov. 2.—The biggest sur-

ATHLETICS ARE TO BLAME FOR IT ALL

THEY THOUGHT THE BRAVES AN EASY PROPOSITION.

Awoke to the Job on Hand After Being Beaten in First Game, but Alas It Seems Too Late. Now.

BOSTON, Mass., Oct. 12.—No matter how the World's Series of

Plank (left) won 21 games for St. Louis' Federal League club in 1915. Stallings (right) saw his Braves slip to second place in the N.L. that season.

The Federal League

Seeing an opportunity to cash in (literally) on baseball's expanding appeal, the new Federal League fielded four teams in existing big-league cities and four in other sizable venues in 1914 and proclaimed itself a third "major league." Among the key defectors to the new league was former Cubs star Joe Tinker (right), who was signed to manage and play for Chicago's Federal League club. The Feds' offer of big money and their absence of a reserve system proved enticing, but the league soon found the sports dollar was spread too thin among the nation's paying customers. After two seasons of operation, the Federal League threw in the towel.

Late in 1915, baseball peace was realized when the A.L. and N.L. agreed to a payout plan under which the Federal League quit business.

This 1914 Federal game in Chicago marked the debut of the park that became Wrigley Field.

knee. Reinforcements, particularly for the pitching staff, were very welcome. President Lannin rose to the emergency by paying a sum variously estimated from $20,-000 to $30,000 for three of Jack Dunn's Baltimore players, Pitchers Ruth and Shore and Catcher Egan. Just why the Red Sox need another catcher is not apparent, unless on the assumption that a backstop will be let go to Detroit as a part of the Cobb-Speaker dicker which all hands are at present engaged in denying the existence of. It is possible, however, that Dunn insisted on Lannin's taking Egan along with the two pitchers.

Ruth is the man Lannin and Carrigan were particularly anxious to land. He has had a remarkable record in the International League, and as long as Jack Dunn seems to be determined to get rid of his ball players, Boston was only too willing to acquire Baby Ruth, also Shore and Egan.

After all, the Carrigans did have a pretty

July 1914:
Babe Ruth arrives in the majors.

'There's no reason I know of why a pitcher shouldn't hit if he wants to.'

—*Babe Ruth, August 8, 1918*

The birth of a legend

George Herman "Babe" Ruth made an obscure-but-auspicious pro debut in 1914 with the Baltimore club (left) of the International League. Pitching in front of 200 fans, he shut out Buffalo. Two years later, Ruth (below, second from right) won 23 games and had a 1.75 ERA for the World Series champion Red Sox.

MUST BE SO, SINCE BABE SAYS IT

GEORGE (BABE) RUTH

As early as 1918, while still with Boston and not yet a full-time hitter, Ruth was good copy. One writer noted the pitcher/slugger "takes perfect care of himself."

"

"Tell us," the interviewer inquired as he craned his neck to get a line vision on "Babe" Ruth's face, "what's the secret of your ability to hit?" The big Boston slugger and pitcher (a rare combination, that,) bent over that he might be within speaking distance, and answered:

"There isn't any secret, Bud. I just live to hit." ...

"I think good hitters can be developed, but I have always contended that a really great batter was born that way. ...

"I'd rather make one home run than six singles, because I think it's a circus to watch the other fellows chasing the ball around the park. I guess it's just a case of the old saying that what a man likes to do, he does best." ...

Physically, George Ruth is a perfect specimen of an athlete. He stands 6 feet 2 inches with his shoes off and weighs 198 pounds. He drinks little, seldom smokes and takes perfect care of himself. He was asked whether his physique had something to do with the power he gets in his drives. For

answer, he cocked his arm and besought us to "feel."

There'll never be a steel shortage in this country with "Babe" around. ...

Asked who named him "Babe," he replied:

"I don't know. The first day I joined Boston I heard somebody yell, 'Hello, Babe.' It's stuck to me ever since."

He said he has not yet decided what he will do when the baseball season terminates. He has had many offers from ship yards and steel leagues, but has not definitely accepted any of them. But he wants to get somewhere he can hit.

"

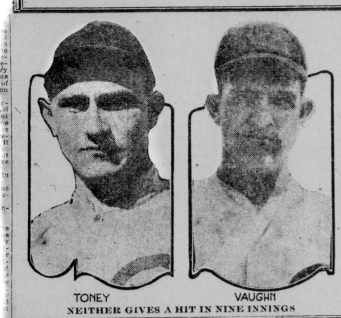

STARS IN RECORD SLAB BATTLE

TONEY   VAUGHN

NEITHER GIVES A HIT IN NINE INNINGS

REDS AND CUBS GIVE FANS A GAME IN CLASS BY ITSELF

There Have Been Many No-Hit Games on One Side, but Never, in Majors, a Contest Where Both Teams Went Hitless for Nine Innings.

RDINARY no-hit games, whether they be of the "revised" kind or otherwise, will

It remains unequaled: After nine innings of a big-league game played in 1917, *neither* pitcher had allowed a hit. The Reds then beat the Cubs in 10 innings as Fred Toney completed a no-hitter. Loser Jim Vaughn gave up two hits in the 10th—the game-winner to football legend Jim Thorpe.

Ty Cobb rolled to his ninth batting crown in a row in 1915, beating runner-up Eddie Collins of the White Sox by 37 points. Only 28, Cobb would take three more titles (1917, '18, '19).

WORLD SERIES 1915, 1916: It took only five games for the Red Sox to capture each Series. First, the Phillies and Grover Cleveland Alexander fell. Then Brooklyn went quietly in a Series highlighted by a 14-inning, complete-game victory by Boston lefthander Babe Ruth.

WORLD SERIES 1917: In a botched rundown play in the fourth inning of decisive Game 6, Giants third baseman Heinie Zimmerman chased Chicago's Eddie Collins across an unattended home plate. The run broke a scoreless tie and helped the White Sox to their second and—through 2000, anyway—last Series title.

WORLD SERIES 1918:
It was memorable in part because of a brief player revolt over the proceeds (for the first time, all first-division clubs received shares). Mostly, though, it was memorable because the Red Sox won the Series for the fifth time— but haven't won it since.

HUG AND HIS YANKS BECOME ACQUAINTED

NEW LEADER PLEASED AT SPIRIT SHOWN BY PLAYERS.

More Space Still Being Given to Herzog Than He's Worth, for a Settlement Would Be Easy.

When little Miller Huggins took over as Yankees manager in 1918, big things were on the horizon for a franchise accustomed to second-division finishes.

Baseball goes

WHY THE AMERICAN ADVANCE WAS DELAYED

A CARTOONIST'S FANCIFUL IDEA OF THE CHECK AT "W ORLDS SERIES HILL"

The specter of war was evident when members of the Browns (left) and Senators (led by Franklin D. Roosevelt, assistant secretary

to war

The impact names in baseball in 1918 weren't, say, Ty Cobb and Walter Johnson. With a world war raging, Newton Baker and Enoch Crowder made the biggest headlines. The secretary of war and draft-lottery director, respectively, Baker and Crowder handed down decisions that classified baseball as a nonessential activity and forced an early end to the season. Those edicts—and manpower losses to the military—were demoralizing, but baseball rebounded. In a fiercely contested World Series that ended on September 11, the Red Sox outfought the Cubs, who were without Grover Cleveland Alexander (right).

BAKER RULE A BLOW TO NATION'S MORALE

NOT ONLY CIVILIANS, BUT BOYS IN SERVICE ARE HIT.

Sports One Big Thing Says George Robbins to Keep Our Heads Up in This War Crisis.

HE'S NEW "CZAR" OF BASEBALL   July

SECRETARY OF WAR BAKER

STILL ONE OF THE BIG GUNS

ALEXANDER IN SOLDIER UNIFORM

ALEXANDER'S DRAFT CAME LIKE THUNDERBOLT FROM CLEAR SKY

CUB FANS HELD HOPE UNTIL LAST

GROVER TAKING LUCK AS IT COMES

Wants it Known He Hadn't Tried to Evade Call and Is Ready to Make the Suprema Sacrifice.

CHICAGO, Ill., April 13.—

Late News Items

ALEXANDER LIKELY TO STAY UNTIL MAY

This Is Latest Information That Comes as to Draft Status of National League's Star Performer.

of the Navy) conducted symbolic marches before games.

JOY IF REDS WIN—

Precursor to

Eddie Collins (third from left) went all out for the Sox. As for (left to right) Buck Weaver, Swede Risberg and Chick Gandil. ....

WORLD SERIES 1919: Shoeless Joe Jackson batted a Series-leading .375 for the Chicago White Sox. Buck Weaver contributed a .324 average. Chick Gandil twice delivered game-deciding hits. And Ed Cicotte, with his team one loss from elimination, came through with a 4-1 victory. But something seemed amiss, particularly after a shift in some of the betting odds toward the Cincinnati Reds. Still, the Reds were a formidable bunch capable of winning baseball's showcase event. Win it they did, and few people questioned the outcome. At least not right away.

ONE LONESOME SOX HERO

PITCHER DICK KERR

While Cincinnati glories in a wealth of World's Series heroes, there is rather a dearth of them for Chicago. The only one who stands out prominently is Little Dicky Kerr, who pitched the only win for the Sox in the first five games and upon whom depended the last ditch chance of the Sox—and Kerr was so little considered by his manager that it was not until the 1919 season was well along that he was given a regular place on the pitching staff. Kerr is another evidence that it does not take a big man to make a great pitcher, for he is one of the smallest athletes in the big show.

KERR THREW $160,000 IN

Little lefthander Dickie Kerr pitched with dogged determination in the '19 Fall Classic, recording two complete-game victories against Cincinnati.

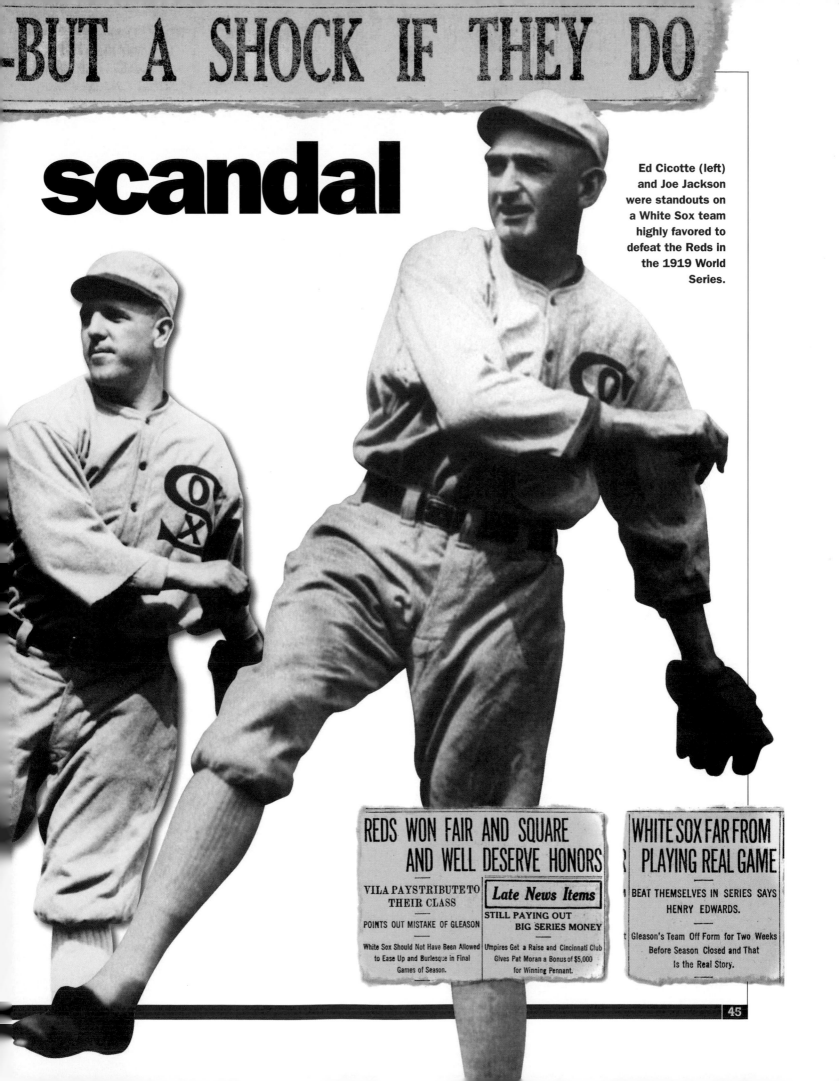

scandal

Ed Cicotte (left) and Joe Jackson were standouts on a White Sox team highly favored to defeat the Reds in the 1919 World Series.

REDS WON FAIR AND SQUARE AND WELL DESERVE HONORS

VILA PAYS TRIBUTE TO THEIR CLASS

POINTS OUT MISTAKE OF GLEASON

White Sox Should Not Have Been Allowed to Ease Up and Burlesque in Final Games of Season.

Late News Items

STILL PAYING OUT BIG SERIES MONEY

Umpires Get a Raise and Cincinnati Club Gives Pat Moran a Bonus of $5,000 for Winning Pennant.

WHITE SOX FAR FROM PLAYING REAL GAME

BEAT THEMSELVES IN SERIES SAYS HENRY EDWARDS.

Gleason's Team Off Form for Two Weeks Before Season Closed and That Is the Real Story.

45

1920
THE JUDGE, THE

1928
BABE AND THE YANKEES

Left to right: Lou Gehrig, Kenesaw Mountain Landis and Babe Ruth.

It's remembered fondly as the Roaring Twenties—the decade of jazz, flappers, speakeasies, dance marathons, raccoon coats, the Charleston and those scandalous gangsters who gave us bootleg whiskey and our first taste of organized crime. Some women were dames, others were libertarians who exercised their newly granted right to vote. A new Ford might cost you $290, a pack of cigarettes 10 cents. Life was fun, naughty, unpredictable and filled with technological innovation and wonder.

In retrospect, the social atmosphere of the period might have been choreographed by the baseball gods. This was a time of sadness, indecision and healing for a nation finally emerging from the dark cloud of World War I, unsure whether to mourn its terrible losses or to celebrate its greatest victory. This was a period of crisis and desperation for baseball, which was

Babe Ruth and Lou Gehrig

1 9 2 0	1 9 2 1	1 9 2 2
The 19th Amendment to the Constitution gives women the right to vote. Sinclair Lewis' *Main Street* is published.	The first Miss America is crowned.	*Reader's Digest* magazine is founded. The American Professional Football Association changes its name to the National Football League.

mired in scandal and looking toward an uncertain future. Only a savior could rescue the national pastime from the consequences of its grievous sins.

When the New York Yankees purchased Babe Ruth from cash-strapped Boston Red Sox owner Harry Frazee on January 5, 1920—12 days before the beginning of Prohibition—*The New York Times* hailed him as "the game's greatest slugger," not as its ultimate savior. But nobody could possibly foresee the incredible impact the young moon-faced lefthander would have on baseball—physically and emotionally. Ruth had helped pitch the Red Sox to two World Series championships, but his major league-record 29 home runs while serving as a part-time outfielder in 1919 had generated national headlines while arousing the curiosity of the Yankees.

The Bambino was a 25-year-old full-time right fielder when he began ushering baseball into a new era of prosperity. And he did it with flair. Ruth was loud, showy and outrageous, much like the long home runs he consistently launched, and he was always looking for a good time—220 pounds of raw personality on the prowl. Being around him was like watching a marching band parade through your living room. He hit the ball higher and longer than any player before him, and he related to the fans who flocked through the gates to watch him play.

Kenesaw Mountain Landis

Ruth pounded an unbelievable 54 home runs in his first season with the Yankees, finishing his onslaught in late September, just as indictments were being returned by a Cook County grand jury against eight members of the Chicago White Sox, who were accused of conspiring with gamblers to lose the 1919 World Series to the Cincinnati Reds. As Ruth was gearing up to make his run at immortality, the integrity of the game was being challenged in a Chicago courtroom.

Only the mysterious disappearance of key evidence late in the trial, including the signed confessions of Eddie Cicotte, Shoeless Joe Jackson and Lefty Williams, kept the players from being convicted of criminal charges by a Chicago jury. But by that time there was little doubt the allegations were true. Baseball took its first important step toward forgiveness with an unqualified admission of guilt—the 1921 hiring of Kenesaw Mountain Landis as the game's first commissioner, a leader with dictatorial powers to replace the long-ruling three-man commission.

The scowling, no-nonsense former federal judge immediately performed surgery on the sagging image of America's national pastime. Displaying the iron-fisted discipline he would bring to the game over the next two decades, Landis handed the eight "Black Sox" a shocking

---

lifetime ban from baseball for consorting with gamblers, a clear message that deviation from league policy would no longer be tolerated.

With the ban, the new commissioner gave baseball a much-needed conscience. Ruth took care of the rest, attracting the fans back to the ballpark while single-handedly changing the style of the game from speed and finesse to instant offense.

The Bambino was incorrigible, a high-living night owl who would tour the best restaurants and saloon districts at night and then hit prodigious home runs during the day. Ruth butted heads several times with Yankee officials over his lavish ways, and Landis suspended him when he ignored the commissioner's barnstorming ban. But his escapades only added to a growing legend, as did a 59-homer season in 1921 and the magical 60-homer plateau he reached in 1927 for what many consider the greatest team in baseball history.

It's no coincidence that the emergence of Ruth signaled the rise of the Yankees from an also-ran franchise that had never won anything to the greatest winning machine in baseball history. The team,

Bob Meusel and Rogers Hornsby (below)

under the direction of diminutive manager Miller Huggins, won its first A.L. pennants in 1921 and '22, losing World Series both years to the Giants. The 1923 Yankees, playing in spectacular new Yankee Stadium, exacted sweet revenge over the Giants when they won the team's first Series. And the 1927 Yankees, with a lineup featuring the Murderers' Row of Ruth, Lou Gehrig, Bob Meusel and Tony Lazzeri, won 110 games and swept the overmatched Pittsburgh Pirates in the fall classic. The 1928 Yankees won 101 times and swept the St. Louis Cardinals.

Ruth's power displays triggered a philosophical revolution that swept through baseball like a monstrous tidal wave. Instead of the speedy, bat-control players who dominated the dead-ball era, team owners began looking for the muscular hitters who could determine the outcome of games with one swing of the bat. And rules that had previously favored pitchers (the allowing of spitballers, for example) were changed to meet the demands for more excitement from offense-minded fans.

1926

Silent film star Rudolph Valentino dies at age 31.

Ernest Hemingway's *The Son Also Rises* is published.

George Sisler

From the Ruthian power influence rose such hitters as Rogers Hornsby, Mel Ott, Jimmie Foxx, Cy Williams, Hack Wilson, Al Simmons and, of course, Gehrig, the Yankees' durable Iron Horse. But the 1920s also featured two of the best single-season batting performances in baseball history—St. Louis Browns first baseman George Sisler hit .420 in 1922 and Cardinals second baseman Hornsby batted .424 in 1924—and the pitching exploits of such future Hall of Famers as Carl Hubbell, Lefty Grove, Waite Hoyt, Stan Coveleski, Dazzy Vance and Walter Johnson.

Other seeds of change took longer to germinate. When Harold Arlin handled baseball's first radio broadcast for Pittsburgh station KDKA in 1921, critics panned the idea as a gimmick. Crusades continued in many cities against Sunday baseball.

And when Branch Rickey unveiled baseball's first farm system for the St. Louis Cardinals, Giants manager John McGraw branded it a "stupid idea."

The 1920s will forever be remembered as a period of unprecedented growth and the securing of baseball's foundation as the national pastime. It was now a sport that attracted U.S. presidents to throw ceremonial first pitches, the once-standoffish gentility to mingle with its stars and regional fans with greater transportation mobility.

One of this Golden Age's great ironies is that it closed on an ominous note, just as Ruth was deeply involved in negotiations to become the first six-figure star in baseball history. As Ruth haggled with Yankees owners in 1929, the nation plunged into a deep financial abyss when the stock market crashed, triggering the Great Depression.

1927

Charles Lindbergh flies nonstop across the Atlantic Ocean, from New York to Paris.

Considered the movies' first significant "talkie," *The Jazz Singer* opens in New York.

1928

Penicillin is discovered. It is in general use by 1946.

Steamboat Willie, Walt Disney's first film short with sound, features Mickey Mouse.

Babe finds a new home

When Red Sox owner Harry Frazee, a strapped theater man, needed cash in January 1920, he unloaded the new home run king, Babe Ruth, to the Yankees for $125,000. After hitting a record 29 homers for Boston in 1919, Ruth set the game on its ear with 54 for the Yanks in 1920.

Although Ruth still did some pitching in '19, he was settling in as a full-time outfielder/slugger.

Ruth starts his awful swing.

The finish. Here Ruth practices the through taught in golf.

Ruth reaching for a high one. Trying to maintain a level bat.

LITTLE MAN WHO LANDS BIG GAME

MILLER HUGGINS

With Ruth adding unheard-of power to the lineup, the future looked brighter for New York manager Miller Huggins.

Browns first baseman George Sisler (above) set a one-season record of 257 hits in 1920, a year in which he batted .407. Two years later, he topped that average by 13 points and hit safely in 41 straight games.

HIS NEW RECORD---THE PRICE

GEORGE "BABE" RUTH

Paying an enormous sum to obtain one player isn't anything new—the Yankees did it more than 80 years ago for Babe Ruth (left).

BOSTON MAY DAY GAME NEW RECORD IN MAJORS

The May 1, 1920, game went a record 26 innings. Even more amazing, pitchers Joe Oeschger (Braves) and Leon Cadore (Dodgers) pitched complete games— and matched zeroes over the last 20 innings. The 1-1 tie was halted by darkness.

RAY CHAPMAN DIES FROM BLOW BY MAYS

Shortstop Ray Chapman (below), a key player on an Indians team headed for its first American League pennant, was struck and fatally injured by a pitch thrown by the Yankees' Carl Mays in an August 16, 1920, game at the Polo Grounds. Chapman, 29, was in his ninth season with Cleveland. He is the only player to die of an injury incurred in a big-league game.

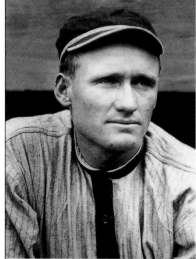

Cardinals second baseman Rogers Hornsby (below) batted .402 (1,078 hits in 2,679 at-bats) from 1921 through 1925.

The stellar career of Walter Johnson (above) was winding down as the 1920s dawned, but he still had two 20-victory seasons in that decade.

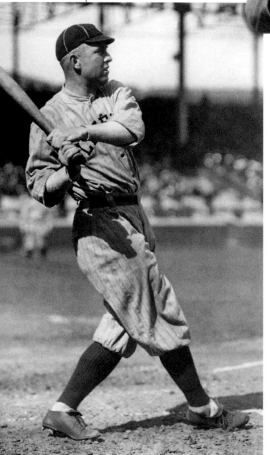

Player/manager Tris Speaker (above) led by example, batting .388 for a 1920 Cleveland team that went on to win the World Series.

Spitball banned

"

(Clark) Griffith, backed by (Connie) Mack, forced the discussion on the spitball and freak deliveries. Griffith at first proposed that the spitball be eliminated at once. Joe Cantillon's report of the excellent effect the outright abolition of the spitter had on American Association play in 1919 evidently confirmed Griffith in his attack on the salivary seducer. Barney Dreyfuss, who has not one spitball pitcher on his team, generously advocated a reprieve of one year for recognized spitballers, the men to be certified to by the presidents of their leagues. The National League certified 12. ... The American League did not turn in its list. If a certified major leaguer changes clubs or leagues, his certification will follow him. The major league clubs will not be permitted to certify spitball pitchers recruited from the minor leagues. The shine, emery, mud, chewing gum, chipped, cut, roughened ball is outlawed, without recourse, at once. Umpires will be instructed to rub even the natural shine off the new balls before submitting them to the pitchers. No player (pitcher included) can rub a ball on his glove, clothing, person, or dirt, grass, etc., or throw a ball to any other player to be soiled, etc. Umpires may use dust to destroy the natural shine on ball covers. The penalty for violation of these rules, against freak deliveries, will be removal from the game and ten days' suspension for the offending player or players. Drastic enough in all truth.
—February 19, 1920

"

In February 1920, the spitball was officially barred. Recognizing that some pitchers made their living with the spitter, baseball went beyond a one-year reprieve and certified 17 big-leaguers as legalized spitballers—meaning they, but no newcomers to the majors, could use the pitch for the remainder of their careers.

HERRMANN, TIRED OF CRITICISM, CHUCKS HIS COMMISSION JOB

When August "Garry" Herrmann quit early in 1920 as chairman of major league baseball's ruling body, the three-man National Commission, it was big news. But bigger news was yet to come: The game soon would adopt a governing structure under which one man would exert full control.

"There, take it and keep still!"

When Babe Ruth slammed his 54th and last homer of 1920 (above), it topped his former record by 25.

In June, the manufacturer of the majors' baseballs had said the ball "is the same as used last year and several seasons before. ... No effort has been made to turn out a livelier ball."

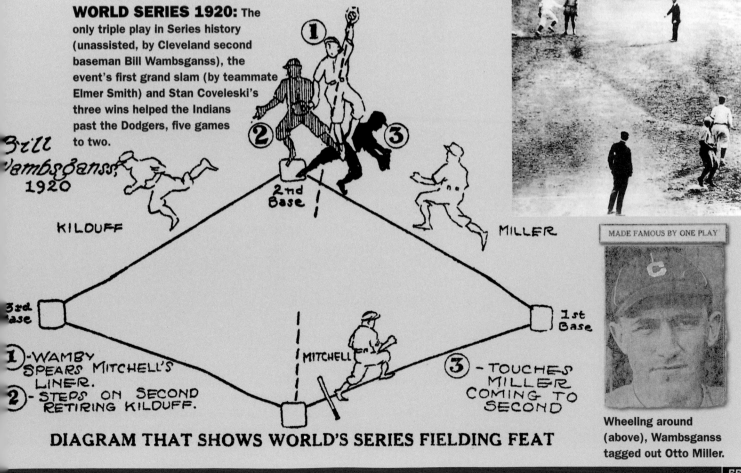

WORLD SERIES 1920: The only triple play in Series history (unassisted, by Cleveland second baseman Bill Wambsganss), the event's first grand slam (by teammate Elmer Smith) and Stan Coveleski's three wins helped the Indians past the Dodgers, five games to two.

Bill Wambsganss, 1920

KILDUFF

MILLER

2nd Base

3rd Base

1st Base

MITCHELL

①—WAMBY SPEARS MITCHELL'S LINER.

②—STEPS ON SECOND RETIRING KILDUFF.

③—TOUCHES MILLER COMING TO SECOND

DIAGRAM THAT SHOWS WORLD'S SERIES FIELDING FEAT

MADE FAMOUS BY ONE PLAY

Wheeling around (above), Wambsganss tagged out Otto Miller.

The Black Sox

As soon as news of the indictments of the "Black Sox" was made public on September 28, 1920, White Sox owner Charles Comiskey (below) announced he was suspending the seven implicated players still on the club's roster. (Chick Gandil was no longer with the team.)

Comiskey said he would reinstate any player cleared of wrongdoing, but he also emphasized that he would seek a permanent ban from major and minor league baseball for any player found guilty.

GRAND JURY INQUIRY INTO THROWN GAMES WILL LEAD TO INDICTMENTS

MEN ON INSIDE KNEW IT WOULD COME OUT

CHICAGO A SAMPLE OF REST OF FANDOM

Almost one year after the favored Chicago White Sox were upended by the Cincinnati Reds in the 1919 World Series, a Cook County (Ill.) grand jury returned indictments against eight members of the losing team. The players were charged with complicity in a conspiracy with gamblers to fix the outcome of the Series.

The indicted players were:

Ed Cicotte, pitcher. (Compiled a 1-2 record in the Series.)
Hap Felsch, outfielder. (Batted .192 with three RBIs.)
Chick Gandil, first baseman. (Batted .233 with five RBIs.)
Joe Jackson, outfielder. (Hit .375 with one homer, six RBIs.)
Fred McMullin, utility player. (Had one hit in two at-bats.)
Swede Risberg, shortstop. (Batted .080 with zero RBIs.)
Buck Weaver, third baseman. (Batted .324 with zero RBIs.)
Lefty Williams, pitcher. (Was 0-3 with 6.61 ERA.)

GRAND JURY HAS YET TO REACH BIG MEN IN GAME'S SCANDAL

Indictment of Eight White Sox Players Only One Phase of Inquiry That Judge McDonald Says Will Continue Until There Is Real Cleanup.

The headline suggesting that the investigation of the 1919 World Series might reach—and eventually implicate—some of the game's so-called "big men" turned out to be off the mark, but the forecast of an overall cleanup of baseball proved to be an accurate assessment.

scandal

Three of the eight Black Sox were enjoying outstanding careers. Shoeless Joe Jackson, who once hit .408 and .395 in consecutive years, had a .356 career batting mark. Ed Cicotte had won 208 games over 14 seasons, and Claude "Lefty" Williams had compiled an 82-48 record in seven years in the majors.

FIX THESE FACES IN YOUR MEMORY

"CHICK" GANDIL

"HAP" FELSCH

JOE JACKSON

ALL PHOTOS © BY UNDERWOOD & UNDERWOOD

EDDIE CICOTTE

CLAUDE WILLIAMS

FRED McMULLIN

"SWEDE" RISBERG

"BUCK" WEAVER

EIGHT MEN CHARGED WITH SELLING OUT BASEBALL

GRAND JURY INQUIRY CLIMAXED BY PROOF THAT COMISKEY WAS TOLD

In November 1920, baseball turned to a tough U.S. District Court judge, Kenesaw Mountain Landis, to run the game in the newly formed position of commissioner. News accounts defined his office as a "one-man court of last resort."

Landis' appointment marked the formal end of the three-man National Commission that had ruled baseball since 1903.

Landis officially took over in January 1921.

The judge takes control

Judge Landis was no stranger to major league baseball. In 1915, the Federal League brought a suit before Landis for an injunction against the American and National leagues. His handling of the case helped effect a peace agreement between the game's warring factions.

LANDIS GIVEN ALL POWERS ASKED FOR TO KEEP BASEBALL CLEAN

REICHOW, THE ORIGINAL LANDIS MAN, PAYS TRIBUTE TO HIS CHOICE

The Black Sox scandal cast a pall over baseball, but not everyone took a gloom-and-doom attitude. An American League umpire, for one, remained upbeat, and he shared his optimism about the game with The Sporting News in the issue of October 28, 1920.

NOW WE SHALL SEE IF PUBLIC PREFERS CHEATING TO HONESTY

Any Fan Giving Support to Black Sox Naturally Indicates That He Doesn't Object to Crookedness in Baseball and Is Willing to Be a Party to It.

CHEER UP, OLD GAME!

BY GEORGE J. MORIARTY
American League Umpire

Come, Father Baseball, lift your weary head,
And face with hope, the sunrise glowing red,
All is not lost because the tempters' gold
Has snared the weak and erring from the fold;
In spite of wayward lads who sold their fame,
Today, you are by far the greatest game.

Yea, lift your head, and once again be proud,
You're gazing at a disappearing cloud.
Sometime the mud is splashed upon the pane,
But when wiped off, we see clear skies again.
Each army great, has traitors, yet we find
It's honest soldiers on to victory wind.

Cheer up, Old Game! just think of politics,
And other earthly games so full of tricks;
The profiteers, a menace to our land—
If only they were governed by your hand
So Spartan-like in seeking out the thief,
'Twould fetch to this old troubled world relief.

Convinced that you are free from grimy stains,
And confident that honest baseball reigns,
The faithful fans have flocked in by the herds
To see Spoke's Indians fight Robby's birds,
Condemning not the loyal with the few
Black sheep that strayed and broke their faith with you.

O, Father Baseball, you will live because
You cherish honesty and rout the flaws.

(Copyright, 1920, by G. Moriarty.)

BROOKLYN, N. Y., Aug. 8.—As High Commissioner of Organized Baseball, Judge Landis has barred the Black Sox, acquitted by a Chicago jury, from participating in major league games. Secretary John Farrell of the National Association, which represents the minor leagues, has announced they are barred from his organization. All that remains now is to see whether the Black Sox are barred by the fans. Organized Baseball has made its stand plain.

In August 1921, a jury found the Black Sox players not guilty, contending there was no evidence of a clear conspiracy to fix the 1919 World Series between the White Sox and Reds. But Commissioner Landis viewed the verdict as flawed. He said that—conspiracy or not—the players' "crookedness" was shown time and again during the trial. Accordingly, Landis banned the eight players for life.

It didn't take long for Landis to show everyone—eight wayward players included—that he would rule baseball with an iron fist.

New York, New York

GIANTS AND YANKEES RISE UP AND KNOCK OUT THE KNOCKERS

The two tenants of the Polo Grounds, the Yankees (below) and the Giants, silenced their critics in and out of New York by winning pennants in 1921. The American League championship was the first in Yankees history.

"BABE" RUTH'S HANDS AND HIS SLUGGER

Here are the powerful hands and wrists and the powerful bat that set a new record this season for home runs. They brought "Babe" his wonderful 59.

LOUISVILLE SLUGGER
HILLERICH & BRADSBY CO.
LOUISVILLE, KY.
TRADE MARK REG. U. S. PAT. OFF.

It is significant that the bat "Babe" used to make his 59 and the bats used by every other player in the 1921 World's Series, both Giants and Yankees, bear the same trade mark—*Louisville Slugger*.

Ask The Bat Boy — He Knows
HILLERICH & BRADSBY CO., Inc. - Louisville, Kentucky
THE LOUISVILLE SLUGGER — THE WORLD'S SERIES BAT

Babe Ruth's 59 homers helped power the '21 Yanks into the World Series—and they helped with endorsements, too.

Waite Hoyt (above) won 19 games for the Yankees in 1921 and didn't allow an earned run in 27 innings of World Series pitching. The Yanks fell in the Series despite Hoyt's heroics.

BROTHERS IN SERIES AGAIN

Robert Meusel

WORLD SERIES 1921: The Giants, led by Emil "Irish" Meusel's .345 average and seven RBIs, won their first Series since 1905 by beating the Yankees, whose lineup included Meusel's brother Bob. Jesse Barnes and Phil Douglas each won twice for the Giants, and Art Nehf pitched a shutout in the clincher.

Emil Meusel

NOT CONSCIENCE ALONE THAT CAUSED RUTH TO CHANGE TACK

Defying an edict laid down by Commissioner Landis (middle), Babe Ruth and Bob Meusel (right) barnstormed after the 1921 season and drew suspensions. They were reinstated three weeks into May in 1922. The '22 season was a stormy one for Ruth, who constantly quarreled with umpires and Yankees officials after his return. Also, he incurred the wrath of previously adoring New York fans when he failed to match his exploits of his first two years with the Yankees.

Charlie Robertson, whose career record in the big leagues wound up at 49-80, tossed a perfect game for the White Sox against Detroit on April 30, 1922. It would be 34 years until the majors' next perfect game.

YANKS BID GOOD BYE TO POLO GROUNDS WITH GREAT ECLAT

PLAYERS' UNION IMPOSSIBLE EVEN IF THERE WAS ANY SUCH

In the early 1920s, the time wasn't right for players to unionize. Still, the desire for a players group was talked about even then. (Three decades earlier, major leaguers had formed the union-like Brotherhood, which led to the short-lived Players League.)

In a record-smashing game (right) played at the Cubs' park at Clark and Addison streets in 1922, the hometown team edged the Phillies, 26-23. Still-existing big-league marks were set for total runs (49) and hits (51) in one game. Despite erupting for 10 or more runs twice in the first four innings, the Cubs had to hang on for the win.

The Yankees, who had been tenants of the Giants at the Polo Grounds (below) since 1913, made their last season at the famed horseshoe a noteworthy one by winning their second consecutive American League pennant in 1922. The gate appeal of Babe Ruth and the Giants' desire to oust the popular Yankees from their park were among the factors in the Yankees' decision to build their own stadium in the Bronx.

The Yankees' Ruth and the Browns' George Sisler (below, right) were longtime American League rivals and two of the game's brightest stars. In 1922, Ruth's New Yorkers won the A.L. flag by one game over Sisler's team, but the St. Louis standout took some consolation by putting up dazzling individual numbers. Sisler finished with a .420 batting average (only four points shy of the highest mark recorded in the 20th century), collected 246 hits and drove in 105 runs.

Red Sox shortstop Everett Scott (left) reached the 1,000 mark in consecutive games played in 1921 and, as a member of the Yankees four years later, extended his then-record figure to 1,307 before sitting out a game.

As the '20s began to roar, President Warren G. Harding continued the tradition of throwing out the first ball of the season.

DEFEAT OF YANKS PUTS WOLVES ON TRAIL OF HUGGINS AGAIN

WORLD SERIES 1922: Babe Ruth's year worsened. After dropping off to 35 homers and 99 RBIs and playing in only 110 games because of various suspensions and indiscretions, Ruth batted .118 in the Series. The Giants, playing with attitude (Irish Meusel, right, jumped on the plate after a home run), dealt the Yankees their second postseason setback in a row, this one four wins to none (with one tie). It was the last Series title for Giants manager John McGraw. Meanwhile, adversary Miller Huggins was feeling some heat.

Yankee Stadium opens

Yankees president Jacob Ruppert (right, with his manager, Miller Huggins, and Boston manager Frank Chance, and above, left to right, with Red Sox owner Harry Frazee, Commissioner Landis and Yankees partner Tillinghast Huston) was a proud man on Yankee Stadium's opening day, which was capped by the Yanks' 4-1 win over Boston. The franchise had come a long way since its early New York days at wooden Hilltop Park (1903-1912).

Hailed then (as it often is now) as the world's greatest sports arena, Yankee Stadium was built in just 185 working days and opened on April 18, 1923. Babe Ruth christened the "House That Ruth Built" with the park's first home run.

FAULTS ARE FOUND WITH NEW BALL PARK OF THE YANKEES

DIAMOND IS TOO CLOSE TO GRAND STAND

Right Field Too Short and Idea of Cinder Track Around Outfield Something That Merits Criticism.

The stadium deemed perfect in most observers' eyes drew surprising criticism in the critique of one correspondent for The Sporting News. The park was a month away from opening.

Detroit's Harry Heilmann won four batting titles—and was a terror each season. He hit .394 in 1921, .403 in 1923, .393 in 1925 and .398 in 1927.

YANKEE STADIUM AS IT'S "BUILT FOR RUTH"

Yankees officials and their stadium architects made certain the House That Ruth Built would be a structure built for Ruth—that is, the massive ballpark would be configured in a manner designed to fit the Bambino's home run stroke. Sure enough, the original distance from home plate to the right field wall at Yankee Stadium was 296 feet.

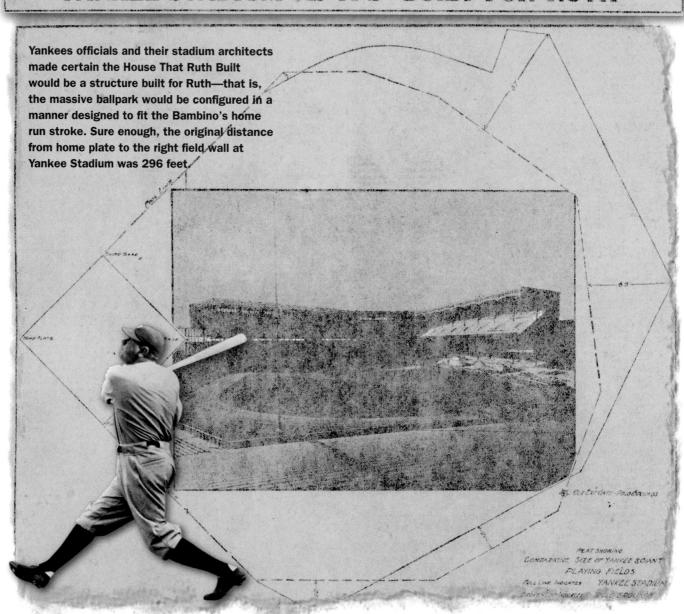

First-time Series champs: the Yanks

WORLD SERIES 1923: It was a breakthrough year for the New York Yankees: the opening of their magnificent stadium, a romp to the pennant, their first Fall Classic crown. With Babe Ruth back in form, the Yankees exacted revenge on the Giants in six games. Ruth hit three home runs, a triple, a double and two singles, drew eight walks and batted .368. All this after a season in which he batted .394 with 41 homers and 131 RBIs.

Yankees lefthander Herb Pennock won Games 2 and 6 of the '23 Series against the Giants, who got outstanding play from center fielder Casey Stengel (inset). Stengel hit the first Series homer in Yankee Stadium history, an inside-the-park smash that won Game 1, and batted .417 in the Fall Classic for the N.L. champions.

The Babe

'I had a better year than he did.'

—Ruth's response during a holdout when a writer reminded him that he already was earning more money that President Herbert Hoover.

'Geez, it sure is hot, ain't it, Prez.'

—The Babe making small talk with President Calvin Coolidge before a season-opening game in Washington.

"Babe Ruth was a man of gargantuan achievements. ... When he wasn't setting home run records, Ruth was shattering all known gastronomic marks. A quart of chocolate ice cream and pickled eels were standard fare between games of a doubleheader. A breakfast might consist of a pint of bourbon and ginger ale, a porterhouse steak, four fried eggs, fried potatoes and a pot of coffee. Ruth ... could party all night, drive cars at breakneck speed, consume enormous portions of food and drink and then perform as the demigod of the diamond. Babe was in a class by himself as a gate attraction."

—The Sporting News' book,
*Cooperstown/Where Baseball's
Legends Live Forever*

Fans everywhere reached out to the Babe, whose immense popularity transcended age, gender and race. Not even stints out of the lineup due to suspension (1922, for ignoring an edict on barnstorming), major illness (1925, an intestinal abscess), minor illness (more than a few stomachaches) or rifts with authority hurt Babe in the eyes of his fans.

'I looked around for a hitter to copy after. Cobb, Speaker and Eddie Collins weren't my type, but Jackson had the smoothest, easiest swing ... so I watched his every action. '

—*Ruth, on modeling his hitting technique after that of Shoeless Joe Jackson.*

The streetwise Ruth (with Yankees teammate Al DeVormer) cut a dapper figure as a man about town.

McGraw's Giants dominate

Manager John McGraw (above) and the Giants would prove in 1924 that they still were in the driver's seat in the National League, winning a record fourth consecutive pennant. Led by first baseman George "High Pockets" Kelly's .324 average, the Giants batted .300 as a team. Kelly also drove in 136 runs.

.424

TOPS ALL HITTERS OF 1924

Not only did Cardinals second baseman Rogers Hornsby lead all big-league batsmen in '24, his average that year was the highest in the majors in the 20th century. Hornsby finished at .424, collecting 227 hits in 536 at-bats. Hornsby exceeded .400 two other times, and his career mark of .358 ranks behind only Ty Cobb's figure of .367.

12 RBIs

Cardinals first baseman Jim Bottomley had one of the greatest individual days in major league history on September 16, 1924. He hit two home runs, a double and three singles in a game at Brooklyn—and drove in 12 runs. His 6-for-6 day helped St. Louis to a 17-3 triumph.

SENATORS BOAST ONE OF STRONGEST OUTFIELDS IN LEAGUE.

Outfielders (left to right) Earl McNeely, Nemo Leibold, Sam Rice and Goose Goslin helped the Senators go out and get their first pennant in 1924. Goslin batted .344 with 129 RBIs; Rice hit .334; rookie McNeely, in limited duty, finished at .330; and Leibold contributed a .293 mark.

The Browns' Ken Williams was one of the top power hitters of the 1920s. In '22, he smashed 39 home runs and drove in 155 runs.

WORLD SERIES 1924: Washington became the Series champion when, in the 12th inning of Game 7, Earl McNeely's bad-hop grounder bounced over the head of Giants third baseman Fred Lindstrom and scored Muddy Ruel. Walter Johnson, finally getting a chance to pitch in the Fall Classic, got the win in the clincher with four scoreless innings of relief. Second baseman Bucky Harris, 27, was in his first year as manager of the Senators, who were honored with a victory parade.

Penciling Gehrig into the lineup

Games of Monday, June 1.

AT NEW YORK—The Yankees' losing streak continued, despite the return of Babe Ruth to the lineup, the Senators winning, 5 to 2. Ruth, who has been absent from the game for eight weeks due to illness, played six innings for his first appearance this season in a major league game. Veach replaced the heavy hitter in right field in the seventh, it being considered advisable not to allow Ruth to exert himself. Score:

New York.	AB.	R.	H.	O.	A.	Wash'ton.	AB.	R.	H.	O.	A.
Wanninger, ss	5	0	0	1	2	Rice, cf	5	2	5	0	1
*Gehrig	1	0	0	0	0	S.Harris, 2b	4	1	1	2	4
Hoyt, p	0	0	0	1	6	Judge, 1b	4	1	0	12	0
Dugan, 3b	4	0	1	0	6	Goslin, lf	4	1	2	4	0
Combs, cf	4	1	2	5	0	J.Harris, rf	3	0	0	1	0
Ruth, rf	2	0	0	2	0	Bluege, 3b	4	0	1	0	9
Veach, rf	0	0	0	0	0	Peck, ss	4	0	0	1	1
Meusel, lf	4	0	1	2	0	Ruel, c	4	0	0	7	3
Pipp, 1b	4	0	1	13	1	W.Jnson, p	3	0	2	0	4
Ward, 2b	3	0	0	0	2	Marberry, p	1	0	0	0	0
Schang, c	3	1	0	3	0						
E Johnson, ss	2	1	1	0	0	Totals	36	5	11	27	12
Jones, p	1	0	0	0	2						
†Witt	0	0	0	0	0						
Totals	31	3	6	27	14						

*Batted for Wanninger in eighth.

When Lou Gehrig, about to turn 22, pinch hit for Pee Wee Wanninger on June 1, 1925, it was the start of something big—a consecutive-game streak that would last until 1939.

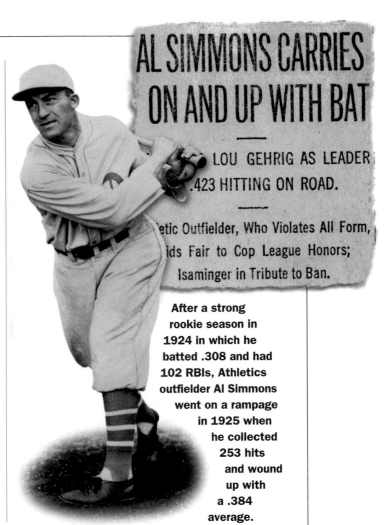

LOU GEHRIG AS LEADER
.423 HITTING ON ROAD.

etic Outfielder, Who Violates All Form,
ds Fair to Cop League Honors;
Isaminger in Tribute to Ban.

Basestealing wizard Max Carey (left) and slick-fielding, hard-hitting third baseman Pie Traynor (top, right) were stalwarts on a 1925 Pirates team that won the National League pennant by 8½ games over the Giants. In the American League, former Indians ace Stan Coveleski helped Washington to the same margin of victory over Philadelphia by winning 20 of 25 decisions.

After a strong rookie season in 1924 in which he batted .308 and had 102 RBIs, Athletics outfielder Al Simmons went on a rampage in 1925 when he collected 253 hits and wound up with a .384 average.

WORLD SERIES 1925: After managers Bucky Harris (Senators, far left) and Bill McKechnie (Pirates) exchanged pleasantries, Pittsburgh went on to become the first team to win a best-of-seven Series after trailing three games to one. Harris counted on aging Walter Johnson, who had excelled in Games 1 and 4, to nail down a second straight Senators crown. But the Big Train jumped the tracks in Game 7, yielding 15 hits in a 9-7 loss. Kiki Cuyler's two-run double decided matters.

PITTSBURG MAKES GREAT FIGHT TO WREST WORLD'S SERIES TITLE

Cards: a flag and a farm

Third-place finishes had been heady stuff for the Cardinals, a franchise that in one five-year run had finished 47½, 63, 55½, 50 and 56 games out of first place. But in 1926, the Cards won their first N.L. pennant, thanks to a lineup that featured seven men with averages of .293 or higher and a pitching staff headed by Flint Rhem, Bill Sherdel, Jesse Haines and newly acquired Grover Cleveland Alexander. The future was bright, too. Branch Rickey was introducing the concept of the farm system, through which the Cards would stockpile talent in an unprecedented manner.

THE END OF PENNANT FAMINE IN ST. LOUIS

A STREET SCENE DURING CELEBRATION OF CARDINAL VICTORY

NATIONAL LEAGUE'S 'MIRACLE MAN' OF 1926

MANAGER ROGERS HORNSBY

The Cardinals, fourth in 1925, rose to the top under the direction of Rogers Hornsby, who had replaced Rickey as manager in '25 (a move that enabled Rickey to focus on front-office duties).

Mr. and Mrs. Alexander found themselves in the spotlight.

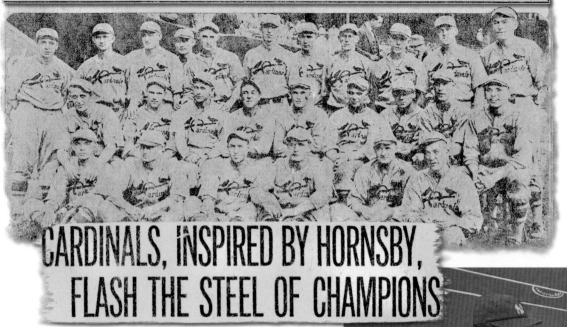

PITCHER GROVER ALEXANDER

CARDINALS, INSPIRED BY HORNSBY, FLASH THE STEEL OF CHAMPIONS

ALEXANDER JOINS IMMORTALS IN CARDINALS' SERIES TRIUMPH

WORLD SERIES 1926: With the Cardinals leading, 3-2, in Game 7 and the bases loaded and two out in the Yankees' half of the seventh inning, rookie Tony Lazzeri strolled to the plate ... and Cardinals manager/second baseman Rogers Hornsby strolled to the mound. Hornsby summoned Grover Cleveland Alexander, 39, to replace starter Jesse Haines. Alexander had pitched a complete-game victory the day before, and there was talk that he had celebrated well into the night. After all, there was no way he would be called upon to pitch in Game 7. Wrong. Alexander, obtained on waivers from the Cubs in June, trudged in and proceeded to strike out Lazzeri. Ol' Pete worked the final two innings as well, the game and the Series ending when Babe Ruth was thrown out while inexplicably attempting to steal second base with the potential winning run at the plate in cleanup hitter Bob Meusel. The St. Louis Cardinals were World Series champions for the first time.

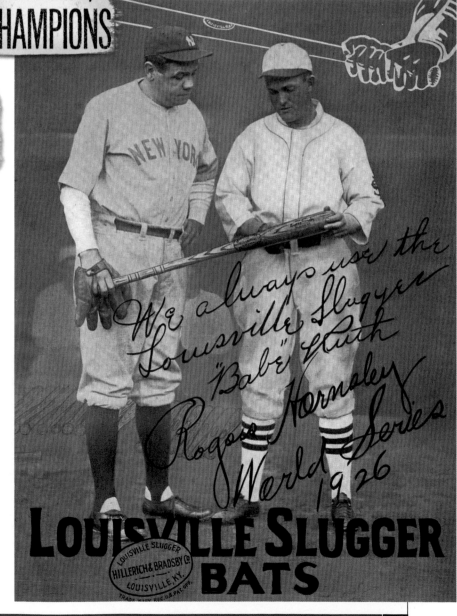

We always use the Louisville Slugger "Babe" Ruth Rogers Hornsby World Series 1926

LOUISVILLE SLUGGER BATS

LOUISVILLE SLUGGER HILLERICH & BRADSBY CO. LOUISVILLE, KY. TRADE MARK REG. U.S. PAT. OFF.

Hornsby packs up

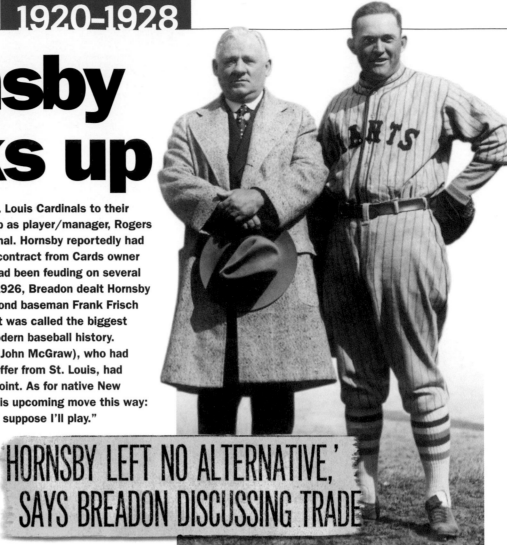

Ten weeks after leading the St. Louis Cardinals to their first World Series championship as player/manager, Rogers Hornsby no longer was a Cardinal. Hornsby reportedly had been insisting on a three-year contract from Cards owner Sam Breadon, with whom he had been feuding on several fronts. Just before Christmas 1926, Breadon dealt Hornsby to the New York Giants for second baseman Frank Frisch and pitcher Jimmy Ring in what was called the biggest and most shocking trade in modern baseball history. Hornsby (with Giants manager John McGraw), who had rejected a one-year, $50,000 offer from St. Louis, had won six batting titles to that point. As for native New Yorker Frisch, he summed up his upcoming move this way: "It's pretty hot out there, but I suppose I'll play."

'HORNSBY LEFT NO ALTERNATIVE,' SAYS BREADON DISCUSSING TRADE

OUTFIELDER HEINIE MANUSH

Tigers outfielder Heinie Manush copped the American League batting title in 1926, batting .378. Manush reached the same figure two years later while with the Browns, but he lost that batting race by one point to Washington's Goose Goslin. Manush's career batting average over 17 seasons was .330.

As The Sporting News put it, Dodgers pitcher Dazzy Vance gave the cameraman a look at how he "holds the pill for the latest piece of deception. Dazzy claims it's some kind of a screwball. ..."

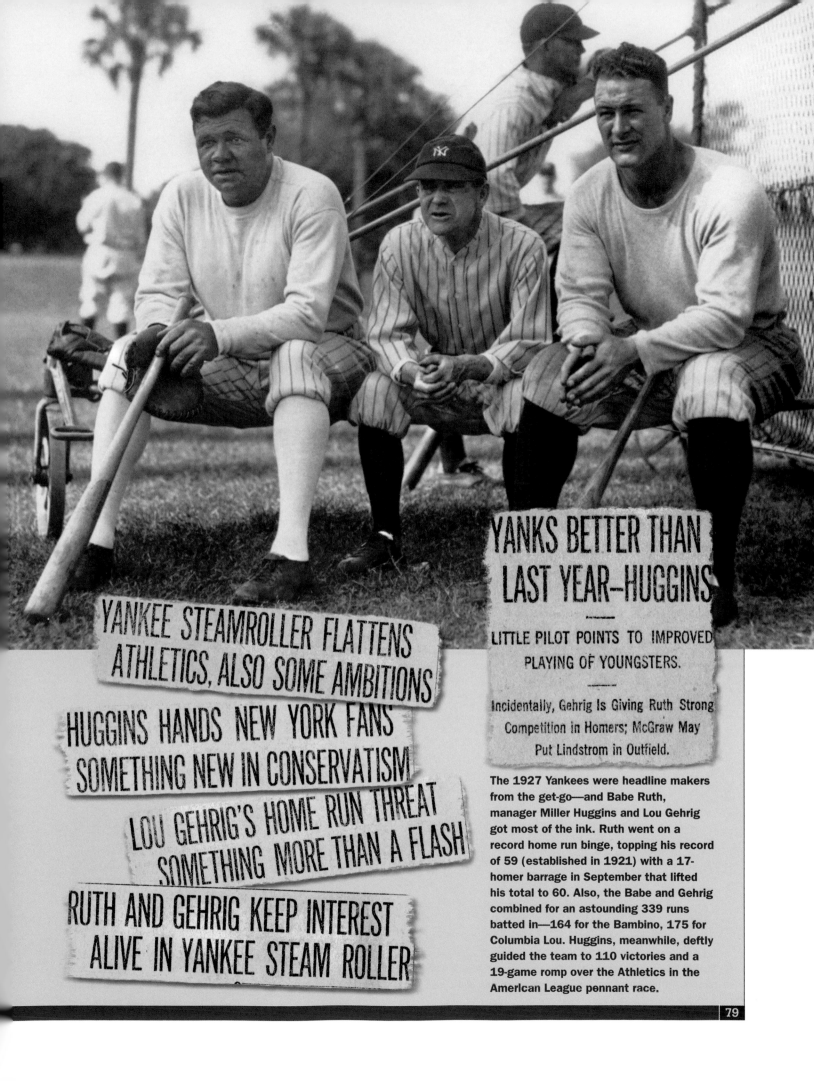

YANKEE STEAMROLLER FLATTENS ATHLETICS, ALSO SOME AMBITIONS

HUGGINS HANDS NEW YORK FANS SOMETHING NEW IN CONSERVATISM

LOU GEHRIG'S HOME RUN THREAT SOMETHING MORE THAN A FLASH

RUTH AND GEHRIG KEEP INTEREST ALIVE IN YANKEE STEAM ROLLER

YANKS BETTER THAN LAST YEAR—HUGGINS

LITTLE PILOT POINTS TO IMPROVED PLAYING OF YOUNGSTERS.

Incidentally, Gehrig Is Giving Ruth Strong Competition in Homers; McGraw May Put Lindstrom in Outfield.

The 1927 Yankees were headline makers from the get-go—and Babe Ruth, manager Miller Huggins and Lou Gehrig got most of the ink. Ruth went on a record home run binge, topping his record of 59 (established in 1921) with a 17-homer barrage in September that lifted his total to 60. Also, the Babe and Gehrig combined for an astounding 339 runs batted in—164 for the Bambino, 175 for Columbia Lou. Huggins, meanwhile, deftly guided the team to 110 victories and a 19-game romp over the Athletics in the American League pennant race.

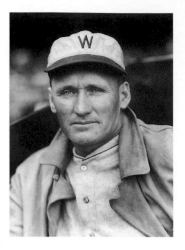

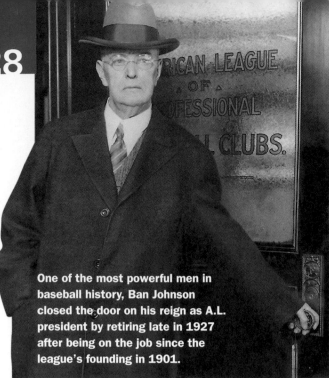

Walter Johnson's major league career came to an end in '27 when he posted a 5-6 record and a 5.08 ERA for the Senators. Johnson hurled one shutout in his final season, increasing his record total to 110. He won 20 or more games in 10 consecutive years and 12 times overall. The Big Train's biggest season was 1913 when he went 36-7, threw 11 shutouts and had a minuscule ERA of 1.14. He went on to manage Washington and Cleveland.

One of the most powerful men in baseball history, Ban Johnson closed the door on his reign as A.L. president by retiring late in 1927 after being on the job since the league's founding in 1901.

The Waner brothers (Paul, right, and Lloyd) were poison to pitchers and standout players for the Pirates' 1927 N.L. champs.

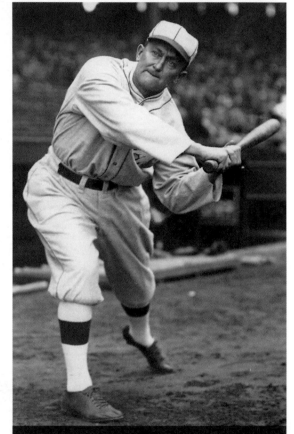

In 1927, Ty Cobb was wearing a different uniform—that of the Philadelphia Athletics. But he displayed the same old hitting stroke, even at age 40. Cobb batted .357 for the A's in '27 and reached 4,000 hits that season. He finished his playing career the next year, compiling a .323 average for Philadelphia in 95 games and increasing his hits total to a final figure of 4,191.

RUTH'S 60th

and everyone of the other 59

WAS MADE WITH

LOUISVILLE SLUGGER BATS

Standard Wherever Baseball is Played

LOUISVILLE SLUGGER HILLERICH & BRADSBY CO. LOUISVILLE, KY.

Phil B. Bekeart Co.
717 Market Street,
San Francisco, California,
Pacific Coast Representatives

Babe Ruth's 60-homer feat in 1927 seemed to get bigger treatment in the ads than it did in the news pages, but by then few of Ruth's exploits took anyone by surprise.

How the Bambino Broke His Record

A NEW HOME run record for Babe Ruth! The great New York Yankee slugger went his mark of 59, established in 1921, one better this season when on September 30 he laced out No. 60 to climax a record month for him in the homer line. He poled out 17 for the circuit during September.

A review of his homers for the 1927 season shows that 19 of his 60 smashes were made against left-handers. Here are his homers as well as his pitching victims:

Date.	Pitcher and Club.	Men on Base
Apr. 15	Ehmke, Philadelphia	0
Apr. 23	Walberg, Philadelphia	0
Apr. 24	Thurston, Washington	0
Apr. 29	Harriss, Boston	0
May 1	Quinn, Philadelphia	1
May 1	Walberg, Philadelphia	0
May 10	Gaston, St. Louis	2
May 11	Nevers, St. Louis	1
May 17	Collins, Detroit	0
May 22	Karr, Cleveland	0
May 23	Thurston, Washington	1
May 28	Thurston, Washington	2
May 29	MacFayden, Boston	0
May 30	Walberg, Philadelphia	1
May 31	Ehmke, Philadelphia	0
May 31	Quinn, Philadelphia	1
June 5	Whitehill, Detroit	0
June 7	Thomas, Chicago	0
June 11	Buckeye, Cleveland	1
June 11	Buckeye, Cleveland	0
June 12	Uhle, Cleveland	0
June 16	Zachary, St. Louis	0
June 22	Wiltse, Boston	0
June 22	Wiltse, Boston	1
June 30	Harriss, Boston	1
July 3	Lisenbee, Washington	0
July 8	Whitehill, Detroit	0
July 9	Holloway, Detroit	1
July 9	Holloway, Detroit	2
July 12	Shaute, Cleveland	0
July 24	Thomas, Chicago	0
July 26	Gaston, St. Louis	1
July 26	Gaston, St. Louis	0
July 28	Stewart, St. Louis	0
Aug. 5	Smith, Detroit	1
Aug. 10	Zachary, Washington	2
Aug. 16	Thomas, Chicago	0
Aug. 17	Connally, Chicago	0
Aug. 20	Miller, Cleveland	1
Aug. 22	Shaute, Cleveland	0
Aug. 27	Nevers, St. Louis	1
Aug. 28	Wingard, St. Louis	0
Aug. 31	Welzer, Boston	1
Sep. 6	Welzer, Boston	2
Sep. 2	Walberg, Philadelphia	0
Sep. 6	Welzer, Boston	1
Sep. 6	Russell, Boston	0
Sep. 7	MacFayden, Boston	0
Sep. 7	Harriss, Boston	1
Sep. 11	Gaston, St. Louis	0
Sep. 13	Hudlin, Cleveland	1
Sep. 13	Shaute, Cleveland	0
Sep. 16	Blankenship, Chicago	0
Sep. 18	Lyons, Chicago	1
Sep. 21	Gibson, Detroit	0
Sep. 22	Holloway, Detroit	0
Sep. 27	Quinn, Philadelphia	1
Sep. 29	Lisenbee, Washington	1
Sep. 29	Hopkins, Washington	3
Sep. 30	Zachary, Washington	1

Simply the best: the '27 Yankees

An extraordinary force, the 1927 Yankees featured a Murderers' Row lineup and four pitchers with 18 or more wins ...

Young Lou Gehrig, who had home run totals of 20 and 16 in 1925 and 1926 (his first two full years with the Yankees), stayed right with Babe Ruth for a good portion of the 1927 season in the battle for the majors' homer crown. In early September, in fact, the two were tied at 44. Ruth went on a tear the rest of the way, though, and Gehrig hit only three more homers.

KEEPING THE BABE COMPANY

FIRST BASEMAN LOU GEHRIG

'That'll cost you $100 ... for breaking up a rally.'

—Miller Huggins, manager of the 1927 Yankees (widely viewed as baseball's greatest team), purportedly to third baseman Joe Dugan after Dugan followed Earle Combs' triple, Mark Koenig's double, Babe Ruth's home run, Lou Gehrig's homer, Bob Meusel's double and Tony Lazzeri's triple with ... a single.

It was mid-March, 1928, and the opening of spring-training camps meant the story lines and storytelling were plentiful. As Rogers Hornsby's cap suggests, the Rajah had been traded again—this time from the Giants to the Braves.

... which made the franchise's 1928 powerhouse less lethal in comparison—but not by much, as opponents discovered.

WORLD SERIES 1927:

After Lloyd Waner (below, left) and brother Paul greeted Babe Ruth and Lou Gehrig, the Yankees said hello and goodbye to Pittsburgh in a hurry. New York's Murderers' Row killed the Pirates softly in the clincher of the four-game sweep, scoring the Series-deciding run when Earle Combs (right, batting earlier in the Series) danced home on a wild pitch. Ruth homered twice in the Series and drove in seven runs, and shortstop Mark Koenig batted .500.

YANKEES' FOUR STRAIGHT VICTORIES TONIC TO GAME, BLOW TO OWNERS

The 10-Man Team

The suggestion made by president John Arnold Heydler of the National League that a permanent job be created for a pinch batter for pitchers is radical enough to provoke debate and logical enough to be accepted as in line with the trend of the game.

It makes a baseball nine a 10-man team because there can be other acceptance of the introduction of a player who can be designated by a manager to do a certain thing all the afternoon. It makes of the pitcher and his man Friday, his batter, a dual compound quite unlike anything that baseball ever has seen. …

… Many baseball men think president Heydler strayed too far from the tradition of baseball in his proposal. No matter how the suggestion may appear to the baseball fan, there are persons who feel that an innovation now and then adds to the zest of things. The present has not been accepted as propitious for a change of the sort advocated, yet there may come a time when such a departure is welcomed without anybody shrinking with fear of the results.

—*December 20, 1928*

"

The designated hitter was an idea whose time had not come in 1928, but the plan nonetheless was advanced that year. Forty-five years later, the DH would become a reality in major league baseball.

YANKEES WON WORLD'S SERIES OF 1928 ON THEIR OWN MERIT

WORLD SERIES 1928: The Yankees cleaned up again, scoring their second straight sweep. This time, St. Louis fell. Lou Gehrig hit four home runs in the Series, and Babe Ruth, who had a three-homer game against the Cardinals in the 1926 Series, did it again. Waite Hoyt won twice for New York. Grover Cleveland Alexander, who had foiled the Yanks two years earlier, got hammered (a 19.80 ERA over five innings).

THE PRIDE OF NEW YORK

BABE RUTH AND LOU GEHRIG

The Yankees' 1-2 punch of Ruth and Gehrig punched out the Cardinals' lights in the '28 Series. Combined, the two sluggers had 16 hits in 27 at-bats (.593), seven home runs and 13 RBIs (nine by Gehrig).

1929

2,130 ... 56 ... 406 ..

1945

AND WAR

Background left to right: Lou Gehrig, Babe Ruth, Ted Williams and Joe DiMaggio. Foreground: Carl Hubbell (left) and Jimmie Foxx.

Left to right: Mickey Cochrane, Al Simmons, Mule Haas and Jimmie Foxx.

Dizzy Dean

It started with a bombshell, devastating news that the world was plunging into economic depression. It ended with real, honest-to-goodness bombs that devastated two cities but moved the rest of the world into a new era of technological prosperity. Somewhere between the stock market crash of 1929 and the end of World War II, baseball learned some important lessons about survival, resiliency and its ever-expanding role in the great American dream.

Survival was on everybody's mind when the nation, amid economic indicators that pointed toward a prosperous future, collapsed into the bleakest period of the 20th century. By 1932, the national income would be cut in half and unemployment would teeter near 25 percent. As Americans scratched and clawed for such necessities as shelter and food, baseball could only tighten its belt and wait for the worst of the Great Depression to pass.

With little money to spend on non-essentials, leisure attention turned toward less expensive pursuits. "Monopoly" was introduced amid a blitz of board games in 1935, and mystery writers like Agatha Christie, Dashiell Hammett and Raymond Chandler topped the list of popular novelists. But nothing filled the nation's leisure hours more comfortably than radio, which introduced the Big Band sound of Benny Goodman, Duke Ellington and Glenn Miller, comedians like Jack Benny and Fred Allen and comedy shows like Amos and Andy, Fibber McGee and Molly and The Shadow.

The radio also kept Americans in close touch with baseball, through the eyes and wonderfully descriptive words of broadcasters like Red

1929

The stock market crashes. Americans begin to endure the Great Depression.

Valentine's Day gangster massacre takes place in Chicago.

The first Academy Awards are presented. *Wings* is selected best picture.

1930

Judge Crater of the New York Supreme Court vanishes, never to be seen again.

1931

The Empire State Building opens in New York.

1932

Charles Lindbergh Jr., 20 months old, is kidnapped and murdered.

Franklin D. Roosevelt is elected President for the first of four times.

Barber, Graham McNamee, Bob Elson, Harry Hartman and Rosey Rowswell. Unable to attend a lot of games, fans still reveled over the larger-than-life (and sometimes exaggerated) exploits of Babe Ruth and Lou Gehrig, St. Louis' rollicking Gas House Gang and a New York Yankees championship machine that marched methodically through the 1930s and '40s.

Baseball battled hard to keep its product afloat. In the early 1930s, gate receipts fell by more than $6 million, putting several franchises under the financial gun. Not long after Philadelphia Athletics owner and manager Connie Mack watched his two-time defending World Series champions lose the 1931 fall classic to St. Louis, he began ridding himself of the best talent on one of the greatest teams ever assembled. Cost-cutting measures became a prerequisite of survival.

As Americans settled into the Depression routine, their hope was rekindled by the reassuring Fireside Chats and New Deal promises of President Franklin D. Roosevelt. And with optimism in the air, baseball began looking for creative ways to get fans back to the ballpark. The first All-Star Game, the brainchild of Chicago sports editor Arch Ward, was played at Comiskey Park in 1933, pitting top American League stars against their National League counterparts. Night baseball, a success at the minor league level, was introduced to the major leagues in 1935, thanks to the vision of Cincinnati general manager Larry MacPhail. The sport's new Hall of Fame named its first class in 1936 and, after decades of sometimes-bitter debate, Sunday baseball finally operated with unanimous approval.

Lou Gehrig and Joe DiMaggio

Leo Durocher

1933

Prohibition ends.

Alcatraz becomes a federal penitentiary.

The nation's first drive-in movie theater opens in Camden, N.J.

WANTED

JOHN HERBERT DILLINGER

$10,000.00
$5,000.00

1934

Bank robber John Dillinger is shot to death by federal agents in Chicago.

1935

Humorist Will Rogers dies in a plane crash in Alaska.

Congress passes the Social Security Act.

The board game "Monopoly" is first distributed by Parker Brothers.

1936

Jesse Owens wins four gold medals at the Berlin Olympics, much to the chagrin of Adolf Hitler.

Lou Gehrig and Babe Ruth

Bob Feller

Losses during the game's Depression years were not confined to the pocketbook. Ruth, the man who powered baseball's emergence from the dead-ball era, retired in 1935 with 714 home runs and teammate Gehrig, baseball's Iron Horse, was struck down by an incurable disease four years later and bid a tear-jerking farewell to a packed house at Yankee Stadium. But an outstanding cast of new talent, headed by Joe DiMaggio, Ted Williams and Bob Feller, arrived to portend another new and exciting era.

Fans in the 1930s were treated to the colorful antics of St. Louis pitcher Dizzy Dean, unofficial spokesman for the Gas House Gang, as well as the power displays of Philadelphia A's slugger Jimmie Foxx, Detroit's Hank Greenberg and Chicago Cubs outfielder Hack Wilson. Foxx hit 58 home runs, two short of Ruth's single-season record, in 1932 and Greenberg matched that performance six years later. Wilson hit a National League-record 56 in a prolific 1930 campaign during which he drove in 191 runs. But the most unbelievable effort was turned in by Cincinnati pitcher Johnny Vander Meer, who in 1938 fired consecutive no-hitters—a feat that has never been matched.

The Yankees' amazing success story continued with seven World Series championships—including a record four straight—in the 12-year span from 1932-43. The Yankee express, without Ruth and Gehrig, was running at full speed when baseball turned the corner on a new, hope-filled decade, secure in the belief that Americans had shed the austerity of the Depression and were ready to open their arms to a prosperous new beginning. But predictions of a profit-filled future were dealt a

1937	1938	1939	1940	1941
The German dirigible Hindenburg crashes in flames at Lakehurst, N.J. Aviator Amelia Earhart is lost in the Pacific Ocean.	Orson Welles' radio dramatization of a Martian invasion panics listeners.	Gone With the Wind and The Wizard of Oz are hits in movie theaters, win critical acclaim.	Disney's Fantasia introduces moviegoers to stereo sound.	Japan bombs American fleet at Pearl Harbor; U.S. declares war.

terrible blow on December 7, 1941, when Japanese planes unleashed their furor on Pearl Harbor, pushing the United States headfirst into World War II. Only a few months after DiMaggio had completed his amazing 56-game hitting streak and Williams had posted the first .400 average since Bill Terry in 1930, the sport would be shoved into an uncertain role in the background of another world crisis.

Baseball, as it had during World War I, hunkered down, prepared to ride out the storm while playing an important role in war relief efforts. But unlike World War I when events were canceled and schedules reduced, Americans were encouraged to use the game as a diversion—and President Roosevelt even issued his "Green Light" letter saying baseball should continue to operate and provide relief from wartime stress.

The game's talent base was depleted with stars like DiMaggio, Williams, Feller, Greenberg, Enos Slaughter and Johnny Mize heeding Uncle Sam's call to arms. But it muddled through a difficult four-year stretch with only a few cancellations and the continued goodwill of the sports-loving public.

As it turned out, the world crisis only stimulated interest and whetted the appetite for baseball. When the fighting ceased and American soldiers returned home to their families, it became obvious that a new wave of technology was ready to fuel a sports explosion. Not even the stunning death in 1944 of commissioner Kenesaw Mountain Landis could delay a new "Golden Age" that would exceed anybody's wildest expectations.

Joe DiMaggio

Hank Greenberg

1942

Casablanca premieres in movie houses.

1943

Oklahoma! opens on Broadway.

1944

GI Bill of Rights is passed.

Bandleader Glenn Miller's plane disappears on a flight over the English Channel.

1945

U.S. drops atomic bombs in Japan, hastening the end of World War II.

The United Nations Charter is drawn up in San Francisco.

You can't tell the players without ...

The Yankees, in 1929, were the first club to wear large numbers on the back of their uniforms on a permanent basis, home and away. They based numbers on batting-order position. Above, cleanup man Lou Gehrig greets No. 3 hitter Babe Ruth.

RADIO HIKES SERIES ALL OVER CONTINENT

THE most extensive radio hook-up ever carried out was effected by the two leading national broadcasting companies — the National and Columbia—to put the World's Series games on the air. Through the intricate chain network of the two companies it was expected that the descriptive stories of the games would reach every section of the North American continent.

Graham McNamee was at the microphone for the National Broadcasting Company, while Ted Husing described the details for Columbia.

Here are some of the larger sta-

You didn't have to be there to be plugged in to the action. Thanks to ever-expanding radio coverage, fans from Portland, Maine, to Portland, Ore., were able to stay on top of baseball's major events.

Connie Mack, whose A's last played in the Fall Classic in 1914, had a gifted 1929 team ready to meet the Cubs of Joe McCarthy (right). Mack's standouts included Jimmie Foxx, Al Simmons, Mickey Cochrane, Lefty Grove, George Earnshaw and Rube Walberg.

Mr. Mack returns to the Series

EHMKE REAL HERO OF OPENER, FANNING 13 CHICAGO BATTERS

WORLD SERIES 1929:
Surprise starter Howard Ehmke (right) got Philadelphia going in Game 1 with a record strikeout performance, then the A's took the heart out of the Cubs with a 10-run seventh inning in Game 4 that overcame an 8-0 deficit. The A's closed out the Series in Game 5, scoring all their runs in the bottom of the ninth in a 3-2 win. Mule Haas had a three-run inside-the-park home run in that big A's uprising in Game 4, and he hit a game-tying homer in the clincher.

EHMKE'S GREAT WIN INSPIRATION TO A'S

VETERAN HELPS TO ERASE SCHEDULE ADVANTAGE OF THE CUBS.

Grove Also Plays Important Part in Role of Relief Pitcher; Ten-run Inning Shows Punch of Macks.

GIANT LIGHTS PROVIDE VISION FOR NIGHT PLAY

Attempts at staging night baseball had been made in the past, but the advanced lighting system introduced by the Des Moines club in the Western League in 1930 turned some doubters into believers. The quality of play didn't suffer, and fans were afforded more chances to attend games. Soon, other minor league venues experimented with nighttime baseball. Major league officials watched with increased interest as permanent light standards went up. But Senators owner Clark Griffith, for one, wasn't impressed. "Night baseball is just a step above dog racing," he said. Another Griffith-ism: "Baseball was meant to be played in the Lord's broad sunshine. There is no chance of night ball becoming popular in the big cities. People there are educated to see the best. High-class baseball cannot be played under artificial lights. ..."

Test at Des Moines Regarded as Success

Minor Magnates Express Enthusiasm Over Trial

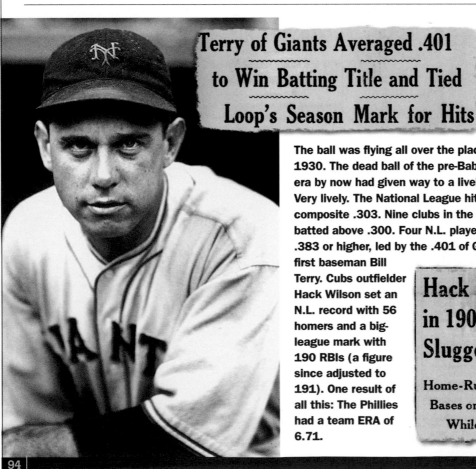

Terry of Giants Averaged .401 to Win Batting Title and Tied Loop's Season Mark for Hits

The ball was flying all over the place in 1930. The dead ball of the pre-Babe Ruth era by now had given way to a lively ball. Very lively. The National League hit a composite .303. Nine clubs in the majors batted above .300. Four N.L. players hit .383 or higher, led by the .401 of Giants first baseman Bill Terry. Cubs outfielder Hack Wilson set an N.L. record with 56 homers and a big-league mark with 190 RBIs (a figure since adjusted to 191). One result of all this: The Phillies had a team ERA of 6.71.

Hack Wilson Bats in 190 Runs, Tops Sluggers in N. L.

Home-Run King Has Most Bases on Balls, Strikeouts While Setting Mark

Baseball Will Never See Another $80,000 Salary

RUTH AND RUPPERT COMPROMISE WHEN BABE SIGNS FOR TWO YEARS

NEW SALARY REPRESENTS $80,000 PER ANNUM

RUTH NEAR MILLION MARK IN EARNINGS

AT THE end of the 1931 season, Babe Ruth, as a result of his

Average 52 home runs and 151 RBIs over the previous four seasons and reign as baseball's box-office king and good things will happen to you. A particularly good thing happened to Babe Ruth preceding the 1930 season: He signed a two-year contract calling for an unprecedented $80,000 each year. After working out the deal with Yankees owner Jacob Ruppert, Ruth went out and had another banner season in '30: 49 homers, 153 runs batted in and a .359 batting average.

WORLD SERIES 1930, 1931: They were powerhouse teams of their era, so when the A's and Cardinals met in successive Fall Classics, it wasn't surprising. In 1930, the A's got great pitching from George Earnshaw and Lefty Grove (far right, with catcher Mickey Cochrane and manager Connie Mack) and won their second straight Series. Earnshaw allowed St. Louis only two earned runs over 25 innings, and Grove yielded just three in 19 innings. Jimmie Foxx provided the big blow in the six-game Series, breaking a scoreless tie in Game 5 with a two-run homer in the ninth inning. The Cards rode the performances of Pepper Martin, Burleigh Grimes and Bill Hallahan to victory a year later. Center fielder Martin collected 12 hits, batted .500 and stole five bases. Grimes and Hallahan each won two games.

WORLD SERIES 1932: It was Game 3, and the Wrigley Field throng was picking on the big guy. Babe Ruth had incurred the wrath of Cubs fans for derogatory comments about the Chicago club after it had voted a former Ruth teammate, Mark Koenig, only a half-share of the '32 Series pot after Koenig batted .353 in 33 games after being obtained from the minors. Also stirring emotions was former Cubs manager Joe McCarthy's return to Wrigley as manager of the vaunted and hated Yankees.

The Yanks had won the first two games of the Series in New York, and this game was tied, 4-4, with one out in fifth as Ruth awaited the first pitch from the Cubs' Charlie Root. The Babe, who had hit a three-run homer off Root in the first inning, took a called strike. Root then missed with two pitches. Another called strike followed, and Ruth acknowledged it—just as he had strike one—with a raised arm. The crowd noise intensified. Ruth then seemingly gestured toward center field, as if to say the next pitch was headed in that direction. That's exactly where it went—over the fence near the base of the flagpole.

Nearly 70 years later, no one really knows what Ruth's gesture meant. (Babe was always coy about it.) But everyone knows that the Yankees, featuring Ruth and Lou Gehrig (who homered after Ruth's "called shot" and also hit two in that game), were an irresistible force. They won Game 3 by a 7-5 score and went on to a sweep.

BATS THAT LEFT CUBS BATTY

LOU GEHRIG   BABE RUTH

M'CARTHY GAINS SWEET REVENGE IN BEATING CUBS FOUR STRAIGHT

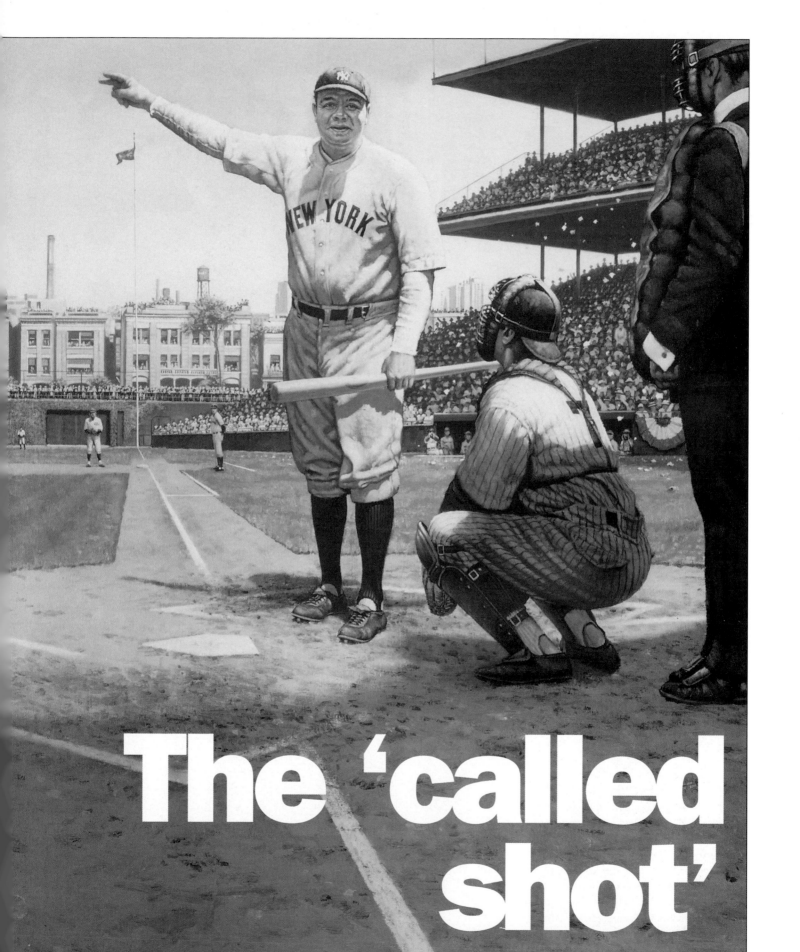

The 'called shot'

MAJORS' ALL-STARS MEET

Leading Representatives of American and

Although the Giants' Carl Hubbell (left) and the Athletics' Lefty Grove were expected to start the first All-Star Game (as The Sporting News reported in a headline, right page), they actually pitched in relief in the 1933 midsummer classic. Grove hurled shutout ball over three innings; Hubbell worked two scoreless innings. The starting pitchers turned out to be Cardinals lefthander Bill Hallahan for the National League and the Yankees' Lefty Gomez for the American League.

IN 'GAME OF THE CENTURY'

National Leagues to Test Strength on Field

FANS' DREAM OF GREATEST GAME COMES TRUE AT CHICAGO ON JULY 6

Americans Hold 13-Point Hitting Advantage Over Nationals; Game Will Start as Southpaw Battle, With Grove and Hubbell on Mound; 49,000 Expected to Attend

Wanting a major sports attraction to be part of Chicago's Century of Progress Exposition in 1933, Chicago Tribune sports editor Arch Ward dreamed up the idea for a major league Dream Game that would match American League stars against their counterparts in the National League. Commissioner Kenesaw Mountain Landis and club owners bought into the idea, although not with great exuberance.

If baseball's executives were lukewarm to the plan, the game's fans were not. Given the opportunity to determine the makeup of the teams, they voted with considerable zeal. And 47,595 turned out at Comiskey Park for the All-Star Game, which matched special managerial selections Connie Mack and the retired John McGraw.

Babe Ruth, now 38, cracked the first home run in All-Star history, hitting a two-run shot in the third inning. Mack, obviously out to win, made only one change among his position players in the entire game. The A.L. won, 4-2.

A fashion note: A.L. players wore their regular home uniforms; the N.L team was dressed in special uniforms with "National League" spelled out on the front.

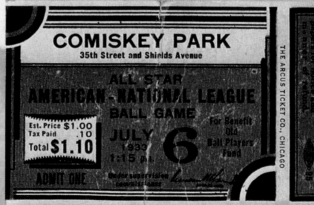

HONOR PAID NEW ENDURANCE KING OF MAJORS

TRIBUTE to Lou Gehrig's achievement in surpassing the continuous service record of Everett Scott of playing in 1307 consecutive games was paid the New York Yankee first baseman at Sportsman's Park, St. Louis, Mo., August 17, when he participated in his 1308th successive contest. President William Harridge of the American League was present for the occasion and Lou was presented with a trophy, emblematic of his feat, on behalf of The Sporting News by its editor, E. G. Brands. Scott was invited to attend, but he found it impossible to do so.

Third Baseman Sewell of the Yankees, shown in the picture, held the second highest consecutive mark until Gehrig came along. He played in 1103 games without a miss and, like Gehrig, performed his trick with one club. Sewell put over his string with Cleveland, while all of Gehrig's games have been played with New York. Scott, in making the old record, was with two clubs, the Boston Red Sox and Yankees. His string was stopped on May 6, 1925, and on June 1, the same year, Gehrig began his remarkable run.

The presentation of the trophy is pictured above, showing, from left to right: President Harridge, E. G. Brands, Lou Gehrig and Joe Sewell.

Everett Scott, baseball's iron man. At least that was Scott's distinction until August 1933 when former teammate Lou Gehrig played in his 1,308th consecutive game (left). Scott, a shortstop, had appeared in 1,307 straight games for the Red Sox and Yankees in a streak that ended in 1925—the same year that Gehrig began his run. In fact, Gehrig began his streak less than four weeks after Scott's came to an end.

JOE DiMAGGIO'S *61*-GAME STREAK

Playing his first full season of minor league ball at age 18—and playing it only one rung below the major league level—outfielder Joe DiMaggio reeled off a 61-game hitting streak in 1933 for San Francisco of the Pacific Coast League.

GIANTS ASSERT RIGHT TO RANKING AS ONE OF GREAT CLUBS OF GAME

WORLD SERIES 1933: Playing in their first Series without John McGraw (first baseman Bill Terry had succeeded McGraw as manager in June 1932), the Giants dispatched the Senators in five games. Carl Hubbell won two games, not allowing an earned run in 20 innings. Young slugger Mel Ott batted .389 for New York and hit a Series-deciding home run in 10th inning of Game 5, which 43-year-old reliever Dolf Luque won with 4⅓ innings of shutout relief. Washington, managed by 26-year-old shortstop Joe Cronin, was making its last Series appearance in franchise history.

NEW YORK GIANTS---THE 1933 CHAMPIONS!

Carl Hubbell: the star of stars

If anyone questioned whether the All-Star Game concept would fly—wondered if there would be compelling drama in this extravaganza—all doubt was erased in 1934 when Giants lefthander Carl Hubbell struck out, in succession, Babe Ruth (Yankees), Lou Gehrig (Yankees), Jimmie Foxx (Athletics), Al Simmons (White Sox) and Joe Cronin (Senators). Four of Hubbell's victims (below, left to right, Simmons, Gehrig, Ruth and Foxx) gathered before the game in anticipation of a victory, which they got despite Hubbell's efforts. The American League rallied for a 9-7 victory at the Polo Grounds, Hubbell's home park.

The Gas House Gang

WORLD SERIES 1934: The Cardinals were boisterous, colorful, aggressive, immensely talented ... and fearless. Trailing the Tigers, three games to two, as the Series moved back to Detroit, they knew that winning twice in the Tigers' ballpark would take some doing. This brash gang—this Gas House Gang—had the wherewithal to do it. In Game 6, St. Louis rookie pitcher Paul Dean tossed a seven-hitter and delivered a game-winning single. Then it was brother Diz's turn. In the winner-take-all game, Dizzy Dean, who notched 30 victories in the regular season, tossed a six-hitter and got 17-hit support in an 11-0 romp that deteriorated into a mess. The Cards struck for seven runs in the third inning, the outburst spiced by manager Frankie Frisch's three-run double. In the sixth, Joe Medwick (right)

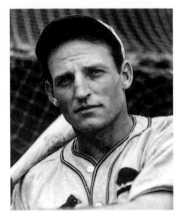

CARDINALS WIN FROM THE TIGERS IN SIXTH MILLION-DOLLAR SERIES

knocked in a run with a triple, a play on which he slid hard into third baseman Marv Owen. When Medwick returned to his left field station, disgruntled Tigers fans hurled bottles, fruit and vegetables in his direction. It wasn't pretty. Nor was the way Detroit played in the final two games.

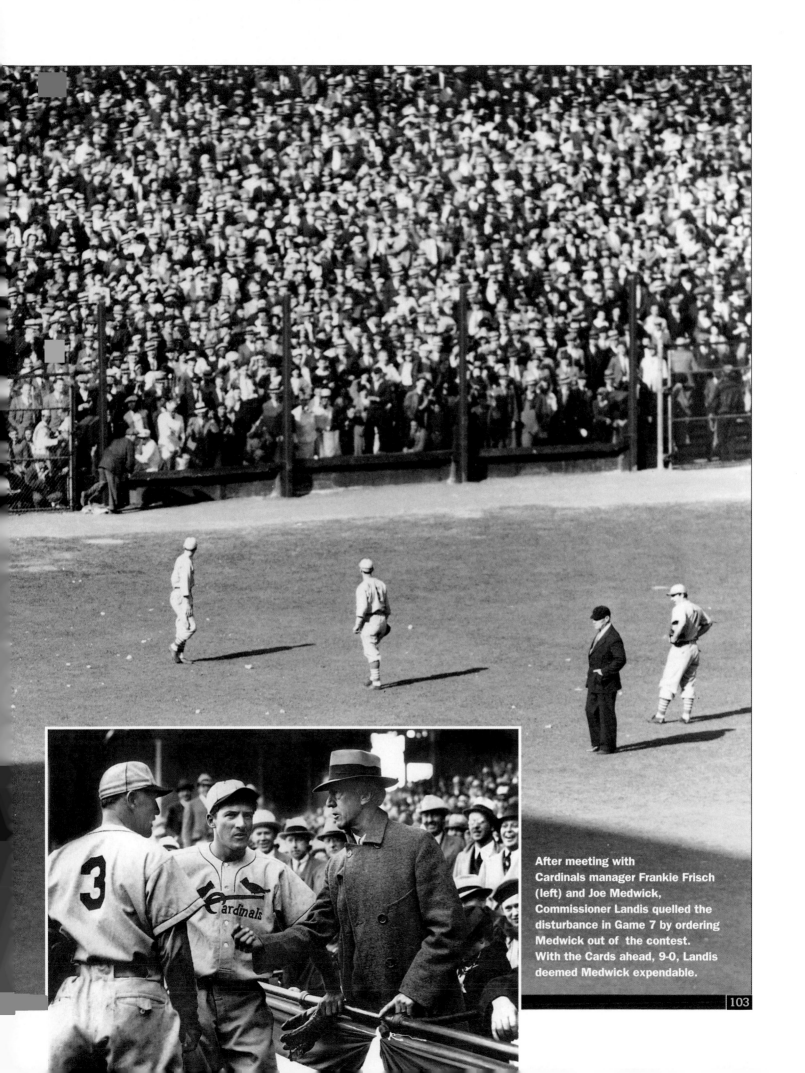

After meeting with Cardinals manager Frankie Frisch (left) and Joe Medwick, Commissioner Landis quelled the disturbance in Game 7 by ordering Medwick out of the contest. With the Cards ahead, 9-0, Landis deemed Medwick expendable.

Connie Mack, wheeler-dealer

Athletics owner/manager Connie Mack was never one to sit idly by. Two decades earlier, he had dismantled his A's team in the wake of an upset loss to the Braves in the World Series. Now, trying to survive in tough Depression-era times, he began disassembling his club shortly after it lost the 1931 Series to St. Louis. In a series of sales and trades, Al Simmons and Mule Haas went to the White Sox in September 1932, Lefty Grove, Max Bishop and Rube Walberg to the Red Sox in December 1933, Mickey Cochrane to the Tigers and George Earnshaw to the White Sox, both also at the end of '33, and Jimmie Foxx to the Red Sox in December 1935.

A BIG GAME HUNTER'S DREAM

RED SOX CORRAL

FOXX

TOM YAWKEY

KRENZ

—Courtesy Philadelphia Record and New York Post

Jimmie Foxx: off to Boston

It was understandable that Red Sox owner Tom Yawkey had visions of slugger Jimmie Foxx dancing in his head (cartoon, page 104). After all, Foxx had hit 58 home runs for Philadelphia in 1932 and won the Triple Crown in 1933—and his powerful swing seemed a perfect fit for Fenway Park and its cozy left field wall. Yawkey's dream was realized after the 1935 season when a trade with the Athletics put Double X in a Boston uniform. Joining the Red Sox at age 28, Foxx had six banner seasons in Beantown—none better than 1938, when he pounded 50 homers, drove in 175 runs and batted .349.

So long, Babe...

A National League arbiter for 37 seasons, Bill Klem umpired in 18 World Series and 104 Series games, both records.

Babe Ruth (with Lou Gehrig) finished his sensational 15-year run as a Yankee in 1934, then ended his active career in 1935 by playing 28 games for the Boston Braves. The Babe went out in style, hammering three home runs for the Braves in one game at Pittsburgh's Forbes Field in his final week as a player.

WORLD SERIES 1935:

Saying a rabbit's foot might not provide enough good luck in the Fall Classic, Tigers outfielder Goose Goslin (below) hauled out a whole live rabbit. Misfortune struck nonetheless when Detroit superstar Hank Greenberg suffered a wrist fracture in Game 2 and missed the last four games against the Cubs. Still, the Tigers prevailed as Goslin, in the 129th and last Series at-bat of his career, singled home the decisive run in the bottom of the ninth inning of Game 6. It was Detroit's first World Series title in five tries.

B.P.S. PAINTS
MANUF'D BY
THE PATTERSON-SARGENT CO.
CHICAGO, CLEVELAND, NEW YORK,
KANSAS CITY, St. PAUL

Cincinnati Lights the Way in Big League Style

President Roosevelt Assists in Epochal Event from Capital

Five years after night ball was introduced in the minor leagues, the Reds brought arc lights to the majors. Cincinnati general manager Larry MacPhail, who had found nighttime games to be a huge success when he ran the Columbus franchise in the American Association, and owner Powel Crosley Jr. helped flip the switch on May 24, 1935. The Reds edged the Phillies, 2-1.

LIGHTS A BEACON ALONG THE RHINE

POWEL CROSLEY

106

...Hello, Joe!

With Ruth in retirement and Lou Gehrig nearing his 33rd birthday, the Yankees' next great player arrived in 1936 when Joe DiMaggio (left, with Dizzy Dean at the '36 All-Star Game) joined the club. DiMaggio, who in 1935 had batted .398 with 154 RBIs for his hometown San Francisco Seals of the Pacific Coast League, reacted badly to heat treatments at the Yankees' spring-training camp and didn't make his major league debut until May 3, 1936. Even so, he had a 29-homer, 125-RBI rookie season.

When voting results were announced in 1936 for the first class of inductees into baseball's Hall of Fame, only five former players—Ty Cobb (the leading vote-getter), Babe Ruth, Honus Wagner, Christy Mathewson and Walter Johnson—were named on the required 75 percent of the ballots. The Hall of Fame and Museum didn't become a physical reality in Cooperstown, N.Y., for another three years, at which time 10 members of the Hall got together (below, front row, left to right: Eddie Collins, Ruth, Connie Mack and Cy Young; back row, from left: Wagner, Grover Cleveland Alexander, Tris Speaker, Nap Lajoie, George Sisler and Johnson).

Dizzy Dean: larger than life

'It ain't bragging if you can do it.'

—*Dizzy Dean*

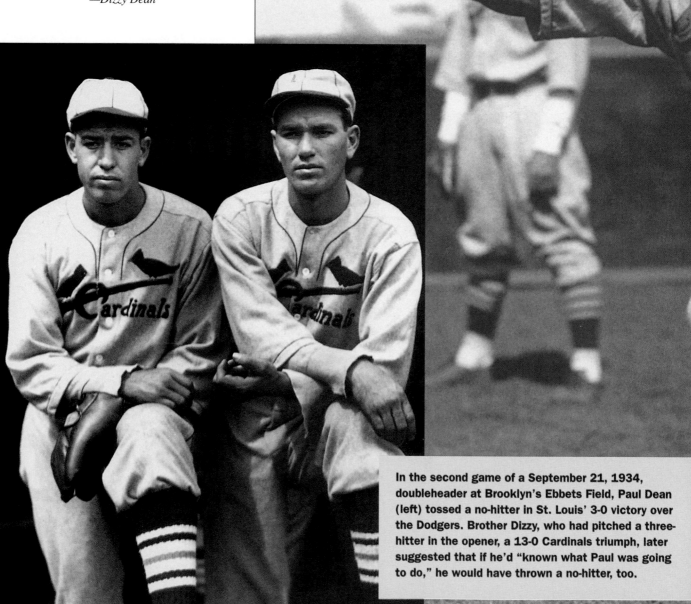

In the second game of a September 21, 1934, doubleheader at Brooklyn's Ebbets Field, Paul Dean (left) tossed a no-hitter in St. Louis' 3-0 victory over the Dodgers. Brother Dizzy, who had pitched a three-hitter in the opener, a 13-0 Cardinals triumph, later suggested that if he'd "known what Paul was going to do," he would have thrown a no-hitter, too.

'The doctors X-rayed my head and found nothing.'

—Dizzy Dean

When Dean pinch ran for the Cardinals' Spud Davis in Game 4 of the 1934 World Series, he bolted for second base on a ground ball off the bat of Pepper Martin. Tigers shortstop Billy Rogell threw to first on the play, but Dean forgot to duck as he barreled into second. The ball caromed off his forehead and landed in right field.

Dean later announced— or so the legend goes—the findings of the X-rays.

Dizzy Dean always talked a good game. More important, he pitched it, too.

In his first five full seasons with the Cardinals (1932 through 1936), Dean won 18, 20, 30, 28 and 24 games. He led the N.L. in strikeouts in four of those seasons.

The last National Leaguer to win 30 games in one season—he achieved the feat in 1934, when he and brother Paul combined for 49 victories—Dean saw his career falter in 1937. Pitching in the All-Star Game at Washington, he suffered a toe fracture when struck by Earl Averill's line smash. Only 26, Dean apparently tried to come back too soon and put stress on his arm. He won only 17 more games in the majors (16 of them for the Cubs, to whom he was traded in April 1938).

DIZZY FOGS CHICAGO WITH ARM MYSTERY

—

WITHDRAWS WITH AILING FLIPPER, LATER SAYS IT'S HIS LEG

'The good Lord was good to me. He gave me a strong body, a good right arm and a weak mind.'

—Dizzy Dean

Rapid Robert

The kid's name was Bob Feller, and he was from Van Meter, Iowa. The Indians nailed down his contract rights only after commissioner Kenesaw Mountain Landis approved their methods of outmaneuvering other clubs for his services. Bypassing the minor leagues, young Feller burst upon the major league scene in spectacular fashion in 1936. After six relief appearances, he got his big chance on August 23—and made the most of it:

> AT CLEVELAND—Bob Feller, 17-year-old Cleveland rookie right-hander, came within one strike-out of equaling the league record and two whiffs of tying the modern major league mark when he fanned 15 Brownies, yielded six blows and the Indians won, 4 to 1, for a clean sweep of the three-game series.
> Feller, who was making his first start in the majors, averaged two strike-outs an inning for the first seven frames, and had 14 to his credit going into the eighth. The Tribe recruit failed to fan any of the St. Louisans in that inning and it was not until after two were out in the ninth that he notched his fifteenth victim, striking out Lyn Lary to end the game. Of the 11 Brownies who faced Feller at the plate, only Harlond Clift and Ray Pepper failed to fan at least once.
> After successive doubles by Beau Bell and Lary accounted for the lone St. Louis run in the sixth, the Tribe took advantage of a streak of wildness by Earl Caldwell, who issued three passes, coupled with a double by Averill and a single by Vosmik, to score three tallies in their half of the stanza. Score:
> St. Louis. AB.R.H.O.A. | Cleveland. AB.R.H.O.A.

Three weeks later, Feller turned in a 17-strikeout game against the Philadelphia Athletics.

HIS SMOKE LEAVES WHIFFS

ROBERT FELLER

Stengel's dismissal irks Brooklyn fandom

Charles Dillon Stengel was anything but a smashing success in his first go-round as a major league manager. After minor league managerial jobs at Worcester and Toledo and a two-year stint as a Dodgers coach, Casey was named Brooklyn manager. He guided the Dodgers in 1934, 1935 and 1936, years in which the club finished sixth, fifth and seventh. Successful? No. Popular? Yes. Brooklyn fans had taken to the affable, fun-loving Casey when he was a Dodgers outfielder two decades earlier, and the bond was still there.

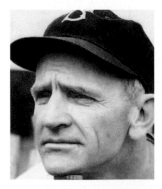

Dodgers' Failure Laid to Shortage of Talen

Tommy Holmes Contends Casey Did as Well as Any Manage
Could Have Done With Flatbush Follies; Burleigh Grimes
Favored to Win Ebbets Field Appointment

President Franklin D. Roosevelt, with Senators owner Clark Griffith and managers Bill Terry (Giants) and Joe McCarthy (Yankees), threw out the first ball at the 1937 All-Star Game at Washington's Griffith Stadium.

WORLD SERIES 1936, 1937: It was Subway Series time—both years. Playing their first Fall Classic without Babe Ruth and their first with Joe DiMaggio, the Yankees won in six games in 1936. The Yanks' Tony Lazzeri, who clubbed two bases-loaded home runs in one game in the regular season, hit a grand slam and drove in five runs in the American Leaguers' 18-4 romp in Game 2. Bill Dickey also had five RBIs. Lou Gehrig's two-run shot off Carl Hubbell in Game 4 put the Bronx Bombers into a commanding three games-to-one lead. Lefty Gomez won two games for the Yanks. In '37, the Yankees prevailed in five games, with Gomez again chalking up two victories. The tone was set for the Giants' quick demise in Game 1 when the Yankees, getting bases-loaded singles from DiMaggio and fellow outfielder George Selkirk, broke loose for seven sixth-inning runs.

Greenberg races time and Ruth mark

When Detroit's Hank Greenberg connected for two home runs in the second game of a September 27, 1938, doubleheader against the St. Louis Browns, he moved within two of Babe Ruth's record of 60 in one season.

The schedule was running out, though. Greenberg had five games remaining to tie or surpass Ruth. He did neither. In fact, the big first baseman was blanked the rest of the way.

Still, Greenberg's 58 homers tied Jimmie Foxx's 1932 total as the third-highest figure in major league history (behind Ruth's 60 in 1927 and the Bambino's 59 in 1921).

A prolific run-producer, Greenberg knocked in 146 runs in '38 after finishing with 183 RBIs in 1937. In 1935, he had 170—103 of them by the All-Star break.

DETROIT CHECKS UP AS TIGERS CHECK OUT

—

TEAM NEEDS OVERHAULING IF IT IS TO BECOME CHALLENGER

—

18 Youngsters Recalled in Hope of Finding Replacements; Hank Greenberg Falls Two Short of Homer Mark

Greenberg got plenty of offensive support in '38 from Tigers second baseman Charlie Gehringer (next to Greenberg). A Detroit fixture since 1926, Gehringer drove in 107 runs.

BOMBERS SET ALL-TIME RECORD BY CAPTURING THIRD TITLE IN ROW

Crushing of Cubs in Four Straight Tilts Accomplished Through Superior Pitching, Fielding and Timely Hits; McCarthy's Second Quick Conquest of His Old Club

WORLD SERIES 1938:

The Cubs' big moment had come a week before the Series when, with darkness descending upon Wrigley Field, manager Gabby Hartnett (left) hit a two-out, ninth-inning home run against Pittsburgh that moved Chicago past the Pirates and into first place. Then true darkness descended: The Cubs were swept by the Yankees in the Series. Red Ruffing won Games 1 and 4 for the Yankees, who got a .400 average and six RBIs from Joe Gordon but zero RBIs from Lou Gehrig (who had slipped to a .295 batting mark in the regular season). Pitching mostly on guile, the Cubs' Dizzy Dean fought off the Yanks for seven innings in Game 2 but gave up a decisive two-run homer in the eighth to Frank Crosetti. Gehrig (above, right) and Joe DiMaggio chatted with New York mayor Fiorello La Guardia before Game 1 in Chicago.

An Iowa Air Ace

Ronald (Dutch) Reagan

A THOROUGH knowledge of the game, a gift for narrative and a pleasant voice have won 25-year-old Ronald (Dutch) Reagan, sports announcer for Station WHO, Des Moines, Ia., a wide following among fans, and the real scope of his popularity is brought out by his showing as a prominent contender in THE SPORTING NEWS popularity contest for broadcasters.

After graduation from Eureka College, Eureka, Ill., where he was active in athletics, Reagan was a life guard for seven years. During his periods of cogitations between rescues, he decided he wanted to

Vander Meer: two no-hitters in a row

Reds lefthander Johnny Vander Meer was a promising pitcher, all right. In 1936, he had been named The Sporting News' Minor League Player of the Year after striking out 295 batters in 214 innings in the Piedmont League; in '37, he showed excellent potential in a stint with Cincinnati. But what Vander Meer did in 1938 was unfathomable: He threw consecutive no-hitters. First, he shackled the Boston Bees on June 11 at Cincinnati's Crosley Field, then he held the Dodgers hitless on June 15 in the first night game played at Brooklyn's Ebbets Field (left).

The Iron Horse breaks down

It seemed as if nothing could stop Lou Gehrig. Nothing that in any way could be described as ordinary. He had overcome illness, injury and fatigue in putting together a consecutive-game playing streak that reached 2,130 games on April 30, 1939. Coming off what for him what had been a down season in 1938 (29 homers, 114 RBIs and his first sub-.300 average since 1925, all accompanied by suggestions that he wasn't the Gehrig of old), the Iron Horse got off to a horrendous start in '39 with four hits in 28 at-bats. He appeared lethargic, and his coordination seemed a little off.

After an off-day on May 1, Gehrig took himself out of the Yankees' lineup on May 2 in Detroit (lower left). He never appeared in another game in the major leagues.

It later was disclosed that Gehrig was suffering from a terribly debilitating disease, amyotrophic lateral sclerosis. Or, as we know it today, *Lou Gehrig's disease.*

GEHRIG SLUMP BIG
NEW YORK MYSTERY

Gehrig Falls Below .300

OLD IRON HORSE NOT WHAT HE USED TO BE

Larrupin' Lou Goes Hitless in Ten Trips on 35th Birthday; Giants Run Into Sink-Holes on Ho

WITHDRAWAL OF GEHRIG, DIMAG INJURY JAR YANKS

Larrupin' Lou Benches Himself in Detroit After Playing in 2,130 Consecutive Games; Joe May Be Out for Weeks;

Lou Gehrig Day (left) honored a man whose baseball skills, work ethic, humility, kindness and courage had won the admiration of millions. But in an emotional ceremony at packed Yankee Stadium on July 4, 1939, Gehrig paid his own tribute to fans and former teammates (including members of the 1927 Yankees) by saying, in part:

"Fans ... you have been reading about a bad break I got. Yet today I consider myself the luckiest man on the face of the earth. I have been in ballparks for 17 years, and have never received anything but kindness and encouragement from you fans. Look at these grand men (old teammates). Which of you wouldn't consider it the highlight of his career just to associate with them for even one day? ..."

Gehrig died on June 2, 1941.

"

A Spartan in courage, a willing worker, loyal to his club and teammates, a clean liver and a lovable character, Lou Gehrig sheds distinction on the game while he is gaining credit for himself, and his name is certain to live long in the annals of the sport.

—*August 24, 1933, on Gehrig's impact during the prime of his career.*

"

Cooperstown Cavalcade Marked by Greatest Galaxy of Past and Present Diamond Stars Ever Assembled

The Hall of Fame had a physical presence in Cooperstown, N.Y., in 1939, the year the shrine was dedicated. Inducted in '39: Al Spalding, Eddie Collins, Cap Anson, Willie Keeler, Buck Ewing, Hoss Radbourn, George Sisler, Charles Comiskey, Candy Cummings and ailing Lou Gehrig (for whom the waiting period was waived).

BOMBERS' FOURTH TITLE IN ROW WON IN SECOND STRAIGHT 'SLAM'

Timely Home-Run Hitting, Stout Pitching, Sparkling Defense Feature Run-Over of Reds; Top Honors Taken by Rookie Keller, With 19 Total Bases on Seven Safeties

WORLD SERIES 1939, 1940: The Reds fell in yet another Yankees sweep in '39 as New York won its fourth straight Series title. Yanks rookie Charlie Keller batted .438 with six RBIs. In Game 4, Joe DiMaggio singled home the winning run in the 10th inning, then circled the bases when catcher Ernie Lombardi lay dazed after a collision with Keller. In '40, the Reds beat Detroit when Bucky Walters pitched a shutout and homered in Game 6 and Paul Derringer won a tight Game 7.

Red Barber interviewed Dodgers manager Leo Durocher (right photo) on August 26, 1939, after New York experimental station W2XBS carried the first telecast of a major league game. Reds manager Bill McKechnie (1) also was interviewed. The game was the opener of a doubleheader at Ebbets Field.

Ted arrives ... and so does TV

Just days away from his making his official big-league debut, Red Sox newcomer Ted Williams (left) takes a cut against the Boston Braves in an exhibition game at Braves Field in April 1939. The game was the first in Boston for Williams, who was coming off a monster season (43 homers, 142 RBIs, .366 average) at Minneapolis of the American Association.

Pvt. Hank Greenberg, U.S. Army

Drafted into the Army, Tigers icon Hank Greenberg left his club in May 1941. Unwilling to seek a deferment (he didn't want to be labeled a shirker, nor did he want the press hounding him about his draft status), Greenberg said he welcomed entry into the service. He also said he expected to be back with Detroit in 1942.

"It is not as if I am through with baseball for life," Greenberg said. "I'll be back next year, and there is no reason why I shouldn't be as good as I ever was."

When Pearl Harbor was attacked and the United States was thrust into World War II, virtually everyone's plans changed—including Greenberg's. He remained in the Army until mid-1945.

Greenberg's service to his country (middle photo, right, and sketch, bottom) turned the already highly popular athlete into an endearing figure.

DI MAG HOT AT GATE, AS WELL AS PLATE

—

RECORD HITTING STREAK TURNS JOE INTO BOX-OFFICE ATTRACTION

Giuseppe Pushes Willie Keeler's Mark Into Discard With Dramatic Homer; Odell Hale Helping Giants

DI MAG TOUCHES OFF BOMBER TIME FUSE

—

WHOLE TEAM RIDES WITH JOLTING JOE ON RECORD HIT STREAK

19-Year-Old Record of Sisler
Falls Before Relentless Drive
Of Yankees' Great Outfielder

Starting May 15, Coast Italian Hits in 41st and 42nd Games, June 29, to Surpass Standard for Sustained Hitting; Work Makes Him Standout for Month of Brides

ag's 56

Joe DiMaggio had won American League batting titles in 1939 and 1940, so his ability to mount a lengthy batting streak came as no surprise in 1941. But when the string extended into the 30s ... then the 40s ... and finally into the 50s, the American sporting public was disbelieving.

The Yankee Clipper, who broke George Sisler's American League record (and modern major league mark) of 41 on June 29 and shattered Willie Keeler's all-time high of 44 on July 2, kept right on hitting. He stretched his streak to 56 games on July 16 at Cleveland Stadium. The next night, he was stopped by Indians pitcher Al Smith and Jim Bagby Jr.—and by third baseman Ken Keltner, who made two outstanding plays on ground balls.

DiMaggio batted .408 during the streak, hit 15 home runs and drove in 55 runs.

So how did Joltin' Joe react to having his record achievement end? He went out and hit safely in his next 16 games.

67,468 CROWD SEES DIMAGGIO STOPPED

THE greatest night crowd of baseball history, 67,468 shouting fans, flocked to Municipal Stadium, Cleveland, the night of July 17, and while it sadly witnessed the 4 to 3 defeat of the Indians by the rip-snorting Yankees, the fans saw something they can relate to their grandchildren—the termination of the longest batting streak in major league annals. The great Joe DiMaggio's consecutive-game skein finally was stopped at 56, 12 above Wee Willie Keeler's former record, by Al Smith and young Jim Bagby of the Cleveland staff. Batting against Smith, DiMaggio twice was retired by sharp fielding by Ken Keltner and the other time Joe walked. Facing Bagby with the bases full in the eighth, Joe's long streak ended a bit ignominiously as he slapped to Lou Boudreau for a double play. By an odd coincidence, the great streak, which was started against Ed Smith of the White Sox, May 15, was ended by another Smith two months and three days later. After the Yankees built up a 4 to 1 lead for Lefty Gomez, the Indians then treated

.406

As his week-to-week batting averages show, Boston's Williams was well on his way to challenging the .400 mark once he got cranked up in late May.

HUB THUMPING TUB OVER THUMPER TED

—

WILLIAMS' BATTING OVERSHADOWS BOSOX' HILL IMPROVEMENT

——

Outfielder's Hot Pace at Plate Follows Change in Attitude; Art Johnson's Pitching Solaces Braves

THUMPING TED TAGS ALL BASES FOR .406

—

COULD HAVE SAT OUT TO PROTECT AVERAGE, BUT REFUSED

——

Six Hits in Double-Header Which Ended Season for Red Sox All Legitimate; Braves Will Not Sell Miller

Hitting .400 is one thing. Accomplishing the feat in the gutsy manner displayed by Ted Williams in 1941 is quite another.

Boasting a .39955 batting average as he prepared for the Red Sox's season-ending doubleheader against the Philadelphia Athletics, Williams had the option of sitting out the games. He still would have been credited with a .400 average.

Watching from the dugout was never an option for Theodore Samuel Williams. "I want to have more than my toenails on the line," he said.

In a remarkable pressure-situation performance, Williams collected four hits in five at-bats in the opening game and improved his average to .4039. He surely had earned the right to sit now. But he didn't. In the second game, he went 2-for-3 and boosted his figure to .4057—which computes to .406 in the record book. A record book that still lists Ted Williams as the majors' last .400 hitter.

MAY 8	.368	JUNE 26	.412	AUG. 14	.408
MAY 15	.339	JULY 3	.403	AUG. 21	.414
MAY 22	.375	JULY 10	.405	AUG. 28	.407
MAY 29	.421	JULY 17	.395	SEPT. 4	.411
JUNE 5	.434	JULY 24	.397	SEPT. 11	.413
JUNE 12	.410	JULY 31	.409	SEPT. 18	.405
JUNE 19	.416	AUG. 7	.408	SEPT. 25	.401

Williams had a
magical season in 1941.
In the All-Star Game at
Detroit, he hit a game-
winning, three-run homer
with two out in the ninth
inning. American League
president Will Harridge
was pleased.

Owen's gaffe

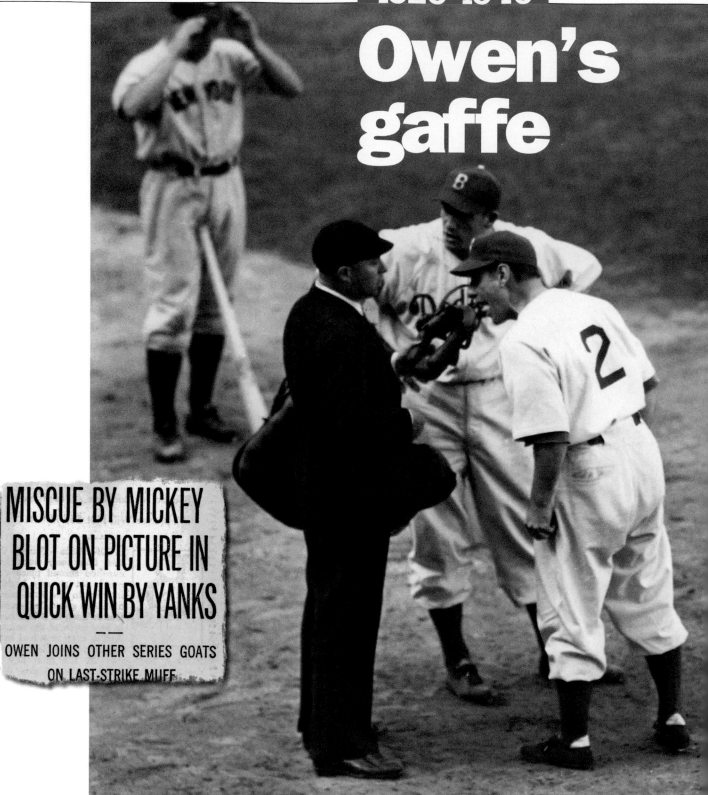

MISCUE BY MICKEY BLOT ON PICTURE IN QUICK WIN BY YANKS
—
OWEN JOINS OTHER SERIES GOATS ON LAST-STRIKE MUFF

WORLD SERIES 1941: When the Yankees' Tommy Henrich went down swinging for the third out in the ninth inning of Game 4, it meant—well, should have meant—that the Dodgers had tied the Series at two games apiece with a 4-3 victory. There was one little technicality, though: The ball got away from catcher Mickey Owen. Henrich made it safely to first base, Joe DiMaggio followed with a single and Charlie Keller sent both runners home with a double. The Yankees went on to win, 7-4, before a stunned Ebbets Field crowd, and they closed out the Dodgers the next afternoon (a day that included a heated protest, above, of a called ball by frustrated Dodgers manager Leo Durocher, right, and pitcher Whitlow Wyatt).

'Lou Can Do It', Admirers Say of Star Shortstop, Recognized as Leader Since College Days

Became Uncrowned Captain of Cleveland Indians as Early as Spring of 1940; Only 24 Now, But He'll Be 'At Least Two Years Older When Next Training Season Is Over'

After the 1941 season ended, shortstop Lou Boudreau (left) was named manager of the Indians—at age 24. He succeeded Roger Peckinpaugh, who late in the 1914 season had become the youngest manager in major league history when he took over the Yankees at 23.

Musical With Bat

Stanley Frank Musial

Headliners

Lefty Spahn of Evansville, 19, Pitches Four Shutouts in Row

EVANSVILLE, Ind.—Bob Coleman, who has groomed many a pitcher for major league stardom during the 20 years he has managed minor league teams, has another one tagged for early delivery. He is Warren Spahn, 19-year-old Buffalo, N. Y., southpaw.

Spahn, who stands approximately six feet and weighs 168 pounds, is the hottest slabster the Three-I has seen in some time. He has won 11 and lost three, and four of his victories were successive shutouts. He started a string of 40 scoreless in...

Boston Braves prospect Warren Spahn was a player to watch in 1941, compiling a 19-6 record and a 1.83 ERA for Evansville of the Three-I League.

A pitcher when he broke into the Cardinals' organization in 1938, Stan Musial was converted into an outfielder and reached the majors by September 1941. And he broke in with a bang, playing 12 games for St. Louis and getting 20 hits in 47 at-bats (.426).

When the United States went to war in December 1941, some of baseball's greatest players went off to serve their country. The Yankees' Joe DiMaggio (left, left photo) spent all of the 1943, 1944 and 1945 seasons in the service, and he was in his prime (28 years old) at the time of his departure.

President Franklin D. Roosevelt gave baseball a tremendous lift early in 1942 with his "Green Light" letter to commissioner Kenesaw Mountain Landis, a missive in which he urged the game to stay in operation during the war as a much-needed recreation activity and morale booster for the U.S. citizenry.

'Green Light' letter

Cleveland strikeout king Bob Feller, a 25-game winner in 1941, missed the next three seasons while serving in the U.S. Navy and pitched in only nine games for the Indians in 1945.

THE WHITE HOUSE
WASHINGTON

January 15, 1942

My dear Judge:-

Thank you for yours of January fourteenth. As you will, of course, realize the final decision about the baseball season must rest with you and the Baseball Club owners -- so what I am going to say is solely a personal and not an official point of view.

I honestly feel that it would be best for the country to keep baseball going. There will be fewer people unemployed and everybody will work longer hours and harder than ever before.

And that means that they ought to have a chance for recreation and for taking their minds off their work even more than before.

Baseball provides a recreation which does not last over two hours or two hours and a half, and which can be got for very little cost. And, incidentally, I hope that night games can be extended because it gives an opportunity to the day shift to see a game occasionally.

As to the players themselves, I know you agree with me that individual players who are of active military or naval age should go, without question, into the services. Even if the actual quality of the teams is lowered by the greater use of older players, this will not dampen the popularity of the sport. Of course, if any individual has some particular aptitude in a trade or profession, he ought to serve the Government. That, however, is a matter which I know you can handle with complete justice.

Here is another way of looking at it -- if 300 teams use 5,000 or 6,000 players, these players are a definite recreational asset to at least 20,000,000 of their fellow citizens -- and that in my judgment is thoroughly worthwhile.

With every best wish,

Very sincerely yours,

Franklin D Roosevelt

Hon. Kenesaw M. Landis,
333 North Michigan Avenue,
Chicago,
Illinois.

REDBIRDS' VICTORY RANKS AMONG GREAT UPSETS OF GAME'S HISTORY

Bombers Bow in Blue Ribbon Classic for First Time Since '26; Freshman Beazley Gains Premier Honors for Winners, While Rizzuto Stars for New Yorkers

WORLD SERIES 1942: The Cardinals had won 43 of their last 51 regular-season games and finished 106-48. Still, they were underdogs against the Yankees, who were playing in their sixth Series in seven years. The Yanks won Game 1, but the Cards then went on a four-game title blitz. Rookie Johnny Beazley won Game 2 despite allowing 10 hits, then pitched a seven-hitter in the clincher, Game 5, which was tied when Whitey Kurowski hit a two-run homer in the ninth. The Series loss was the first since 1926 for the Yanks, who had won eight times since then. Playing in his first Fall Classic, Cards outfielder Stan Musial (left photo, with Yankees outfielder Charlie Keller) batted .222.

WORLD SERIES 1943:

Joe McCarthy ran his Series championships as Yankees manager to seven. New York exacted revenge on the Cardinals, ousting them in five games as Spud Chandler yielded one earned run in two starts. The five pitchers employed by the Yankees in this Fall Classic had a combined ERA of 1.40, which helped overcome an anemic New York offense (17 runs and a .220 average). It was the first Series heavily affected by wartime manpower losses. The Yanks were without Joe DiMaggio, Phil Rizzuto and Red Ruffing; the Cards persevered minus Enos Slaughter, Terry Moore, Howie Pollet and Johnny Beazley. The Cards' lone victory came in Game 2, when Mort and Walker Cooper carried on despite the death of their father earlier in the day. Mort, pitching to batterymate Walker, tossed a six-hitter. In Game-3 action (right), St. Louis' Danny Litwhiler, hustling past Yankees first baseman Nick Etten, beat out an infield hit.

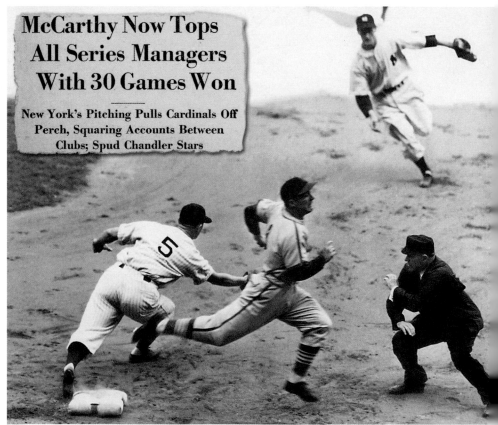

McCarthy Now Tops All Series Managers With 30 Games Won

New York's Pitching Pulls Cardinals Off Perch, Squaring Accounts Between Clubs; Spud Chandler Stars

WAR AND SPORT: Cartoonist Willard Mullin's glimpse at tight situations in baseball as viewed by fighting men in life-and-death situations showed the bond between the game and its followers, who tuned in Red Barber and the World Series wherever they were.

Death takes Landis at top of power

Became National Figure By Stern, But Just Reign

Named as Supreme Authority After Exposure of 1919 World's Series, Commissioner Was Re-Elected Three Times by Owners to Whom He Dictated

"

From the beginning, Landis took the side of the players, and he was swift to act when he felt their rights and privileges were involved. Honesty of the game also was a fundamental principle with him, and any act that threatened its name resulted in severe penalties against offenders. ...

Landis always looked with aversion on the operations of the vast farm chains, and studied their moves closely to keep them within the baseball law. Hundreds of players were given their free agencies during his incumbency. ...

—*November 30, 1944, on the death of commissioner Kenesaw Mountain Landis.*

"

THE 75 YEAR OLD SLUGGER IS NOT ONLY STILL IN THERE SWINGING, BUT THE SLICKEST CLUB OWNERS AREN'T SNEAKING A SINGLE PITCH PAST HIM — NO MATTER HOW HARD THEY'VE TRIED TO GET HIM OUT RECENTLY!

KENESAW

MOUNTAIN

THE NIGHT BALL VERDICT AND THE WAIVER PLAYER DECISIONS SHOW THE JUDGE STILL TAGS 'EM EVERY TIME THEY GET OFF BASE!!

ALTHOUGH BASEBALL ASKED HIM TO SIGN FOR FIVE MORE YEARS, MAYBE THE JUDGE WOULD FIND SPARE TIME TO FOLLOW CORUM'S TIP TO KEEP AN EYE ON THE PRO GAME I...

Chandler to Be Active Leader; He'll Travel and Talk for Game

Sen. Albert "Happy" Chandler of Kentucky was chosen by major league club owners to succeed Landis as commissioner, and he took over on April 24, 1945. Like Landis, Chandler was resolute—a man who didn't back down when he thought owners, managers or players were out of line. And he quickly and forcefully demonstrated that he would champion the integration of Organized Baseball.

Now Pitching for the Yanks!

Six Leagues Halt on D-Day

Some Games Called Off in Other Loops

Following President Roosevelt's suggestion that Americans stay at home or visit churches whenever news of an Allied invasion came, baseball effectively shut down on June 6, 1944, when troops under the command of Gen. Dwight D. Eisenhower (below) stormed the beaches at Normandy.

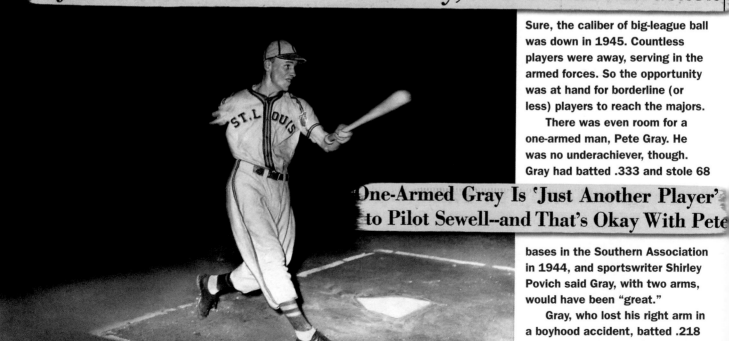

Outfielder Must Make Grade on Ability, Not as Gate Attraction

Sure, the caliber of big-league ball was down in 1945. Countless players were away, serving in the armed forces. So the opportunity was at hand for borderline (or less) players to reach the majors.

There was even room for a one-armed man, Pete Gray. He was no underachiever, though. Gray had batted .333 and stole 68

One-Armed Gray Is 'Just Another Player' to Pilot Sewell--and That's Okay With Pete

bases in the Southern Association in 1944, and sportswriter Shirley Povich said Gray, with two arms, would have been "great."

Gray, who lost his right arm in a boyhood accident, batted .218 in 77 games for the '45 St. Louis Browns.

Growing Pains

WHEN DO I GET LONG PANTS?

BASEBALL

PACIFIC COAST LEAGUE

PCL denied the label of distinction

Seeking the "major league" label after World War II, the Class AAA Pacific Coast League failed in bids to attain such a ranking.

The PCL, a preparatory stop for many major leaguers-to-be and long a haven for players just past their big-league prime, was told by baseball's hierarchy that it lacked the population, parks and other "essentials" to be classified as a big league.

On the verge of a population explosion in its member cities, the PCL hoped status as a baseball grownup was just a matter of time. (As it turned out, Los Angeles/Hollywood, San Francisco, Seattle, Oakland and San Diego eventually wound up with big-league clubs through relocation or expansion.)

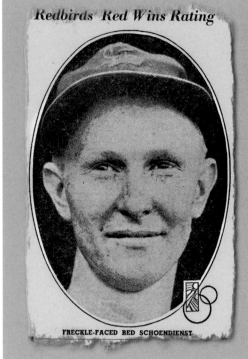

Redbirds' Red Wins Rating

FRECKLE-FACED RED SCHOENDIENST

In only his second year of pro baseball, Cardinals farmhand Red Schoendienst won Most Valuable Player honors in the International League in 1943. Playing shortstop for Rochester, he batted a league-leading .337. Schoendienst would be converted into a second baseman before his second major league season, 1946.

Big Inning Gives Cards Final Game and Series

WORLD SERIES 1944: The Browns played in their first Series, an all-St. Louis affair, and won the opener when Denny Galehouse tossed a seven-hitter and George McQuinn hit a two-run homer. But the Cardinals, Sportsman's Park tenants of the long-suffering Browns, won in six games. Trailing two games to one, the Cards took the next three as starters Harry Brecheen, Mort Cooper and Max Lanier and reliever Ted Wilks limited the Browns to two runs. No Cardinal had more than two RBIs in the Series. McQuinn was the hitting star (.438, five RBIs).

Gabby Street to Return; Dean Out as Play Gabber

By EDGAR G. BRANDS

Two broadcasts, instead of one, will simultaneously cover the home games of the Cardinals and Browns this season, but Dizzy Dean will not be among the play-by-play broadcasters. Both daylight and night games will be aired over WIL and WTMV, the latter an East St. Louis, Ill., station.

France Laux and Johnny OHara, with one other announcer to be named, will be at the microphone for WTMV, with the Hyde Park Brewery as sponsor. Harry Caray and Gabby Street will handle the games for WIL under the sponsorship of the Griesedieck Bros. Brewing Co.

In 1945, a newcomer teamed on radio with Gabby Street (story, left) to describe St. Louis games. Three years later, WGN in Chicago initiated Cubs telecasts and Ernie Harwell joined the Dodgers' broadcast team. In 1949, Russ Hodges became voice of the Giants. And in '50, Brooklyn hired a new play-by-play man: Vin Scully, 22.

On the warfront

Two down!

With two of the Axis powers (Italy and Germany) having surrendered, it wouldn't be long until the third, Japan, was defeated. The coming end of World War II meant the troops—and the ballplayers therein—soon would be coming home. Although Senators star Cecil Travis (headline, below) managed to get into 15 games in '45, the Yankees' Joe DiMaggio didn't resume his career until 1946.

Joe DiMag, Travis Due Back Soon

—

Other Service Heroes Likely to Take Hand in Stirring Pennant Scramble

Parks Close in Tribute to Memory of Roosevelt

All ball parks were closed the afternoon of April 14 in tribute to President Franklin D. Roosevelt, and in some cases, teams eliminated exhibition games for three days. The Senator-Yankee game scheduled for Washington, April 16, dedicated to the late chief, had to be postponed because of bad weather and was reset for April 20.

The Pacific Coast League called

FDR, 'baseball's savior,' is dead

After President Roosevelt died on April 12, 1945, an editorial in The Sporting News said "no other Chief Executive concerned himself so much about the life and the welfare of the national pastime." TSN believed "so close was his contact with the sport, so tremendously important his friendship and support ...," that FDR deserved a place in Cooperstown. It said the President's "Green Light" letter in 1942 enabled baseball to preserve its very existence.

Cubs reach Series, take Tigers to Game 7 ... then are devoured

PRETTY GOOD.... WHAT THERE WAS OF IT!

WORLD CHAMPS

CUBS

WORLD SERIES 1945: The Cubs, thanks largely to Hank Borowy, made it to the Series—their last such visit of the century. Obtained from the Yankees in late July, Borowy won 11 of 13 decisions for Chicago (and was 21-7 overall). Series rival Detroit had clinched the A.L. flag on the final day of the season when service returnee Hank Greenberg hit a ninth-inning grand slam against the Browns. The last war-era Series, the Tigers-Cubs clash wasn't sterling but had its moments: Borowy threw a shutout in Game 1; just out of the Navy, Detroit's Virgil Trucks (left, with Greenberg) won Game 2, in which Greenberg hit a three-run homer; the Cubs' Claude Passeau fired a one-hitter in Game 3; and Chicago, with Borowy hurling four scoreless relief innings, took a 12-inning thriller in Game 6. Borowy, making his third start of the Series, didn't retire a hitter in Game 7, and Detroit rolled to the title with a 9-3 win.

Pitching Trio, Greenberg Bat Tip the Scale

Detroit Grabs Second Title by Halting Cubs, 9 to 3, in Seventh Game

'Why not now? I want to win.'

—Branch Rickey, when asked in October 1945 about his timing in the signing of a black player.

Branch Rickey

N. Y. State Law Cited by Rickey

However, Robinson, Signed For Montreal, Unlikely to Play for Dodgers

By DAN DANIEL
NEW YORK, N. Y.

Branch Rickey

Branch Rickey's action in signing John Roosevelt (Jackie) Robinson, age 26, Negro, born in Georgia, all-round athlete at U. C. L. A. and shortstop of some promise, for the Montreal farm of the Brooklyn club, has developed a vast number of repercussions.

Robinson was signed at Montreal, October 23, by Hector Racine, president of the International League club; Lt. Col. Romeo Gauvreau, vice-president of the Royals, and Branch Rickey, Jr., in charge of Brooklyn farms, in the office of the Royals.

It is quite conceivable that the story as received far more attention than worth ...

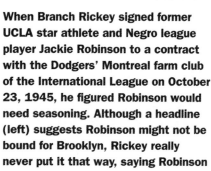

When Branch Rickey signed former UCLA star athlete and Negro league player Jackie Robinson to a contract with the Dodgers' Montreal farm club of the International League on October 23, 1945, he figured Robinson would need seasoning. Although a headline (left) suggests Robinson might not be bound for Brooklyn, Rickey really never put it that way, saying Robinson "is not now major league stuff." As for legal problems involved in introducing a black player, Rickey noted that an anti-discrimination law had taken effect in New York state in July—thereby easing the path for blacks to play throughout the state at major league and minor league levels. (Three International League teams were based in New York state.)

'Guess I'm Just a Guinea Pig,' Says Jack Robinson; Realizes His Responsibilities in Montreal Tryout

Rickey was a master teacher whose grasp of a player's talent, potential and character seldom was off the mark. Reluctant to rave about Robinson at the outset lest he put added pressure on him, Rickey nevertheless thought Jackie was just the man—in terms of skill and temperament—to send into the heat of the integration fight.

1946

THE GAME'S CHA

The Sporting News newspaper:

Day-by-Day National League Schedule... See Page 21

BASEBALL — BASEBALL

The Sporting News

THE BASE BALL PAPER OF THE WORLD

Section One — In Two Sections

VOLUME 126, NUMBER 25 — ST. LOUIS, JANUARY 26, 1949 — PRICE: TWENTY CENTS

STAN AND TED GO TO BAT IN HASH LEAGUE

Atlanta Fandom Okays Jackie's Visit

Klan Leader's Protest Fails to Create Stir

Polls Favor Appearance of Dodger Negro Pair in April Exhibitions

Over the Fences of Prejudice — By Mack

Musial Buys Interest in Restaurant

Williams Reported About to Become Partner in Cambridge Cafe

C'MON JACKIE, LET'S SEE YOU HIT A HOMER

SOUTHERN BALL PARKS

136

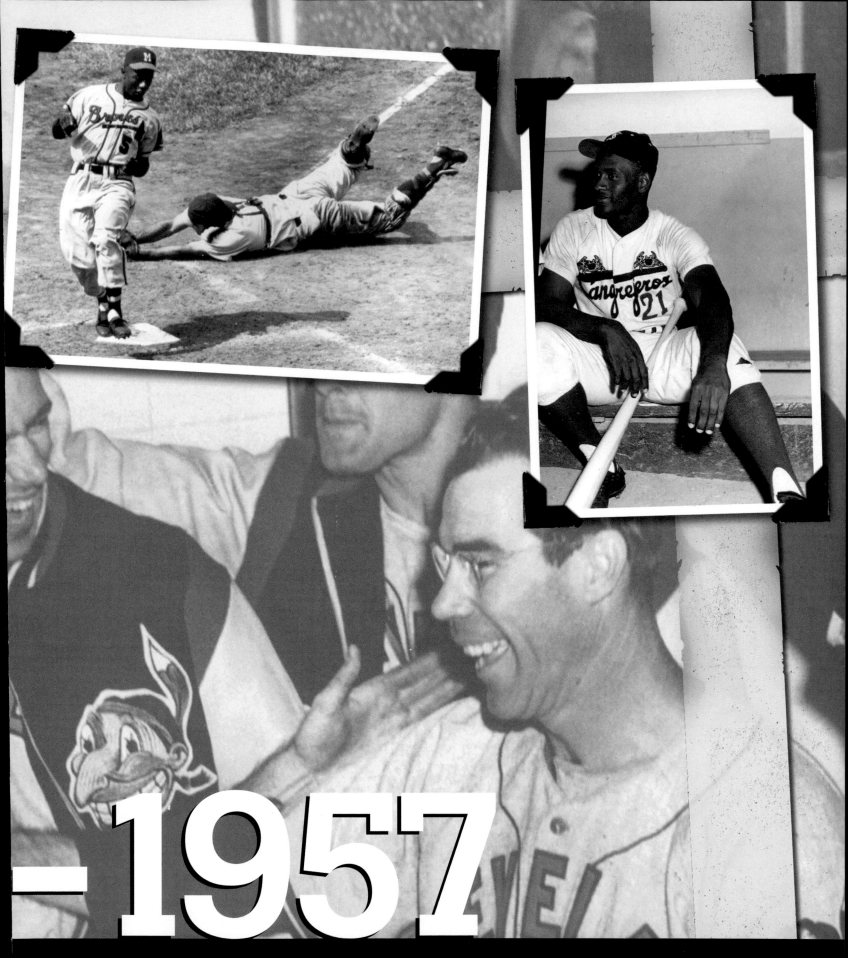

1957

NG FACE: JA KIE, TV

Left to right: Bobby Avila and Willie Mays; Walter
Alston, Walter O'Malley and Pee Wee Reese; Hank
Aaron; Roberto Clemente in winter ball. Background:
Cleveland Indians clubhouse celebration, 1948.

L ike a butterfly emerging from its dark cocoon, a war-weary nation looked at the changing world with wide-eyed wonder. Modern medicine already had been revolutionized by the discovery of penicillin, and everything pointed toward a technologically enhanced future filled with advancements in television, communications, transportation and air travel. Soon the nation would be linked from coast to coast, triggering a population shift west and to the suburbs.

There was no rest for the weary in this fast-paced transition to the modern era. At the end of World War II, 5,000 television sets were in American homes, many of which did not even have indoor plumbing. By 1951, 17 million sets had been sold. Within a decade, baseball was competing for consumer affection with Milton Berle, Ed Sullivan, Lucille Ball, Ozzie and Harriet, Davy Crockett, Roy Rogers, drive-in movies, Hula-Hoops, rock 'n' roll music and a popular teen dance show called *American Bandstand*.

This was a period of discovery, social as well as physical. The lessons and redefined values of the 1940s and '50s would take root and blossom in the decades to come.

Blacks who had fought for freedom alongside whites in the war began fighting for justice in their own country. Baseball helped break the racial ice when Jackie Robinson played his first game for the Brooklyn Dodgers in 1947, removing a color barrier that had existed for more

1946	**1947**	**1948**	**1950**
It's a Wonderful Life connects with moviegoers.	The Polaroid camera is patented. Flying-saucer sightings are reported in the U.S. Broadway hands out its first Tony awards.	Harry Truman is re-elected President in an upset of Thomas E. Dewey.	President Truman orders U.S. forces to Korea. Charles Schulz creates the "Peanuts" comic strip.

than 60 years. By 1959, every team would have at least one black player and Americans would be teetering on the edge of a civil-rights movement that would change the face of society.

If integration seemed like a monumental step forward, the unionization of players was more subtle. The organized labor movement, which had seriously threatened to invade the baseball world in 1946, succeeded in 1954 with the creation of the Major League Baseball Players Association—a minor blip on the expanding economic map. It wouldn't be minor for long.

The postwar focus was all about financial empowerment. And the driving force was that little box with a picture tube. Those who didn't grasp the power of television remained locked in the dark ages. Its equipment and techniques were crude and its programming lacked direction in the baby-boom 1940s, but that would change quickly. As it became clear that television could provide baseball with the portal to a prosperous future, major league officials began courting the medium at the expense of their minor league brethren. The bottom-line payoff would be big.

Ted Kluszewski

Jackie Robinson

Everyone flinched when the Gillette Safety Razor Co. announced in 1950 that it had agreed to pay $6 million over six years for television rights to the All-Star Game and World Series. But that was just the tip of the iceberg. As suddenly prosperous major league owners jockeyed for position and players began lobbying for a bigger piece of the financial pie, it became clear that baseball's infatuation with television also would expose a distasteful side to the "new game."

With the promise of untapped riches and the exodus to the suburbs, baseball owners began looking for more fertile markets. Fertile as in big. When the Boston Braves moved to Milwaukee

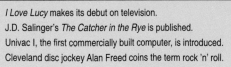

1951
I Love Lucy makes its debut on television.
J.D. Salinger's The Catcher in the Rye is published.
Univac I, the first commercially built computer, is introduced.
Cleveland disc jockey Alan Freed coins the term rock 'n' roll.

1952
The Today Show makes its debut on NBC-TV.

1953
Korean War armistice is signed.
The Corvette makes its debut.
TV Guide hits the checkout counters.

before the 1953 season, it marked baseball's first franchise shift in half a century. The St. Louis Browns followed the Braves' lead later that year by moving to Baltimore, and the Philadelphia Athletics fled to Kansas City after the 1954 season. Baseball's new big-business mentality would redefine the boundaries and values of a sport in transition.

While the economics of the game were undergoing revolutionary change, baseball's power structure remained constant. In the 11-year span from 1947-57, the New York Yankees claimed nine American League pennants and seven World Series championships, including an unprecedented five in a row under colorful manager Casey Stengel. To say the road to baseball superiority passed through New York was a major understatement. The Brooklyn Dodgers won six National League pennants and a World Series title during that span, and the Giants won two N.L. pennants and a World Series crown.

The Bronx Bombers and Brooklyn's Boys of Summer might have dominated the standings, but they didn't monopolize the headlines. St. Louis outfielder Enos Slaughter immortalized his career with a mad dash around the bases that gave the Cardinals a championship in 1946—after they had defeated the Dodgers in baseball's first pennant playoff—and the most dramatic home run in baseball history, Bobby Thomson's "Shot Heard 'Round the World," gave the Giants a 1951 pennant playoff win over the hated Dodgers.

The 1950s also will be remembered for the appearance of Bill Veeck's midget in a major league game and the five-homer doubleheader barrage of St. Louis' Stan Musial. One of the great performances in baseball history was staged in 1956 by Yankees pitcher Don Larsen, who posted the first perfect game in World Series history.

The 1940s introduced us to such outstanding hitters as Musial, Robinson, Roy Campanella, Yogi Berra, Ralph Kiner and Duke Snider, but no period in history produced a better power-hitting class than the 1950s. Hank Aaron, Mickey Mantle, Willie Mays, Frank Robinson, Ernie Banks, Eddie Mathews and

1954

Racial segregation in public schools is ruled unconstitutional by the U.S. Supreme Court.

Dr. Jonas Salk begins inoculating children against polio.

The Air Force Academy opens in Colorado.

Swanson introduces TV dinners.

1955

Rosa Parks refuses to yield her seat to a white man on a Montgomery, Ala., bus, triggering events that begin the civil-rights movement.

Actor James Dean dies in a car crash.

1955

Gunsmoke makes its premiere on TV.

Disneyland, America's first major amusement theme park, opens in California.

Harmon Killebrew joined hands in their march toward the magic 500-homer club and baseball's ultimate honor, the Hall of Fame.

The only real glitch in this period of prosperity occurred in the early 1950s, when Americans were forced to endure another war. But the Korean conflict did not force undue hardship on the game, and the manpower drain was negligible. Players like Ted Williams, Don Newcombe, Mays, Jerry Coleman, Bob Kennedy and Curt Simmons lost time to military service, but there was never any threat beyond a minor drop in star power.

The Korean War was a fading memory in 1957 when circumstances in New York and Brooklyn set the stage for one of the most important developments in the game's evolution. With the vast improvements in air travel opening up horizons well beyond the Mississippi River, baseball looked longingly toward the greener pastures of the West Coast and braced for the sport's first modern expansion. Any remaining misconceptions that baseball "was only a game" would be shot down faster than a guided missile could reach Los Angeles or San Francisco.

1956

Elvis Presley has four No. 1 hit records, the first being "Heartbreak Hotel." His appearance on *The Ed Sullivan Show* leaves viewers all shook up.

The interstate highway system is inaugurated.

1957

President Eisenhower sends federal troops to Little Rock, Ark., to ensure the enrollment of nine black students at Central High School.

American Bandstand makes its network-TV debut. And *Leave It to Beaver* becomes a favorite with viewers.

Beat-generation author Jack Kerouac writes *On the Road*.

The great debate

As the 1946 major league season wound down, the Red Sox's Ted Williams and the Cardinals' Stan Musial were adding to their impressive résumés and sparking debates over who was the better player. Williams, who had led the American League in 1941 with a .406 average and topped the league in 1942 with a .356 mark, was on his way to a runner-up finish in '46 after spending three seasons in the armed forces. Musial, the National League hitting king in 1943 at .357, was headed for a .365 average and his second batting championship. Batting titles alone didn't tell the story in 1946. Williams hit 38 home runs with 123 RBIs and was named the A.L.'s Most Valuable Player. Musial, who was selected the N.L.'s MVP, collected 228 hits (including 50 doubles and 20 triples) and drove in 103 runs. And, by season's end, both lefthanded sluggers had helped lead their teams into the World Series.

'Mexico OK for songwriters, but ... they just don't have it there.'

—Vern Stephens, shortstop for the St. Louis Browns, turning down an offer to stay in the Mexican League (April 11, 1946).

For the first time since the Federal League made player raids more than three decades earlier, the National and American leagues lost talent to an outside force. This time, it was the independent Mexican League, which in 1946 lured such stars as the Cardinals' Max Lanier, the Dodgers' Mickey Owen and the Giants' Sal Maglie.

Browns slugger Vern Stephens also fled south of the border, but he played only two games before rejoining the Browns prior to the start of the season.
Commissioner Happy Chandler barred 18 jumpers (Stephens escaped a penalty) from Organized Baseball for five years, but he lifted the ban in 1949.

Jackie Cracks Homer in Bow

IT MAY NOT BE LONG before Jackie Robinson of Montreal, who is the first Negro infielder to play in Organized Ball in this century, gets a chance with the parent Brooklyn Dodgers. Photo shows him crossing the plate at Roosevelt Stadium, Jersey City, N. J., April 18, after hitting a home run with two runners on the bases in the third inning of the Royals' 14 to 1 opening-day victory over the Jerseys. The blow was one of four by the Negro in the International League inaugural. He is being congratulated by George Shuba, a teammate. The umpire is Art Gore

Jackie Robinson, who in 1946 hit a home run for the Class AAA Montreal Royals in his first minor league game (left), was headed for the majors in 1947 in the view of Montreal general manager Mel Jones. Said Jones: "What can't he do except eat in the dining room at the Waldorf?" Robinson previously played for the Kansas City Monarchs in the Negro leagues.

Tragedy in the minors

In the worst accident in professional baseball history, nine members of the Spokane team of the Western International League were killed on June 24, 1946, when their bus careened off a narrow road in the Cascade Mountains. One player, Jack Lohrke, had gotten off the bus at its last stop after receiving notice to report to San Diego of the Pacific Coast League. Lohrke went on to play in the majors for the Giants and Phillies.

Two years later, five players for the Duluth club of the Northern League died when their bus and a truck collided near St. Paul, Minn.

First Pennant Playoff in History of Majors

WITH the National League deadlocked at the end of the regular 1946 championship season, September 29, the St. Louis Cardinals and Brooklyn Dodgers each having 96 victories and 58 defeats, the first playoff series in major league history became necessary. In 1908, the Cubs won the National League flag by defeating the Giants in a post-season game, but that historic game of October 8 was not a playoff but a replay of a September 23 New York-Chicago contest, in which Fred Merkle failed to touch second as the Giants' "winning run" was driven home in the ninth inning. This replay was ordered by former National League President Harry Pulliam, in which action he was supported by the league's board of directors.

The National League constitution provides for the playing of a best two-out-of-three series in the event of a deadlock, such as existed at the close of the regular 1946 season. It also stipulates that the games and records of such a series shall go into the final standing of the clubs and the season's official averages. Getting Sam Breadon, president-owner of the Cardinals, and Leo Durocher, manager of the Dodgers, on two telephones, Ford Frick, league president, flipped a coin to decide which club would have the choice of the first game. Breadon called it incorrectly, and Durocher asked that the first game be played in St. Louis, which would give him the second and third games in Brooklyn, in the event a third contest was necessary.

However, whatever benefit Durocher expected to gain by playing a possible third game at home was lost when the Cardinals took the series in two successive games, winning in St. Louis, October 1, by a score of 4 to 2, and repeating in Brooklyn, 8 to 4, October 3. In both games, the Redbirds looked like the fresher, stronger club, and clearly demonstrated their season-long superiority over Flatbush's famous "Bums."

Eddie Dyer, St. Louis manager, won the first game with Howard Pollet,

Slaughter's mad dash

It was a 3-3 score in the bottom of the eighth inning of Game 7 of the 1946 World Series when the Cardinals' Enos "Country" Slaughter tore around the bases and scored from first on a hit (ruled a double, not a single) to left-center by Harry Walker. Slaughter's hustle dealt the Red Sox their first Series loss (Boston had won in 1903, 1912, 1915, 1916 and 1918).

WORLD SERIES 1946: Slaughter (above, second from left) celebrated with (left to right) manager Eddie Dyer, George "Red" Munger, Whitey Kurowski and rookie catcher Joe Garagiola. Meanwhile, Boston star Ted Williams (bottom, far left) commiserated with teammate Mickey Harris in the losers' clubhouse. While St. Louis fans hailed their heroes with a confetti-laced parade, Red Sox shortstop Johnny Pesky (bottom, middle) was being second-guessed for hesitating before making a relay throw to the plate on Slaughter's dash. Williams also took some heat, hitting .200 in the Series with one RBI. It would be the first of four Game-7 World Series losses for the Red Sox since their last Series win in 1918.

Dodgers Split on Robinson

Many Oppose Graduation of Negro to Big Tent

"

Jackie Robinson declares he does not want to play for the Dodgers if there is an undertow of resentment toward him. That feeling would only disrupt the morale of the club, he said, and hurt its chances of winning the pennant.

"I got along fine in Montreal," he went on. "I made friends there. The team, I am sure, did not suffer by my presence. We won the pennant by as big a margin as we pleased and went on to win the Junior World's Series.

"That couldn't have happened if Montreal's morale was not as high as it should be. No sir. Morale is mighty important. If the Dodgers don't want me, there would be no point in my forcing myself on them. I am in the Dodger organization and naturally I want to see them win. I wouldn't want to feel that I was doing anything that would keep them from winning."

—*April 2, 1947*

"

A shrewd judge of talent, Dodgers president Branch Rickey thought Robinson had the right stuff to excel. It didn't take long for Robinson to prove Rickey correct. He batted a league-high .349 for Class AAA Montreal in 1946 and went on to win Rookie of the Year honors in the majors in 1947 when he hit .297 for Brooklyn and topped the National League with 29 stolen bases.

CROUCH STANCE THAT AIDS HIS HITTING...

Never afraid to stir it up, Dodgers manager Leo Durocher stirred it up a little too much with his off-the-cuff remarks and off-the-field associations and drew a one-year suspension for overall misconduct in April 1947 from commissioner Albert "Happy" Chandler. Among other transgressions, Durocher had accused Yankees general manager Larry MacPhail of having alleged gamblers in his box at a March exhibition game in Havana—a charge that didn't sit well with MacPhail or Chandler.

Stan Musial and the Cardinals went from World Series champions to second-place finishers in the National League in 1947. The Cards' decline proved extensive—they wouldn't play in another Fall Classic until 1964, the year after Musial retired. Stan the Man kept on hitting, though. Beginning in '48, he captured four batting crowns in five years.

Name "The Man" "Stosh" Polish	Position	Bats	Throws VE-2-3060
Musial, Stanley Frank	OF-1B	L	L
Born-Place	Date November 21, 1920		Married Yes
Donora, Pa.		Height 6'	Weight 175
Address 85 Trent Drive Ladue, Mo. 63124			

Teams Played With
Monessen 9/37-for 38-rel.to Greensburg /38-opt to Williamson,W.Va. 6/38-rec.and rel.to Columbus,Ga. /38-rel.to Albany,Ga. 9/38-res.for 39 bus,Ga. /38-rel.to Albany,Ga. 10/39-rel.to Ashe-susp.list 4/39-rein.7/39-opt.to Williamson,W. Va. 7/39-rec.by Albany,Ga. 10/39-rel.to Ashe-ville 10/39-40-opt.to Daytona Beach 5/40-rec. by Asheville 9/40-rel.to Columbus,O. 9/40-res for 41-opt.to Springfield,Mo. 4/41-opt.trfd.to Rochester 8/41-rec.by Columbus,O. and rel.to

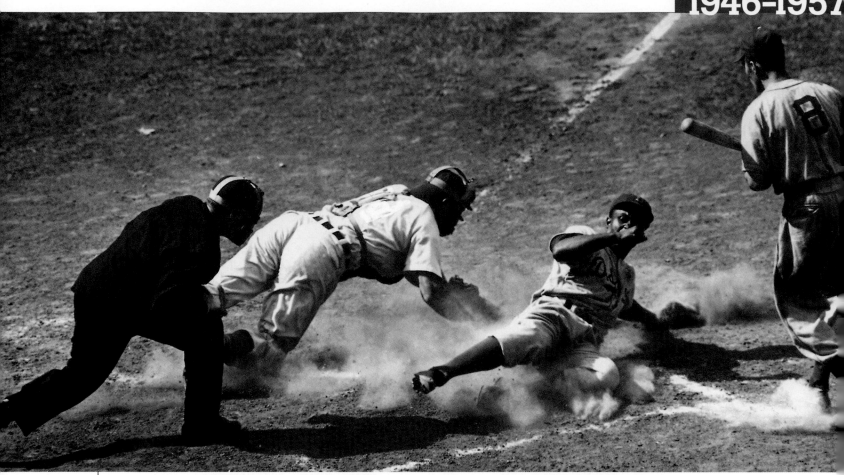

Jackie breaks the color barrier

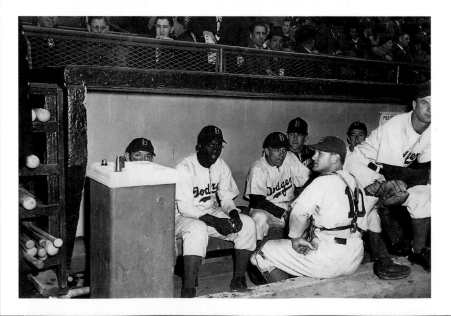

'I look for this thing to take its natural course. ... The signing of a Negro will be no more news than the signing of a white boy.'

—Branch Rickey, June 23, 1947

The Negro Player Steps on the Scales

Five years ago, during the early part of the war, when it appeared there would be a shortage of satisfactory major league players caused by calls to the colors, there were indications that teams in need of talent might utilize the service of Negro players.

Although Commissioner K.M. Landis never went on record on the question, no Negro player was brought up during wartime. THE SPORTING NEWS, however, carried an editorial on August 6, 1942, which expressed the opinion that use of mixed teams in baseball would benefit neither the Negro nor white professional game, because of the possibility of unpleasant incidents. ...

THE SPORTING NEWS has not changed its views as expressed in 1942, but feels that with the majors having taken the step of introducing a colored player into their ranks, the situation calls for tolerance and fair play on the part of players and fans.

The 1942 editorial said in part:

"There is no law against Negroes playing with white teams, or whites with colored clubs, but neither has invited the other for the obvious reason they prefer to draw their talent from their own ranks, and because the leaders of both groups know their crowd psychology and do not care to run the risk of damaging their own game. Other sports had their Joe Louises, Jesse Owenses, Fritz Pollards, and like notables, respected and honored by both races, but they competed under different circumstances from those predominating in baseball.

"The baseball fan is a peculiar creature. We believe no one will question that fact. He deems it his inalienable right and privilege to criticize and jeer in words that not always are the choicest or the most gentlemanly. Not even a Ted Williams or a Joe DiMaggio or a Babe Ruth is immune. It is not difficult to imagine what would happen if a player on a mixed team, performing before a crowd of the opposite color, should throw a bean ball, strike out with the bases full or spike a rival. Clear-minded men of tolerance of both races realize the possibilities and have steered clear of such complications, because they realize it is to the benefit of each and also of the game."

—Excerpt from editorial, May 21, 1947

JACKIE ROBINSON, who failed to get a hit in three official trips in his major league debut, rolling to Third Baseman Bob Elliott in the first inning. The Dodgers beat the Braves, 5 to 3.

After Brooklyn's Jackie Robinson became the first black player in modern major league baseball on April 15, 1947, Larry Doby (above, right, with Robinson) broke the color barrier in the American League a little more than 2½ months later. Doby made his debut with the Cleveland Indians on July 5, 1947, and went on to a Hall of Fame career highlighted by two A.L. home run championships. Three other black players appeared in the majors in 1947: Henry Thompson and Willard Brown, both of the Browns, and Dan Bankhead of the Dodgers.

Debut 'Just Another Game' to Jackie
Negro Star Did His Thinking Night Before; 'Brooklyn Players Have Been Swell'

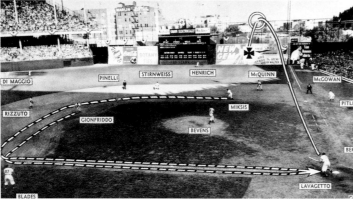

A ninth-inning double by Cookie Lavagetto (top, left) not only ended an oh-so-close bid by the Yankees' Bill Bevens (above, middle, and above, right, with Joe DiMaggio) for the first Series no-hitter, it lifted Brooklyn to a stunning 3-2 win.

The Cookie monster

'Greatest Catch in World's Series History'

AL GIONFRIDDO, substitute left fielder of the Dodgers, shown immediately after making his sensational catch of Joe DiMaggio's home run bid in the sixth game of the World's Series at Yankee Stadium. Note the ball in Gionfriddo's glove, just over the gate that leads to the bullpen. The catch kept DiMaggio from getting a three-run homer that would have tied the score at 8 to 8.

WORLD SERIES 1947: The Dodgers, who had yet to win a World Series, seemed to be living right this time around. They won Game 4 despite going hitless for 8⅔ innings. And they won Game 6 when a defensive replacement who had just entered the game hauled down a long smash by Joe DiMaggio that had a chance to tie the score. But, ultimately, the Yankees, who had won 10 Series crowns in the previous 24 years, were the ones living the high life.

Thanks to sensational relief pitching (five innings of one-hit, shutout ball) by Joe Page in Game 7, the Yankees won a tumultuous Series and were crowned baseball's champions for the first time since 1943.

Strangely, three Series notables never returned to the majors after this Fall Classic: Bill Bevens, the New York pitcher who was on the brink of no-hit fame; Cookie Lavagetto, who broke up the no-hitter with a pinch double; and Brooklyn's Al Gionfriddo, who robbed DiMaggio.

The Sporting News weighed in on Satchel Paige:

"

Many well-wishers of baseball emphatically fail to see eye to eye with the officials responsible for two late developments in the game. These were the call to the minor leagues to set aside Sunday, July 11, as Olympic Day ... and the signing of Satchel Paige, superannuated Negro pitcher, by Bill Veeck, publicity-minded head of the Cleveland Indians, to "save the pennant." ...

In criticizing the acquisition of Satchel Paige by Cleveland, The Sporting News believes that Veeck has gone too far in his quest of publicity, and that he has done his league's position absolutely no good insofar as public reaction is concerned.

Paige said he was 39 years of age. There are reports that he is somewhere in the neighborhood of 50.

It would have done Cleveland and the American League no good in the court of public opinion if Paige were as Caucasian as, let us say, Bob Feller.

To bring in a pitching "rookie" of Paige's age casts a reflection on the entire scheme of operation in the major leagues.

To sign a hurler at Paige's age is to demean the standards of baseball in the big circuits. Further complicating the situation is the suspicion that if Satchel were white, he would not have drawn a second thought from Veeck.

William Harridge, president of the American League, would have been well within his rights if he had refused to approve the Paige contract. ...

—*Editorial by J.G. Taylor Spink, July 14, 1948*

"

Satchel Paige (left, with Larry Doby) proved his critics wrong, fashioning a 6-1 record and 2.48 ERA for the 1948 Indians and helping them to the A.L. pennant. He pitched two shutouts.

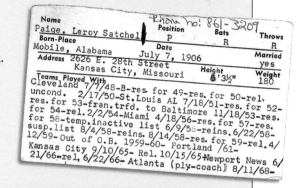

In a shocking managerial move, Leo Durocher took his firebrand style from the Dodgers to the rival Giants midway through 1948. He had been suspended for the 1947 season for conduct detrimental to the game.

Burt Shotton, who had stepped in for Durocher as Dodgers manager in '47, replaced him again in July 1948. One of Shotton's promising players in '48 was rookie catcher Roy Campanella.

'The big fellow's gone, leaving a big heartache'

—August 25, 1948

America's psyche was numbed on August 16, 1948, with the death of Babe Ruth, who had transcended baseball with his extraordinary appeal to the masses. The greatest slugger and gate attraction the game had known, he did everything in style and many things to excess.

Appearing at Yankee Stadium (below, left) on Babe Ruth Day in 1947, the Bambino was in deteriorating health. Having lured throngs a quarter-century earlier with long-ball exploits that helped rescue baseball from the mire of the Black Sox scandal, he even attracted huge crowds in death, as evidenced by the lines that filed past his casket and the people who watched the Babe's funeral cortege.

A. L. Pennant Playoff Game

DUPLICATING the National League's 1946 pennant-race deadlock, the Cleveland Indians and Boston Red Sox completed the 1948 American league season in a first-place tie, October 3, necessitating the second championship playoff in major league history. The two clubs finished the regular season with 96 victories and 58 defeats each—exactly the same record compiled by the St. Louis Cardinals and Brooklyn Dodgers in their stalemate two years earlier.

In contrast to the National League constitution, which provides for a best-out-of-three series in the event of a first-place tie, American League regulations call for only one game. In addition to the Indians and Red Sox, the New York Yankees remained in the flag race until the next-to-last day of the season, October 2, when they lost to Boston to bow out. With a three-way tie for the pennant possible, Will Harridge, American League president, held a coin-tossing ceremony in his Chicago office, Friday, September 24, to determine playoff sites. Ironically, the three clubs involved entered a three-

Gene Bearden (left), who pitched Indians to victory over Red Sox in playoff game for pennant, receiving congratulations from Manager Boudreau.

WORLD SERIES 1948: After Gene Bearden (a five-hitter) and manager Lou Boudreau (4-for-4, two home runs) led Cleveland to victory in the first A.L. pennant playoff, Boudreau (above, arm raised) and club president Bill Veeck (open shirt) soon had more to celebrate—a Series win over the Boston Braves that was sparked by pitchers Bearden and Bob Lemon.

Unsuccessful in earlier managerial stints with the Brooklyn Dodgers and Boston Braves, Casey Stengel was hired to manage the Yankees in '49 after three years of guiding Class AAA Oakland of the Pacific Coast League. Stengel, viewed as a real character throughout his baseball career, appeared somewhat of an odd fit for the regal Yankees. He had managed Oakland to the PCL championship in 1948, though.

"

... Paige's assignment to pitch for the Indians the night of August 13 caused one of the worst jams in the history of Comiskey Park. A crowd of 51,013 got into the stands, and club officials estimated that 15,000 would-be ticket purchasers were turned away. ... The attendance was high for the season and an all-time record for a Chicago night game. ... Just before starting time, the pressure of the crowd at one of the entrances became so heavy that the gates collapsed. Hundreds of fans—whether they had tickets or not—poured through the breach.

—An excerpt from an August 25, 1948, story on the drawing power of former Negro leagues star Satchel Paige, who reached the majors that year at age 42. Paige shut out the White Sox that night.

"

Picture Story of Bizarre Shooting ∴ *of Phillies' Eddie Waitkus*

—Photos by Chicago Sun-Times

CHICAGO POLICEMAN leading distraught Ruth Steinhagen from the Edgewater Beach Hotel after she shot Eddie Waitkus, the Phillies first baseman.

ARTICLES in Miss Steinhagen's room reveal the lovesick typist's hero worship for the baseball star. Framed photo of Waitkus and clippings are shown on bed. Waitkus is shown in inset.

WAITKUS is placed in an ambulance outside the hotel after he was shot in the chest by the 19-year-old girl. The ex-Cub was in Chicago for a series with the Chicago club.

The shooting of Phillies first baseman Eddie Waitkus in a Chicago hotel room in June 1949 jarred the senses. Waitkus, a regular with the Cubs in the previous three seasons, was shot by a 19-year-old woman who had a twisted infatuation with the ballplayer. Waitkus survived the attack, but he missed the rest of the season. After recovering from his injuries, he helped Philadelphia to the 1950 N.L. pennant with a .284 batting average and played in the major leagues through 1955.

WORLD SERIES 1949: Spurred by Tommy Henrich's ninth-inning homer that broke a scoreless tie in Game 1, the Yankees, in their first Series under Casey Stengel, beat Brooklyn in five games. The Yanks prevailed despite Joe DiMaggio's 2-for-18 (.111) hitting.

When manager Fred Haney (right) introduced relatively scanty attire for his Hollywood Stars team of the Pacific Coast League in 1950, eyebrows were raised. Haney insisted that the uniforms, first worn on April 1, would improve speed and make it easier to cope with summer heat. The idea wasn't an April Fool's joke but nonetheless was short-lived.

'Major scouts bid for Billy Martin; $100,000 tag on Oaks' Kid Flash'

—May 4, 1949

On April 19, 1950, The Sporting News printed the minor league broadcast schedules, which listed up-and-comer Jack Buck.

Lots of Gold in Them Thar Medals ∴ By Darvas

Coming off an MVP season in 1949, Jackie Robinson was more popular than ever. As his skills and honors continued to grow, so did his value—as Dodgers president Branch Rickey (left, cartoon) realized.

The Pirates' Ralph Kiner seldom had trouble finding his weapon of choice. He won or shared the National League home run title in seven consecutive seasons, reaching a high of 54 homers in 1949. Kiner, who spent 2½ years in the military and retired at age 33, averaged nearly 37 homers and more than 100 RBIs per season in a 10-year major league career.

The day after becoming the sixth player in big-league history to hit four home runs in one game, the Dodgers' Gil Hodges was saluted by young fans in his Brooklyn neighborhood. Hodges' big game was against the Braves on August 31, 1950.

The Sporting News' coverage of Negro leagues competition wasn't extensive, but TSN did keep readers apprised of the goings-on.

WORLD SERIES 1950: The Phillies were called the Whiz Kids because of their youth and enthusiasm. But they turned into the Fizz Kids in October, losing four straight to the Yankees. In a startling move, Phils relief ace Jim Konstanty started Game 1. He was outdueled by Vic Raschi and lost, 1-0. The Yanks then won by 2-1, 3-2 and 5-2 scores.

Dick Sisler (left) and manager Eddie Sawyer were ecstatic after Sisler's 10th-inning homer against Brooklyn on the last day of the 1950 season clinched the Phillies' first N.L. pennant in 35 years. The Dodgers trailed by one game entering the finale.

Connie Mack retires

After an astonishing 50 years as manager of the Philadelphia Athletics, Connie Mack retired in October 1950 and was honored with "Connie Mack Day" and a parade.

The Grand Old Man, a little more than two months shy of his 88th birthday, had directed the Athletics to five World Series championships and nine American League pennants. His A's were A.L. champions four times in one five-year stretch (1910 through 1914), and they captured three consecutive pennants beginning in 1929.

Having reached the majors as a catcher for Washington of the National League in 1886, Mack got his first managerial assignment late in the 1894 season when he took over the Pittsburgh team. He managed that club for two-plus seasons.

Mack, born Cornelius McGillicuddy, was succeeded as Philadelphia manager by A's coach Jimmie Dykes.

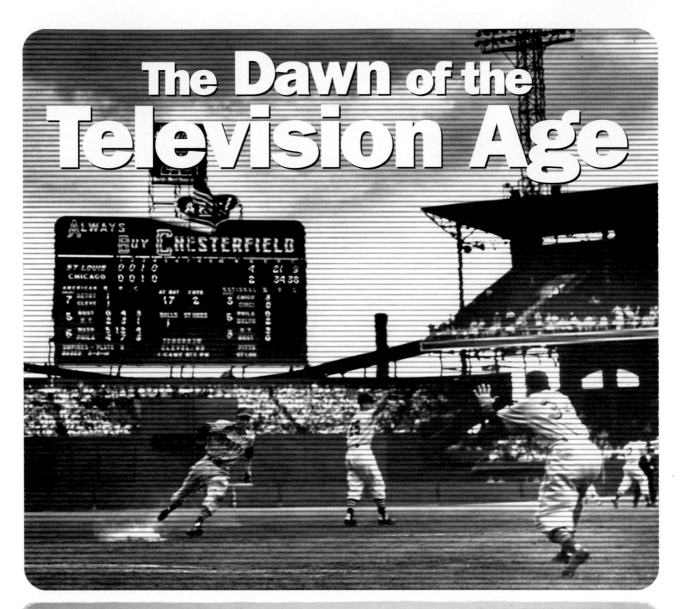

The Dawn of the Television Age

Chandler Wraps Up $6,000,000 Video Deal

"

Completion of negotiations by which telecasts of the World's Series and All-Star games for the next six years will pour $6,000,000 into baseball's treasury was announced by Commissioner A.B. Chandler here, December 26. Chandler collaborated with Joseph P. Spand, Jr., president of the Gillette Safety Razor Co., and Frank White, president of the Mutual Broadcasting System, in announcing that the $6,000,000 contract had been signed, continuing Gillette and Mutual's exclusive telecasts of baseball's foremost attractions.

Chandler said the $6,000,000 will be applied largely to financing the players' annuity and insurance plan, usually called the pension plan.

—January 3, 1951

"

Two-Way Slugger Fitted for Clipper's Shoes

Mickey Raps Homers From Either Side

Dickey, Henrich Schooling Kid Shortstop in Plan to Use Him in Center

By DAN DANIEL

PHOENIX, Ariz.

Mickey Mantle, the 19-year-old who hit .383 for Joplin in the Class C Western Association last season, and is not on Casey Stengel's roster, but who is expected to wind up on the Yankees, if not this year, then in '52, continues to be the talk of the world's champions.

There are many unusual features about this quiet, well-behaved and conceivably quite bewildered youngster from the lead-zinc mine country around Commerce, Okla.

Not the least interesting is the fact that he is a member of an almost extinct tribe—the switch-hitters.

With Joplin in 1950, Mantle hit 14 homers lefthanded and 12 from the third base side of the plate. It may be that somewhere in the record book of minor league achievement there is a counterpart of this odd feat. But, up to now, research experts have not been able to locate it. Usually a switch-hitter has his power from his lower, original stance.

Mantle explains that he is naturally a righthanded hitter. However, he looks slightly better when hitting lefthanded. That's still another oddity.

He's Clothes-Line Clouter

At this writing, Mantle has hit three homers for the Bombers, No. 3 came off the lefthanded Chet Johnson of the San Francisco Seals, and like his two previous wallops, left the park on a line. Mickey doesn't hit looping homers.

Mantle's first four-bagger, at Wrigley Field in Los Angeles, off the right-handed Bob Spicer, smashed into the center field wall some 420 feet from the plate.

Mickey's second out-of-the-park achievement signalled an 11 to 8 victory over Joe Gordon's Sacramento club. Mickey belted that one off Lefthander Harry Grubb.

Mantle is under the personal direction of Professor Thomas Henrich. But his most effusive booster is Bill Dickey.

"I was greatly impressed with Mickey in February, 1950, when we ran a school at Phoenix," Dickey told me.

"Mantle had had only one year of experience, with Independence in the K-O-M League, and had hit .313.

"But during 1950 at Joplin, Mantle grew greatly in baseball and in physical stature. He is stronger, and he drives a ball harder.

"I have heard of some half-formed plan to turn Mantle into a first baseman. If it were up to me, I would not do that. I would let him continue his work in the outfield. His amazing speed would be wasted at the bag."

Best Ever, Says Dickey

Asked if he had seen a switch-hitter so young and so effective, Dickey chuckled, "No. Never. But then, the turnabout feature of his batting is just a minor one."

Not so in the estimation of Casey Stengel. "I know how valuable an asset a player possesses if he is able to shift against right-handers and lefthanders.

"This is especially true today, in our era of specialists. You have outfielders and infielders and catchers who are useful only against southpaws, or exclusively against righthanders.

"This, of course, is nothing new. Back in 1914, when George Stallings won the world's championship with the Miracle Braves, he had the two-platoon system in the outfield. Later John J. McGraw picked up the idea.

"With a proper hitter of the switch type, you don't have to worry about the character of the opposition hurling."

When Mantle reported at Phoenix on February 19, he was there merely for instruction. He had been playing short, and Stengel had decided to convert him

TOMMY HENRICH IS COACHING MANTLE IN THE WAYS OF THE OUTFIELD...

"HE NEEDS A LITTLE TIME TO LEARN JUDGEMENT— BUT HE SHOULD PICK IT UP FAST"

MICKEY IS A BASEBALL RARITY—A SWITCH HITTER WITH NATURAL POWER FROM BOTH SIDES···HE HIT 14 HOME RUNS LEFT-HANDED, 12 RIGHT-HANDED AT JOPLIN LAST SEASON — BATTING .383

JOE DIMAGGIO'S COMMENT WHEN WE ASKED HIM WHO WOULD REPLACE HIM AFTER HE RETIRES NEXT YEAR...

"THERE'S ALWAYS SOME YOUNGSTER COMING UP–THEY'LL FIND SOMEBODY"

—THAT "SOMEBODY" APPEARS TO BE 19 YR. OLD **MICKEY MANTLE** THE SLUGGING CLASS C SHORTSTOP CASEY STENGEL HOPES TO CONVERT TO THE YANKEE CENTER FIELD...

SAYS 'CASE'—"IT'S A BIG RISK TO JUMP A KID FOUR CLASSIFICATIONS ···BUT IF HE HAS WHAT IT TAKES I'LL TAKE THE GAMBLE"

WITH A TRIPLE AND A HOMER IN HIS FIRST EXHIBITION GAME HE GOT OFF TO A FLYING START"

'If He Can Make It, I'll Move to Right or Left'

Greatest Prospect Joe Can Remember

PHOENIX, Ariz.—"Mickey Mantle is the greatest prospect I can remember," declares Joe DiMaggio of his understudy. "Maybe he has to learn something about catching a fly ball, but that's all. He can do everything else." DiMag has shown no resentment over the ballyhoo Mantle has received. "If he's good enough to take my job, I can always move over to right or left," Joe added.

into a center fielder. The plan was to ship Mickey to Binghamton.

However, much has happened since. To begin with, Joe DiMaggio has announced, "This very likely is my last year." That means the Yankees must accelerate the development of a replacement. They believe that Joe still will be around in 1952. But they know they have to be ready with a new center fielder in 1953.

Mantle's all-round achievements have forced a new appraisal of the young Oklahoman. Instead of being shipped to Binghamton, he was signed to a Kansas City contract. But there is still a possibility that he will be kept on the Yankees, under Casey Stengel's surveillance, instead of going to Kansas City.

Mantle has trouble with balls hit over his head. But he is young and fast, and learns quickly.

Mickey looks like the most precocious juvenile player seen in a major camp since Mel Ott, at 16, came up to the Giants, and stuck.

The interesting fact that Mantle is

a turn-around batter has prompted investigations into the number of survivors of this breed in the major leagues, and its origin.

Just when a batter first switched is not set down in the annals of baseball. It would be interesting to trace the genesis of the sect. Undoubtedly, some batter found himself not hitting and decided to try the other side. Mantle says he got into the habit

of switching when he was only ten years old. Even at that early date the family had professional baseball plans for the kid.

In the major leagues, there are only four switch-hitters, pitchers excluded. They don't often count for much, anyway.

In the American League, the lone regular representative of the breed is Outfielder Dave Philley of the White Sox.

Switch batters among the hurlers include Hal Newhouser, Steve Gromek and Early Wynn. The last named with Cleveland, quite often is used as a pinch-hitter.

In the National League there are three outstanding turn-around batters—Red Schoendienst, Cardinal infielder,

It was just a natural, automatic reaction to a determination to get the best results.

Batting against these flingers, Mantle adopted the practice of turning around.

(CONTINUED ON PAGE 4, COL. 3)

THE SPORTING NEWS, APRIL 4, 1951 ★ 3

Dutch-Irish

Name		Position	Bats	Throws
Mantle, Mickey Chas.		SS-OF	L&R	R

Born-Place			Date	Married
Spavinaw, Okla.			10/20/31	Yes

Address			Height	Weight
5730 Watson Circle Dallas, Tex.			5'11	185

Teams Played With

Independence 6/13/49— res. for 50. Rel. to Joplin, 2/7/50- rel. to Binghamton 9/27/50—res. for 51 —Rel.to New York AL 4/15/51—Opt. to Kansas City 7/15/51—Rec. by New York AL 8/20/51—RES. FOR 1952. RES. FOR 1953 RES. FOR 54— Res. for 55—RES. FOR 56—RES. FOR 57. RES. FOR '58. RES. FOR '59 - RES. FOR '60 - RES. FOR '61. RES. FOR '62. RES. FOR '63 disabled list 6/7/63—rein. 7/12/63. RES. FOR '64 RES. FOR '65 RES. FOR '66 RES. FOR '67 RES. FOR '68 RES. FOR '69 VR.list 3/10/69— RES. FOR '70

The Sporting News
Baseball Questionnaire

Date ....

Name: Mickey (First) Charles (Middle) Mantle (Last)

Born in: Spavinaw (City, Town or Township) Oklahoma State.

on October 20 1931 (Month, Day, Year) Present Height 5' 11½" Weight 187

Playing Position: Outfield Bat—R or L Both Throw—R or L R

Date of Marriage and to Whom: Dec. 23 1951 - To Merlyn Johnson

Player's Nickname "Muscles" How did you acquire the nickname I don't know —

Ancestry (check): English ✓; French ...; German ...; Hebrew ...; Irish ✓; Italian ...; Polish ...

Slavish ...; Other .... Color of Hair: Blond Color of Eyes: Grey

Hobby or Hobbies: Hunting & Fishing Name Pronounced Mantle

If a graduate of preparatory school, junior college or college, list name of institution, the years attended or when graduated and degree received ....

Address during off-season: Commerce (Street) Oklahoma (City) 317 So. River (State)

Position during winter months: None

Baseball Experience (List Clubs and Years): Independence Kansas 1949, Joplin Missouri (Miners) 1950, Yankees 1951, Kansas City, Mo. 1951

If in U. S. Service—Date Joined .... Date Discharged ....

Rank .... Branch of Service ....

Organization and Station ....

What do you consider your outstanding performance in baseball: Hitting 2 HR's - a triple a double + single in one game while at Kansas City, against Toledo.

The undersigned grants to the publishers of THE SPORTING NEWS the right to consent to the use of his autograph and above information for publicity purposes as may in its judgment seem desirable, with stipulation that same may in no instance be used as an endorsement for any product, nor carry any advertising matter.

Mickey Mantle

'Mickey Mantle rated top prospect at age 19.'
—January 31, 1951

Mickey Mantle had played shortstop in Class C ball in 1950 and wasn't on the Yankees' roster when spring-training camps opened in 1951, but there was little doubt that the muscle-bound Oklahoman gave new meaning to the term "phenom." Blessed with the rare combination of explosive speed and astounding power, he had hit .383 with 26 home runs, 136 RBIs and 22 stolen bases for Joplin of the Western Association in '50. And with Joe DiMaggio winding down his career, the Yankees were ready to groom Mantle for outfield duty.

♦ DEALS ♦

of the Week

Majors-Minors

━━━ MAJOR LEAGUES ━━━

Pirates—Purchased Pitcher Paul La-Palme from Indianapolis; Optioned Outfielder Ted Beard and Pitcher Bill Pierro to Indianapolis.

Giants — Acquired Outfielder Willie Mays from Minneapolis; optioned Infielder Artie Wilson to Ottawa.

━━━ CLASS AAA ━━━

Columbus, O.—Sold Outfielder Vince Moreci to Houston; released Pitcher John Grodzicki; bought Shortstop Joe Aliperto from Omaha and Pitcher Pete Mazar from Houston; optioned Pitcher Bob Kerce to Columbus, Ga.

Indianapolis—Released Pitcher Elmer Riddle; returned Shortstop Jim Clark to Hollywood; sold Outfielders Culley Rikard to Chattanooga and Whitey Platt conditionally to Syracuse; optioned Pitcher Stanley Milankovich to Ne

Willie Mays (right) was promoted to the Giants in 1951 after hitting .477 in 149 at-bats in Class AAA. He won N.L. Rookie of the Year honors that year (.274 average and 20 homers in 121 games) and helped the Giants mount a miracle rally in the pennant race.

"Buck"   Negro

Name Mays, Willie Howard, Jr.	Position OF	Bats R	Throws R

Born-Place Westfield, Ala.   Date May 6, 1931   Married yes

Address 51 Mt. Vernon Lane   Height 5'10½"   Weight 185
Atherton, California.

Teams Played With
Minneapolis 6/20/50-opt. to Trenton 6/23/50-rec. by Minneapolis 9/7/50-res. for 51-rel. to New York NL 5/25/51-res. for 52-NDS List 5/29/52-53-54-rein 3/2/54-res. for 55-res. for 56-res. for 57-res. for 58-fran. trafd. to San Francisco /58-res. for 59-res. for 60- RES. FOR '61. RES. FOR '62. RES. FOR '63 RES. FOR '64 RES. FOR '65 RES. FOR '66 RES. FOR '67 RES. FOR '68   RES. FOR '69 RES. FOR '70 RES. FOR '71 RES. FOR '72-Traded for pitcher Charlie Williams and

BATS MAY CARRY DODGERS TO FLAG ROMP

Fearsome Flatbush Foursome   *By Darvas*

Saliva Test Suggested If They Flop

If the Dodgers don't finish first, a saliva test will be in order. That's what they are saying here and there around the course as Flatbush sluggers lose baseballs at a faster early pace than any of the great homer teams. They should make a good run for the record, as well as the flag, while they act as if pitching doesn't matter, neither their own nor the other guy's.

—*front-page story, May 30, 1951*

'Short career for midget in Brownie uniform'

—August 29, 1951

In a Bill Veeck promotional gimmick, 3-foot-7 Eddie Gaedel was sent up to pinch hit for the Browns in a 1951 game against Detroit. Gaedel, wearing number ⅛, walked on four pitches from Bob Cain and gave way to a pinch runner. He was released the next day.

Indians righthander Bob Feller enjoyed his last banner season in 1951, pitching the third no-hitter of his career and winning 20 or more games for the sixth and final time (below).

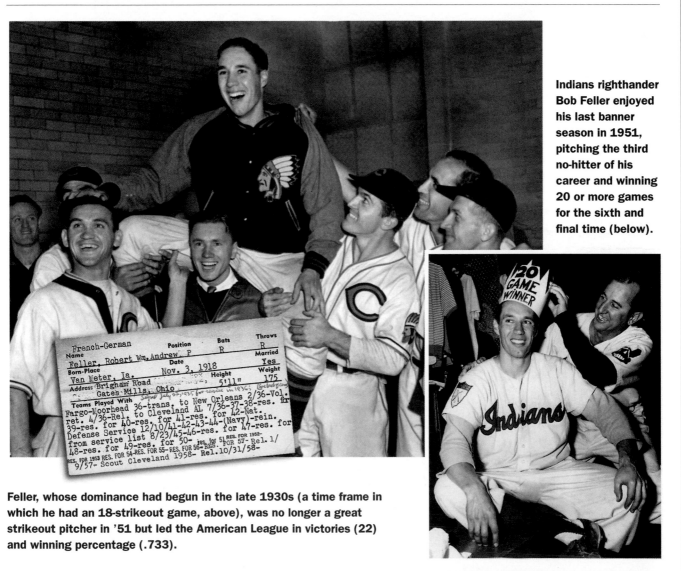

Feller, whose dominance had begun in the late 1930s (a time frame in which he had an 18-strikeout game, above), was no longer a great strikeout pitcher in '51 but led the American League in victories (22) and winning percentage (.733).

The National League hauled out the heavy artillery in the 1951 All-Star Game at Detroit, getting home runs from (standing, left to right) Boston's Bob Elliott, Brooklyn's Gil Hodges, Pittsburgh's Ralph Kiner and St. Louis' Stan Musial in an 8-3 victory over the American League. N.L. manager Eddie Sawyer of the Phillies and league president Ford Frick were part of the postgame celebration. All was not lost for the host city's A.L. fans, who cheered home runs by Tiger favorites George Kell and Vic Wertz.

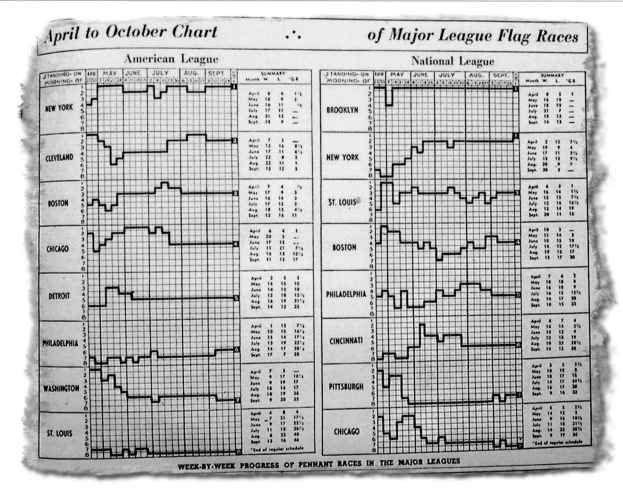

Charting the 1951 season, The Sporting News showed how the Brooklyn Dodgers led almost all the way in the National League pennant race—and how the New York Giants mounted a fantastic finish.

Thomson's home run

It was the greatest moment in baseball history. It was The Shot Heard 'Round the World. It was the Miracle of Coogan's Bluff.

What it was, was this: The Giants vs. the Dodgers in decisive Game 3 of the archrivals' tumultuous playoff series to determine the 1951 National League champion. The Giants, who on August 11 had trailed first-place Brooklyn by 13½ games, trailed in this game entering the bottom of the ninth inning. In fact, the Dodgers, with 20-game winner Don Newcombe pitching a four-hitter, held a seemingly comfortable 4-1 lead at the Polo Grounds. Then came the moment. The shot. The miracle. The Giants' Alvin Dark singled. Don Mueller also singled. After

Monte Irvin fouled out, Whitey Lockman laced a double that scored Dark and sent Mueller to third base. Brooklyn's lead cut to 4-2 and the tying runs on base (Clint Hartung was running for Mueller, who had injured his ankle sliding into third), Dodgers manager Charlie Dressen summoned Ralph Branca from the bullpen. With the crowd in a frenzy, Branca whistled a strike past Giants third baseman Bobby Thomson. Branca (below, right) threw again, and Thomson hit the ball toward the lower left field stands. Dodgers outfielder Andy Pafko (above, left) watched helplessly as the ball sailed over the fence. "The Giants win the pennant!" Giants broadcaster Russ Hodges screamed again and again.

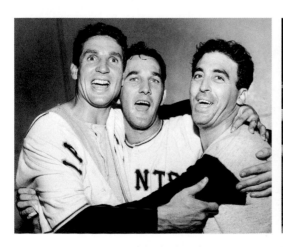

Surprise Party ·.· By Darvas

After the Dodgers blew a big lead in the 1951 N.L. race, their demise underwent considerable scrutiny. But it was the Giants' amazing run—not a Brooklyn collapse—that told the story. The Giants won 16 consecutive games and 37 of their last 44 regular-season contests.

Kisses in Giants' Clubhouse; Tears and Gloom for Dodgers

NEW YORK, N. Y.—In the Giant clubhouse: Clem Labine, Dodger pitcher, came in with Walter O'Malley, president; Chuck Dressen, manager, and Roy Campanella, catcher, to extend congratulations.

Labine put out a hand to Bob Thomson.

"Who are you?" asked the Scot.

"Labine," was the laconic reply of the pitcher who had fanned Thomson in the second game with three aboard.

"Oh, sure," Thomson came in. "I remember you from yesterday."

Dressen was embraced by Durocher, but that was not suspicious, because everybody was kissing everybody else in the room, between sips of champagne, while Eddie Logan, clubhouse man, mournfully regarded his concessions of cokes and beers.

Sal Maglie, often laconic, was verbose for a change. He told stories. "Away back in Philadelphia," he said, "Jansen won a game. It was his fourth while I had won nine. Larry said to me: 'I think I will catch you before this is over.' I said to him: 'If you catch me, we will win the pennant.'"

Sal didn't add the obvious. Jansen won his twenty-third in relief of Maglie, to tie Maglie, and the feat did win the pennant.

NEW YORK, N. Y.—In the Dodger clubhouse: Ralph Branca was sprawled out, sobbing. The air was that of a morgue. Players who had asserted unbounded confidence even when the Giants were three-two-one game behind, were silent, in marked contrast to the jubilant sounds from the Giant dressing room.

Chuck Dressen, manager, acted gracefully. He received reporters and their questions courteously, although he had no answer for several queries. He might have gone out and replaced Branca at the wailing wall.

Instead, he recalled a tale of the early spring, when he and Leo Durocher came on together from California on the same train. "He told me," said Chuck, "that it was one-two between us. But he left it open then as to which of us would be No. 1."

Dressen shrugged. Durocher could not conclude the story when he spoke to Dressen on the train; he did not have to after the third game.

Don Newcombe was surrounded by sympathetic souls, but he could not speak, and dressed and left hurriedly. Newcombe, had Branca delivered, would have been hailed as the pennant-saver for his 24 innings of pitching, at cost of one run, within five days.

But Branca sobbed on, and Newcombe had said his all on the mound.

Cadillacs, Complacency Costly; Dodgers Learn Lesson Hard Way

Forgot Robinson's Warning 'We Have to Go Out and Fight for Every Game'

—JOE KING

Three Errors in Inning--'Wet Grass'

BROOKLYN, N. Y.—It was the wet grass, said Chuck Dressen, which caused the Dodgers to make three errors in an inning in Boston, Sep-

over first base. Pee Wee Reese bobbled a grounder. Carl Furillo, who has the steadiest and most deadly arm in the National League,

'Pride of Yankees too proud to linger for full fadeout'
—December 19, 1951

Alone With His Memories

AFTER ANNOUNCING RETIREMENT

WORLD SERIES 1951: The Yankees stopped the Giants in six games for their third Series win in a row. Joe DiMaggio (with fellow outfielder Hank Bauer) played in his last Fall Classic and homered in Game 4.

The Korean War had less direct impact on baseball than World War I and World War II, but the game still suffered the departure of a few notable players. Red Sox superstar Ted Williams, a fighter pilot, and young Giants sensation Willie Mays (right, with manager Leo Durocher) were among those called to military duty. Williams played only six games for Boston in 1952 and 37 in 1953. Mays appeared in 34 games for New York in '52 and missed all of '53.

TABBING THE KIDS

Signing of a number of high-priced bonus kids by the Red Sox held the spotlight as the major league clubs grabbed the phenoms off the high school and college diamonds for their farm affiliates last week.

Topping the list of prospects inked by the Boston club were Frank Baumann, a lefthanded pitcher of St. Louis, Mo.; Marty Keough, pitcher-outfielder of Pomona, Calif., and Haywood Sullivan, University of Florida catcher. All of these highly-touted prospects received bonuses reported to exceed $50,000, with many of the estimates reaching as high as $100,000.

In getting Sullivan, who lives in Dothan, Ala., Scout Neil Mahoney was the winner of an endurance contest that began when Sullivan graduated from high school three years ago. Ten scouts attended the recent N. C. A. A. tournament, where Sullivan played, and six made outright bids.

Other young talent signed by major league organizations for their minor league affiliates include:

Braves—Henry Aaron, 17-year-old Negro shortstop from Mobile, Ala., who played with the Indianapolis Clowns, for Milwaukee (American Association). Bob McConnell, Boston University captain and second baseman, for Eau Claire (Northern). Infielder Ed Redmond of Springfield College, for Welch (Appalachian). Jack Schlarb, University of Southern California pitcher, and Bob MacNeil, hurler for UCLA, both for Ventura (California).

Browns—Bill Williams, righthander from Jacksonville, Ill., for Independence (K-O-M). Ed Skavy, third baseman from Cathedral High School of Jacksonville, Ill., for Enid (Sooner State).

Cardinals—Milton (Bud) Farley, year-old third baseman-pitcher from Sacramento (Calif.) Junior College, for Lynchburg (Piedmont). Don Hudson, 19-year-old outfielder for Fresno (California).

Dodgers—Tom Cole, 21-year-old pitcher who won eight games and lost one and had a 1.08 earned-run average with Western Michigan University this season, for Fort Worth (Texas); Gerald Didier, second baseman from Baton Rouge, La., for Santa Barbara (California). John Roseboro, catcher from Ashland, O., and a freshman at Wilberforce College, for Sheboygan (Wisconsin State).

Indians—Herbert Score, 19-year-old pitcher from Lake Worth, Fla., where he averaged 18 strikeouts during his scholastic career and hurled several no-hitters, for Indianapolis (American Association). Billy Harrell, 22-year-old Negro outfielder of Siena College, for Reading (Eastern). Wendell Hall, 18-year-old catcher from Greenwood, S. C., for Bakersfield (California). Bob Jones, third baseman from Central High School in St. Louis, for Green Bay (Wisconsin State).

Pirates—Matthew (Mutt) Kuhn, 21-year-old West Virginia Wesleyan pitcher-outfielder, for Hutchinson (Western Association).

Phillies—Bob Donkersley, 22-year-old shortstop from Fresno (Calif.) State College, for Baltimore (International) and optioned to Tri-City (Western International). Leroy Johnson, 20-year-old sandlot pitcher from Milwaukee, Wis., for Grand Forks (Northern). Bob Ciolek, 22-year-old first baseman from Michigan City, Ind., who played with Michigan State College, for Bradford (Pony).

Red Sox—Paul Schulte, 17-year-old southpaw of the Crenshaw Legion team, Glendale, Calif., which won the national championship last year; Roger Johnson, 21-year-old outfielder from Hermosa Beach, Calif., who batted .370 for the University of Arizona this year, and Frank Sisco, pitcher recently discharged from the Army, who won 30 and lost only one, while chalking up seven shutouts, in service play, all for San Jose (California).

Tigers—Francis Oneto, 21-year-old second baseman from Fresno (Calif.) State College, for Jamestown (Pony).

White Sox—Lloyd Jenney, catcher-third baseman from the University of Arizona, and Frank Layana, football and baseball star at Loyola High School of Los Angeles, both for Waterloo (Three-I League). W. Wren, outfielder (Three-

With baseball's amateur draft more than a decade away, the signing of young talent was still wide open in 1952. There were a lot of misses, to be sure, but a June roundup of signings in The Sporting News showed the Boston Braves and Cleveland Indians were tabbing some exceptional kids.

Boasting a typically strong pitching staff, the Indians had three 20-game winners in 1952 (left to right, Mike Garcia, Bob Lemon and Early Wynn) but still fell two games short of the Yankees in the A.L. pennant race.

The downtrodden Browns at least could rally 'round righthander Ned Garver (jacket), who won 20 games for the last-place American League team in 1951.

After seeing their 1950 pennant hopes dashed on the final day of the season and their "cinch" 1951 flag get away, the Dodgers celebrated their return to the top of the National League heap in 1952. Led by such stars as (right) Duke Snider, Jackie Robinson and Pee Wee Reese, Brooklyn had five players with 19 or more home runs, five pitchers with double-figure victory totals and a defense that committed only 106 errors.

WORLD SERIES 1952: Managers Charlie Dressen of the Dodgers and Casey Stengel of the Yankees matched wits in this Series, which the Yankees won despite the robust hitting of Duke Snider (below). Snider slugged four home runs and drove in eight runs, but the Yanks won their fourth consecutive Fall Classic by taking Games 6 and 7 at Brooklyn's Ebbets Field. Yankees second baseman Billy Martin made a big play in the clincher, racing in to catch an unattended bases-full popup off the bat of Jackie Robinson. As usual, Dodgers fans were disappointed but unbowed.

'Major map altered in sudden upheaval'

—March 25, 1953

Milwaukee celebrated its return to majors after 51-year absence by setting an all-time National League attendance record when 1,826,397 jammed new County Stadium (above) in 1953 to cheer transplanted Braves.

"

Personalities Blocked Browns' Transfer, Asserts Veeck

In the 53 year history of the American League, no club president had suffered a knockout punch comparable to that which five of Bill Veeck's associate magnates administered to him in the special league meeting at the Tampa Terrace Hotel, March 16, 1953.

On Veeck's application to transfer the Browns from St. Louis to Baltimore, the league voted a vehement "No" by five to two. Only Hank Greenberg, Cleveland, and Frank Lane, Chicago, supported Veeck.

—March 25, 1953

"

Less than a month before the start of the 1953 season, the National League approved the move of the Braves from Boston to Milwaukee. It was the majors' first franchise shift in 50 years. After drawing only 281,278 fans in Boston in '52, the Braves attracted an N.L.-record 1,826,397 fans to Milwaukee's new County Stadium in '53. As Milwaukee residents celebrated their good fortune (top photo), Baltimore fans' hopes of landing the St. Louis Browns for the '53 season were shot down at a meeting of American League owners.

The Shot That Shook the Records

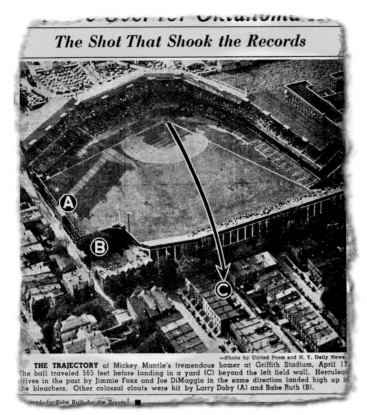

THE TRAJECTORY of Mickey Mantle's tremendous homer at Griffith Stadium, April 17. The ball traveled 565 feet before landing in a yard (C) beyond the left field wall. Herculean drives in the past by Jimmie Foxx and Joe DiMaggio in the same direction landed high up in the bleachers. Other colossal clouts were hit by Larry Doby (A) and Babe Ruth (B).

—Photo by United Press and N. Y. Daily News

Mickey Mantle's strongman reputation grew even larger on April 17, 1953, when the Yankees' emerging star muscled up and hit a 565-foot home run off the Senators' Chuck Stobbs. The switch hitter was batting righthanded in a game at Griffith Stadium.

The Brewer's Big Hosses ∴ *By Mullin*

Anheuser-Busch Stock Rises After Purchase of Cardinals

ST. LOUIS, Mo.—One immediate reaction from the sale of the Cardinals to Anheuser-Busch, February 20, was a rise in the price of the brewery's stock in brisk over-the-counter sales reported that day. From a prevailing price of about $25.50 at the end of trading the previous day, stock reached a high of $27 on February 20, the day the brewery went into the baseball business. At the close of the eventful day the stock had reacted somewhat and closed at about $26.

Saying he acted to ensure that the team would stay in St. Louis, August A. Busch Jr., president of Anheuser-Busch Inc., purchased the Cardinals early in 1953.

West of Hoboken ∴ *By Mullin*

Seven months after their first bid to relocate to Baltimore was denied, the Browns got approval to switch to the Maryland city. A Baltimore syndicate bought the franchise from Bill Veeck.

Ernie Banks (right) and Gene Baker, flanking manager Phil Cavarretta, became the Cubs' first black players in 1953. Banks broke in on September 17, three days ahead of Baker.

Holloman Hurled No-Hitter in First Start

A ROOKIE making his first major league start pitched the lone no-hitter of 1953 in the Big Time. The author of the gem was Alva Lee (Bobo) Holloman, 27-year-old righthander of the St. Louis Browns. He turned the trick in a night game at Busch Stadium in St. Louis, May 6, defeating the Philadelphia Athletics, 6 to 0.

Holloman fanned three and walked five—three in the ninth inning. Most of the fielding plays behind him were routine. The Browns made only one error—by Holloman himself. In the fifth inning Gus Zernial bounced one high and slow to the left of the mound. Holloman leaped to spear the ball, but could not get it out of his glove and finally dropped it for an error. Holloman had another scare in the sixth inning when Joe Astroth topped

Fame was fleeting for Bobo Holloman, who had relieved in four games prior to his no-hitter. With his '53 record standing at 3-7 on July 23, he was sold to Class AAA Toronto.

5 IN A ROW

1953 YANKS

YANKEE CHAMPS OF 1921·'22·'23

YANKEE CHAMPS 1926·'27·'28

CHAMPS 1936·'37·'38·'39

CHAMPS 1941·'42·'43

WORLD SERIES 1953: The '53 Dodgers had stars in (bottom left to right, left photo) Jackie Robinson, Duke Snider, Roy Campanella and Gil Hodges, plus batting champion Carl Furillo. But for the fourth time in seven years, they lost the Series to the Yanks, who won a record fifth straight title. Billy Martin (below, with Eddie Lopat and Mickey Mantle) batted .500 and got the Series-deciding hit. Brooklyn's Carl Erskine (far bottom) struck out a then-Series record 14 batters in Game 3.

Playing for Jacksonville in 1953, second baseman Hank Aaron won the league batting title. While not on the Milwaukee Braves' roster the next spring, Aaron was pressed into major league duty at age 20 when Braves trade acquisition Bobby Thomson suffered a leg fracture. Moved to the outfield, Aaron responded with a solid rookie season.

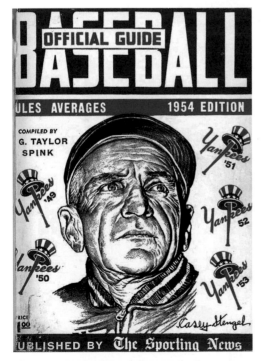

Manager Casey Stengel oversaw the Yankees' unprecedented run of World Series success, making winning old hat for the franchise with the top-hat logo.

By a resounding 7 to 2 decision, the Supreme Court ruled, November 9, that baseball still is a sport, rather than interstate business, and therefore is not subject to federal anti-trust laws.

From Commissioner Ford C. Frick down, baseball men everywhere were jubilant over the reaffirmation of the historic 1922 opinion delivered by Associate Justice Oliver Wendell Holmes. The important ruling—surprisingly handed down less than a month after the high court heard appeals in three suits—means that baseball cannot be challenged in the courts as an illegal monopoly.

It means too, that the reserve clause and other restrictive agreements peculiar to the game will remain in effect unless Congress takes action.

—November 18, 1953

'He Did It in '51, He Can Do It Again'

WILLIE MAYS . . . Whips up pennant fever on Coogan's Bluff.

No. 5 batsman. In 34 games, he hit

'New spirit on club as Mays marches back from Army'

—February 24, 1954

Television's growing impact was evident when the St. Louis Cardinals announced plans to televise all their road games in 1954. Said general manager Dick Meyer: "From everything we have heard, (the telecasts) will be very popular with the fans. We hope the fans enjoy them." The Cardinals' decision came several weeks after a similar arrangement was announced by the Cleveland Indians.

Banks Won't Stick Beyond June, Dykes Wagers Scribe

YUMA, Ariz. — Manager Jimmie Dykes of the Orioles is so positive that Shortstop Ernie Banks will not stick with the Cubs beyond June, that he has wagered a box of golf balls with Edgar Munzel, Chicago Sun-Times scribe and correspondent for THE SPORTING NEWS.

Even when the Cubs demonstrated their faith in Banks by trading Roy Smalley to the Braves, Dykes refused to hedge. "I still say that he won't hit .240, and he'll be out of the National League by June," said Jimmie. HUGH TRADER.

In the spring of '54, not everyone thought young Cubs shortstop Ernie Banks was a keeper.

The Indians (left) dethroned the Yankees as A.L. champs in '54—but the Yanks didn't go quietly. New York won 103 games, topping its victory totals of the five previous title years. Cleveland finished with an A.L.-record 111 wins. Key Indians: (left to right) manager Al Lopez, Al Smith, Bobby Avila, Larry Doby, Al Rosen, Vic Wertz, Dave Philley, George Strickland, Jim Hegan and Bob Lemon.

NATIONAL LEAGUE TEAM DELEGATES talk things over with Ralph Kiner (extreme right), league player representative, when major league players formally organized in Cleveland, July 12. Left to right, Stan Musial, Cardinals; Warren Spahn, Braves; Robin Roberts, Phillies; Carl Erskine, Dodgers; Ted Kluszewski, Reds; Whitey Lockman, Giants; Bob Friend, Pirates, and Kiner.

Formal organization of the Major League Baseball Players Association came in 1954. The union quickly asked a boost in minimum pay ($6,000 to $7,200)—but was rebuffed.

Thirteen years after breaking into the major leagues, Stan Musial was still The Man. He put on an amazing show on May 2, 1954, walloping a record five home runs in a doubleheader against the Giants. The Cardinals' superstar was on his way to another eye-popping season, one in which he batted .330 with 35 homers and 126 RBIs.

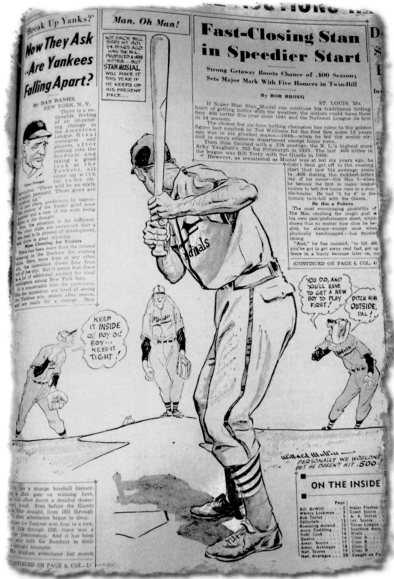

Milwaukee's Joe Adcock (left) got the glad-hand treatment all day on July 31, 1954, at Ebbets Field in Brooklyn. Adcock tied a major league mark with four home runs in one game and set a record with 18 total bases in the Braves' 15-7 rout of the Dodgers. Adcock homered and doubled against Erv Palica and also hit home runs off Don Newcombe, Pete Wojey and Johnny Podres.

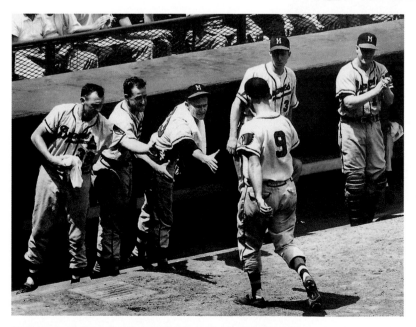

A journeyman minor leaguer, Joe Bauman (below) set a professional baseball record in 1954 when he hit 72 homers for Roswell of the Class C Longhorn League. Bauman, 32, also topped the league in RBIs with a staggering 224 (in 138 games). He hit for average, too—.400.

Senators bonus baby Harmon Killebrew (above, left), 18, and veteran Mickey Vernon took time in '54 to catch up on their reading. Vernon actually is perusing an issue from his early days in the pro ranks.

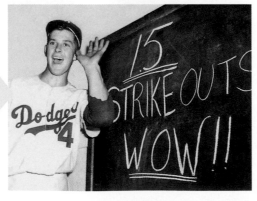

Called up by the Dodgers from Class AA late in the '54 season, lefthander Karl Spooner struck out 15 Giants in his big-league debut and four days later fanned 12 Pirates. He shut out both clubs. Spooner went 8-6 for Brooklyn in 1955, then bowed out of the majors at age 24 because of arm trouble.

With Willie Mays and Don Mueller finishing 1-2 in the batting race, Johnny Antonelli winning 21 games, Hoyt Wilhelm recording a 2.10 ERA in 57 relief appearances and Dusty Rhodes providing offensive punch in a part-time role, the Giants rolled to the '54 N.L. pennant, a symbol of which was rolled out by shortstop Alvin Dark (above, left) and first baseman Whitey Lockman.

WORLD SERIES 1954: Sure, the Indians had set an American League record for wins in one season, but the National League was just happy to see a team other than the mighty Yankees in the Fall Classic. So happy, in fact, that the underdog N.L. champion Giants, seemingly emboldened by Willie Mays' miraculous play (below) in Game 1, dispatched Cleveland in four games. With two Indians on base in the eighth inning of Game 1, the score tied 2-2 and Don Liddle pitching in relief at the storied Polo Grounds, Mays raced to deep center field and, with his back to the plate, made an over-the-shoulder catch of a 460-foot smash by Vic Wertz. Pinch hitter Dusty Rhodes won the game with a three-run homer in the 10th. Rhodes then delivered a game-tying pinch single in the fifth inning of Game 2 and, staying in the game, homered in the seventh. He contributed a two-run pinch single in Game 3. Dusty wasn't needed in Game 4 when Liddle and two relievers closed out the stunned Indians.

The greatest catch in World Series history

When the Pirates drafted outfielder Roberto Clemente out of the Dodgers' organization in November 1954, it didn't cause a big stir. Clemente had batted only .257 in 87 games of Class AAA ball that year.

The major league map changed again after the 1954 season when approval was given for the shift of the Athletics from Philadelphia to Kansas City. The move ended the Mack family's ties to the A's franchise, which had dated to the founding of the A.L. in 1901. Celebrating the relocation of the A's with A.L. president Will Harridge (right) were new owner Arnold Johnson (middle) and Kansas City mayor William Kemp.

Name	Position	Bats	Throws
		R	R
Clemente, Roberto Walker	OF		Married
Born-Place	Date		Yes
Carolina, Puerto Rico	August 8, 1934		Weight
Address Calle 19 #36 Ext. San	Height		170
Agustin, Rio Piedras, P. R.	6'		

Married Usra Cristina Zabala Nov. 14, 1964.

Teams Played With
Montreal 2/27/54-(B) drafted by Pittsburgh 11/22/54-res. for 55-56-57-res. for 58-Military List 10/8/58-59-rein. 3/12/59-disabled list 5/25/59-rein. 7/4/59-res. for 60-res. for 61-res. for 62-Pittsburgh Scout 10/1/62-thru-3/31/63-res. for 63-res. for 64-res. for 65-res. for 66-res. for 67-res. for 68-res. for 69-res. for 70-RES. FOR '71 RES. FOR '72 RES. FOR '73 Died in a plane crash the night of December 31, 1972, near San Juan, Puerto Rico.

Batting .340 for Detroit in 1955, Al Kaline matched the feat of Tigers icon Ty Cobb nearly a half-century earlier by winning a major league batting title at age 20. The A.L. runner-up was Kansas City's Vic Power, who hit .319.

HATS OFF...!

ERNIE BANKS
CHICAGO, Ill.

Not since 1930, when the late Hack Wilson, roly poly outfielder, established a new National League record for home runs with 56 and at the same time shattered all existing marks for runs batted in with 190, have the Cubs enjoyed such a historic season as 1955, insofar as individual batting exploits are concerned.

This year Ernie Banks, only a sophomore in the major leagues, set another homer record that had eluded Wilson as well as the other storied sluggers right on up to the mighty Babe Ruth.

In a night game with the Cardinals, September 19, the fabulous Cub shortstop hit his fifth grand-slam home run of the season. The blow came off Rookie Lyndall McDaniel, who was making his first major league start.

No one in the long history of the game ever had been able to wallop more than four grand-slams in a single year. Banks previously shared that record with ten others.

They included Ruth, Lou Gehrig, Frank Schulte of the famed Frank Chance Cubs, Rudy York, Vince DiMaggio, Tommy Henrich, Ralph Kiner, Sid Gordon, Al Rosen and Ray Boone.

Banks launched his grand-slam attack against Russ Meyer of Brooklyn at Wrigley Field, May 11. He hit No. 2 off Lew Burdette of the Braves at Wrigley Field, May 29. His third jackpot blow came off Ron Negray in Philadelphia, July 17, and his fourth victimized Dick Littlefield of the Pirates, August 2, at Wrigley Field.

The stage was set for Ernie's record-smashing homer in Busch Stadium because of a brilliant stop by Red Schoendienst.

With one out, Dee Fondy singled in the seventh inning. Gene Baker also singled and Fondy stopped at second. Gale Wade then slashed the ball over second base and Schoendienst made a diving stop. It went for a hit, but Red's great save kept Fondy from scoring and thus kept the bases loaded for Ernie's shot into the left field bleachers.

Banks already had entered the record book earlier when he smashed Vern Stephens' mark for most home runs by a shortstop in a season. Vern collected 39 when he was with the Red Sox in 1949.

Ernie reached a total of 44 with that grand-slammer off McDaniel. Wilson is the only Cub who ever hit more than Ernie in a single season and that was Hack's record 56 in 1930.

Just how much the modest, shy Negro youngster from Dallas has meant to the Cubs is almost incalculable. His defensive brilliance at shortstop alone would set him apart as one of the top stars of the major leagues.

But then that is only the half of it. He also is one of the greatest offensive units in the business. The Cubs, who suffered from scoring malnutrition all year, would have dropped right out of the bottom of the league without him.

Frank Lane's tribute to Banks probably should end all discussion of just how valuable the slender shortstop is. Frantic Frankie, who watched Banks jealously for the past two years as an executive of the rival White Sox, said during the summer:

"If you gave me the choice of any player in the National League, I wouldn't hesitate a second. Banks would be my man!" MUNZEL.

This popular essay by broadcaster Ernie Harwell first appeared in The Sporting News on April 13, 1955:

"

The Game for All America

by Ernie Harwell

Baseball is President Eisenhower tossing out the first ball of the season; and a pudgy schoolboy playing catch with his dad on a Mississippi farm.

It's the big league pitcher who sings in night clubs. And the Hollywood singer who pitches to the Giants in spring training.

A tall, thin old man waving a scorecard from his dugout— that's baseball. So is the big, fat guy with a bulbous nose running out one of his 714 home runs with mincing steps.

It's America, this baseball. A re-issued newsreel of boyhood dreams. Dreams lost somewhere between boy and man. It's the Bronx cheer and the Baltimore farewell. The left-field screen in Boston, the right-field dump at Nashville's Sulphur Dell, the open stands in San Francisco, the dusty, wind-swept diamond at Albuquerque. And a rock home plate and a chicken wire backstop—anywhere.

There's a man in Mobile who remembers a triple he saw Honus Wagner hit in Pittsburgh 46 years ago. That's baseball. So is the scout reporting that a 16-year-old sandlot pitcher in Cheyenne is the new "Walter Johnson."

It's a wizened little man shouting insults from the safety of his bleacher seat. And a big, smiling first baseman playfully tousling the hair of a youngster outside the players' gate.

Baseball is a spirited race of man against man, reflex against reflex. A game of inches. Every skill is measured. Every heroic, every failing is seen and cheered—or booed. And then becomes a statistic.

In baseball, democracy shines its clearest. Here the only race that matters is the race to the bag. The creed is the rule book. Color is something to distinguish one team's uniform from another.

Baseball is Sir Alexander Fleming, discoverer of penicillin, asking his Brooklyn hosts to explain Dodger signals. It's player Moe Berg speaking seven languages and working crossword puzzles in Sanskrit. It's a scramble in the box seats for a foul— and a $125 suit ruined. A man barking into a hot microphone about a cool beer, that's baseball. So is the sportswriter telling a .383 hitter how to stride, and a 20-victory pitcher trying to write his impressions of the World Series.

Baseball is a ballet without music. Drama without words. A carnival without kewpie dolls.

A housewife in California couldn't tell you the color of her husband's eyes, but she knows that Yogi Berra is hitting .337, has brown eyes and used to love to eat bananas with mustard. That's baseball. So is the bright sanctity of Cooperstown's Hall of Fame. And the former big leaguer, who is playing out the string in a Class B loop.

Baseball is continuity. Pitch to pitch. Inning to inning. Game to game. Series to series. Season to season.

It's rain, rain, rain splattering on a puddled tarpaulin as thousands sit in damp disappointment. And the click of typewriters and telegraph keys in the press box—like so many awakened crickets. Baseball is a cocky batboy. The old-timer whose batting average increases every time he tells it. A lady celebrating a home team rally by mauling her husband with a rolled-up scorecard.

Baseball is the cool, clear eyes of Rogers Hornsby, the flashing spikes of Ty Cobb, an overaged pixie named Rabbit Maranville, and Jackie Robinson testifying before a Congressional hearing.

Baseball? It's just a game—as simple as a ball and a bat. Yet, as complex as the American spirit it symbolizes. It's a sport, business—and sometimes even religion. Baseball is Tradition in flannel knickerbockers. And Chagrin in being picked off base. It is Dignity in the blue serge of an umpire running the game by rule of thumb. It is Humor, holding its sides when an errant puppy eludes two groundskeepers and the fastest outfielder. And Pathos, dragging itself off the field after being knocked from the box.

Nicknames are baseball. Names like Zeke and Pie and Kiki and Home Run and Cracker and Dizzy and Dazzy.

Baseball is a sweaty, steaming dressing room where hopes and feelings are as naked as the men themselves. It's a dugout with spike-scarred flooring. And shadows across an empty ballpark. It's the endless list of names in box scores, abbreviated almost beyond recognition.

The holdout is baseball, too. He wants 55 grand or he won't turn a muscle. But, it's also the youngster who hitchhikes from South Dakota to Florida just for a tryout.

Arguments, Casey at the Bat, old cigarette cards, photographs, Take Me Out to the Ball Game—all of them are baseball.

Baseball is a rookie—his experience no bigger than the lump in his throat—trying to begin fulfillment of a dream. It's a veteran, too—a tired old man of 35, hoping his aching muscles can drag him through another sweltering August and September. For nine innings, baseball is the story of David and Goliath, of Samson, Cinderella, Paul Bunyan, Homer's Iliad and the Count of Monte Cristo.

Willie Mays making a brilliant World Series catch. And then going home to Harlem to play stickball in the street with his teenage pals—that's baseball.

And so is the husky voice of a doomed Lou Gehrig saying, "I consider myself the luckiest man on the face of this earth." Baseball is cigar smoke, hot-roasted peanuts, The Sporting News, winter trades, "Down in Front," and the "Seventh-Inning Stretch." Sore arms, broken bats, a no-hitter, and the strains of the Star-Spangled Banner.

Baseball is a highly paid Brooklyn catcher telling the nation's business leaders: "You have to be a man to be a big leaguer, but you have to have a lot of little boy in you, too." This is a game for America, this baseball.

"

Bums Not Counting Their Chickens Yet, Just Drooling a Bit

They Realize It's a Long Haul Until September; Setbacks by Giants Check Any Over-Confidence

When the 1955 Dodgers won their first 10 games of the year and 22 of their first 24, Brooklyn fans dreamed their dream again—that "next year" and a first World Series crown just might come *this* year. The fast start helped Brooklyn—led by longtime favorites Duke Snider, Gil Hodges, Roy Campanella, Carl Furillo, Jackie Robinson, Pee Wee Reese, Don Newcombe, Carl Erskine and Clem Labine—run away with the N.L. flag (second-place Milwaukee trailed by 13½ games) and culminated in just the kind of celebration (right) that the Flatbush faithful long had wanted.

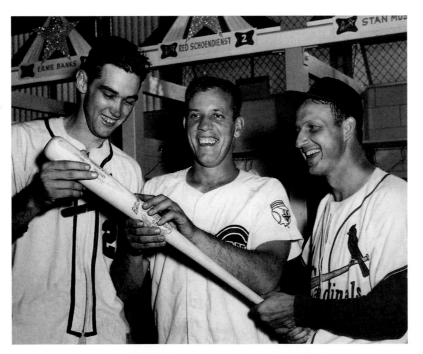

Winning National League pitcher Gene Conley (left, of the Braves) and stellar reliever Joe Nuxhall (Reds) examine the sweet spot of the bat belonging to Stan Musial (Cardinals), whose 12th-inning homer toppled the American League, 6-5, in the '55 All-Star Game.

> **"**
>
> ### Jaunts into Jersey spotlight Dodgers' need of new park
>
> Walter O'Malley, president of the Dodgers, tossed a bombshell into the metropolitan major league picture last week when he announced that seven games on Brooklyn's regular schedule will be played in Jersey City next year. ... In some quarters, the first reaction to O'Malley's action was that it is a covert threat to Brooklyn fans and civic leaders of New York's largest borough that their Dodgers may be moved to another city.
>
> —*August 24, 1955*
>
> **"**

WORLD SERIES 1955: When Sandy Amoros snared Yogi Berra's twisting fly ball (above) with two Yankees on base in the sixth inning of Game 7 and turned it into a double play, Brooklyn took heart. Not just the team; the borough, too. This time, things really could be different for a franchise that was 0-7 in the Fall Classic. Sure enough, with lefthander Johnny Podres protecting his 2-0 lead the rest of the way, the Brooklyn Dodgers at last became World Series champions.

The Dodgers' first of seven home games at Roosevelt Stadium in Jersey City in 1956 was a bust—largely because of the cold. Seemingly intensifying his threat to move from Brooklyn unless civic leaders helped to provide a new park to replace aging, tiny Ebbets Field, owner Walter O'Malley also scheduled eight Dodgers games for Roosevelt in '57. Playing in Jersey City was viewed as a wedge—not a permanent solution.

'Chilly' Jersey Welcome for Brooks

DESPITE ADVANCE BALLYHOO, many vacant seats were evident at the Dodgers' Jersey City "opener" in Roosevelt Stadium, April 19. Although a crowd of 24,000 had been expected, the paid attendance in chill weather was 12,214.

His power pace later tailing off, Mickey Mantle finished with 52 home runs (20 more than the A.L. runner-up) in 1956. Though falling short of Babe Ruth's 60, Mantle had a career year—a Triple Crown season in which he hit .353 and drove in 130 runs.

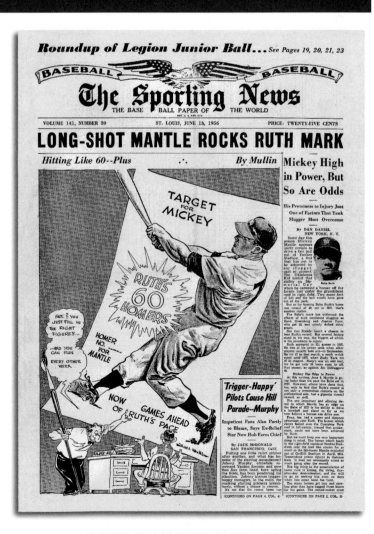

	1	2	3	4	5	6	7	8	9	10	R	H	E
BKLYN.	0	0	0	0	0	0	0				0	0	0
YANKS	0	0	0	1	0	1	0	0			2	5	0

AT BAT 8 POS.
BALL 1 STRIKE 2 OUT 2

The perfect game

With the 1956 World Series tied at two victories each, Don Larsen didn't seem the perfect choice to start Game 5 for the Yankees.

After all, Larsen, 27, still hadn't nailed down a regular spot in the Yankees' rotation despite two seasons of trying. Plus, the righthander had lasted only 1⅔ innings against the Dodgers in Game 2 of the '56 Series. And then there was that 3-21 record he had compiled for the Orioles in 1954. But the *perfect* choice he was. Employing a no-windup delivery, Larsen, incredibly, yielded no hits and allowed no baserunners. Ninety-seven pitches thrown; 27 Dodgers up, 27 down (the last being pinch hitter Dale Mitchell, who took a called third strike). In the first no-hitter in World Series history, it was Yankees 2, Dodgers 0.

WORLD SERIES 1956: The Yanks coasted, 9-0, in Game 7. Bill Skowron (left) had a grand slam, Yogi Berra (right) hit two homers and pitcher Johnny Kucks excelled.

The first Cy Young Award was presented in 1956, and it went to Dodgers ace Don Newcombe (right), who also carted home the N.L.'s MVP plaque. Teammate Don Drysdale won recognition as Brooklyn's top rookie.

'Jackie's goodbye leaves 'em gulping'

—January 16, 1957

In a trade that seemed inconceivable, the Dodgers dealt Jackie Robinson to their hated rivals, the Giants, in December 1956. A month later, Robinson announced his retirement, voiding the swap (in which Brooklyn was to receive pitcher Dick Littlefield and cash).

Robinson, 37, spent 10 seasons in the majors and had a .311 career batting average. One of the most tenacious competitors and unnerving baserunners the game had ever known, he was Rookie of the Year in 1947, the National League's MVP and batting champion in 1949, a two-time stolen base leader, a key player on six pennant-winning Dodgers teams and a member of Brooklyn's only World Series championship club.

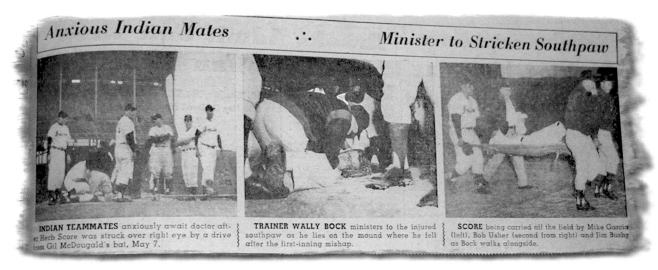

Anxious Indian Mates ∴ *Minister to Stricken Southpaw*

INDIAN TEAMMATES anxiously await doctor after Herb Score was struck over right eye by a drive from Gil McDougald's bat, May 7.

TRAINER WALLY BOCK ministers to the injured southpaw as he lies on the mound where he fell after the first-inning mishap.

SCORE being carried off the field by Mike Garcia (left), Bob Usher (second from right) and Jim Busby as Bock walks alongside.

Indians lefthander Herb Score, on the fast track to greatness, was struck in the right eye by a line drive off the bat of the Yankees' Gil McDougald on May 7, 1957. Score, who had led the American League in strikeouts in 1955 and 1956 (his first two years in the major leagues) and won 20 games in '56, faltered after the injury. Boasting a 38-20 career record at the time of the mishap, he was 17-26 thereafter. Score insisted that arm trouble, not the eye injury, caused his decline.

Stuffing the ballot box

No one was arguing about chads, dimpled or otherwise, in 1957, but Cincinnati fans created a stir when their avalanche of votes resulted in seven Reds winning starting roles in the All-Star Game. Commissioner Ford Frick, thinking more deserving players were victimized, ruled that Hank Aaron and Willie Mays would start in place of Reds outfielders Wally Post and Gus Bell. (In 1956, five Reds had been elected starters in Cincinnati's get-out-the-vote drive.)

Majors' Gate Up, Braves Set Mark in '57

LED BY the Milwaukee Braves, who set a National League attendance record with 2,215,404, the major leagues drew 17,015,819 paid customers during the 1957 season. This represented a gain of 472,569—or 2.86 per cent—over the '56 total. The senior circuit again set the pace with 8,819,601, but the American League, with 8,196,218, enjoyed the biggest increase, 302,535.

The Braves, continuing their fabulous gate showing, went over the 2,000,000 figure for the fourth straight year as they cracked the old N. L. record of 2,131,388 which they set in 1954. Four other National League clubs —St. Louis, Philadelphia, Cincinnati and Brooklyn—exceeded the million mark. The Dodgers remained the circuit's No. 1 road attraction, playing to 1,539,988 in rival parks.

The New York Yankees led the American League in home attendance for the ninth consecutive year with a draw of 1,497,134. Detroit, Boston, Chicago and Baltimore also went over the million figure as all A. L. clubs except Cleveland and Kansas City registered gains. The Tigers enjoyed the biggest increase of any major club, 221,164, while the Yankees boasted the majors' best road attendance, 1,838,424.

The National Association, with 28 leagues, lured a total of 15,544,383 paid fans in 1957, including all-star, playoff and inter-league games. This compared with 17,078,252 for the '56 season when the same number of leagues operated. Buffalo of the International League led all minor league clubs at the gate with 386,071 for the regular season.

The majors' official 1957 figures (minors' attendance shown with respective league averages), plus game and season highs for each club, follow:

The Braves, who had taken the Dodgers to the wire in 1956, beat everyone to the wire in 1957. Milwaukee clinched the pennant before its wildly supportive fans on September 23 when Hank Aaron hit a two-run homer in the 11th inning against the Cardinals. Aaron hit 44 homers and knocked in 132 runs in '57, and Eddie Mathews slammed 32 homers. Midyear acquisition Red Schoendienst provided leadership, and late-July call-up Bob "Hurricane" Hazle batted .403 in 41 games. Warren Spahn won 21 games, Bob Buhl 18 and Lew Burdette 17. Braves victory scenes were plentiful in '57 and again in 1958 (above, left to right, are manager Fred Haney, owner Lou Perini, Spahn, reliever Don McMahon and Aaron).

Attention-getters in 1957 included (left to right) Cincinnati's Frank Robinson, Cleveland's Roger Maris, Boston's Ted Williams and St. Louis' Von McDaniel. Robinson, 1956 N.L. Rookie of the Year when he hit 38 homers, smashed 29 in '57 and batted .322; Maris, an Indians rookie, displayed all-around potential and a home run cut; Williams, 39, hit a league-high .388; and McDaniel, right out of high school, pitched two-hit and one-hit shutouts (but quickly flamed out).

WORLD SERIES 1957: After shutting out the Yankees in Game 7 for his third win of the Series, Milwaukee's Lew Burdette got a hug from catcher Del Crandall as third baseman Eddie Mathews rushed to join the Braves' championship celebration at Yankee Stadium.

NELSON A. ROCKEFELLER (left) shakes hands with Walter O'Malley, Dodger president, September 18, as they discussed a stadium project at a meeting with Mayor Robert Wagner (center). Standing in the rear is John Cashmore, Brooklyn borough prexy.

Rockefeller Plan Snagged, Brooks Turn Eyes to Coast

The future of National League baseball in New York took a big hit in July 1957 when Giants owner Horace Stoneham, citing plunging revenue and fans' relocation to the suburbs, said his team had no chance to survive in the Polo Grounds. Stoneham later announced he was taking the team to San Francisco. And when a plan for a new stadium in Brooklyn encountered opposition in September, the Dodgers were on the brink of bolting, too.

For Outstanding Fielding...

RAWLINGS ANNUAL MAJOR LEAGUE

GOLD GLOVE AWARDS

Recognizing the importance of superior individual fielding performance to the advancement of baseball as America's national game, Rawlings has established Annual Gold Glove Awards beginning with the 1957 season.

Each of the nine Major League players chosen for The Sporting News All-Star Fielding Teams will be honored with a Rawlings Gold Glove Award. Selections will be made by a Committee named by The Sporting News.

Rawlings
"The Finest In The Field!"

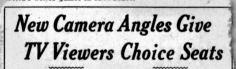

World Series games in Milwaukee.

New Camera Angles Give TV Viewers Choice Seats

Photogs Even Pick Up Catcher's Signals

By CLIFFORD KACHLINE
ST. LOUIS, Mo.

Introducing the center field camera in the 1957 World Series, network television gave fans at home a view of the game to which they have grown accustomed.

Defensive excellence was acknowledged in 1957 with the introduction of the Gold Glove, an award sponsored by the Rawlings Sporting Goods Co. and presented to members of The Sporting News' Major League All-Star Fielding Team.

With Giants owner Horace Stoneham having disclosed plans to move his club to San Francisco, the Dodgers announced officially in October 1957 that they, too, were headed for California (where a Los Angeles welcoming party was ready). The Dodgers still had a loyal fan base in Brooklyn, but the fun at Ebbets Field (left) couldn't offset the minuses of a cramped, deteriorating park. The Giants' attendance had fallen precipitously—to 653,923 in '57—at the Polo Grounds.

Three's Crowd in New York, Says Stoneham

Cheers, Tears, Souvenir Rush at Giants' Farewell to N.Y.

Mob Scene Marks Polo Grounds Wake

Crowd Goes Wild After Game's End

Players Flee to Clubhouse as Fans Swarm Onto Field

Fans Tote Mementoes Away; One-Time Stars of Team on Hand for Ceremonies

By JOE KING
NEW YORK, N. Y.

Probably the strangest scene ever to take place in a baseball park, one of twisted, tangled emotions that would defy analysis by a board of Supreme Court psychiatrists, was staged as the Giants played their final game in the Polo Grounds, September 29.

A crowd turned from orderly array into a roaring mob abruptly as the game ended and swarmed over the field to snatch or uproot any available object as a souvenir. Grand old-timers of the glory days of the Giants were introduced before the game and almost without exception seemed puzzled and quiet by the occasion, which was a sad event for them and for so many others, and no reason for hurrahs.

It is difficult to make a start; there are so many extravagant incidents. However, the day surely had its fitting finale as the last fan left the park. She was Mrs. Blanche S. McGraw, widow of the great manager of Giant glory, and she said, struggling with tears, "I still can't believe I'll never see the Giants in the Polo Grounds again. New York can never be the same to me."

Nor, alas, to so many others, including those who chanted in unison before the center field clubhouse: "We want Stoneham—with a rope around Horace Stoneham, president, was not present at this ceremony which he had arranged as a farewell to the park which the Giants had held longer than any other team in baseball had kept a home.

MEMBERS OF THE GIANTS sprinted to the center field clubhouse as the crowd surged onto the field immediately aft- er the final game at the Polo Grounds, September 29. The crowd then went on a souvenir-hunting rampage.

'Next year for Dodgers means California.'

—October 16, 1957

When Los Angeles plucked the Dodgers out of Brooklyn after the 1957 season, it left a wrenching void in the borough.

1958

WESTWARD HO!

1968

The news sent shock waves through the baseball world. It also triggered the greatest period of growth and prosperity the game has ever known. When the Dodgers and Giants bolted the gray streets of Brooklyn and New York for the greener pastures of Los Angeles and San Francisco, they redefined the physical and financial boundaries of a sport on the move.

With the first pitch of the 1958 season, the baseball map stretched from coast to coast and the game truly had become America's National Pastime. The era of relocation and expansion was at hand, no matter what the cost. If there were any doubts about baseball's big-business aspirations, one needed to look no further than the Borough of Churches, where jilted fans would agonize over the loss

of their beloved Dodgers for decades to come.

In retrospect, it seems odd that the game's corporate personality emerged during a period of social and political upheaval. While Americans protested, rebelled, celebrated, fought, loved and cried during the tumultuous 1960s, baseball transformed itself into a powerful enterprise that would reap the benefits of the coming technological bonanza.

The wild and crazy decade of the '60s was a mad dash from Barbie dolls and G.I. Joes to the once-incomprehensible reality of space travel. In between, baseball provided a welcome diversion as Americans fought an unpopular war in Southeast Asia, protested with the baby-boom generation on college campuses, danced to the music of Elvis and the Beatles, marveled at women's liberation, "made love, not war" with the hippies and mourned the assassinations of three charismatic political leaders.

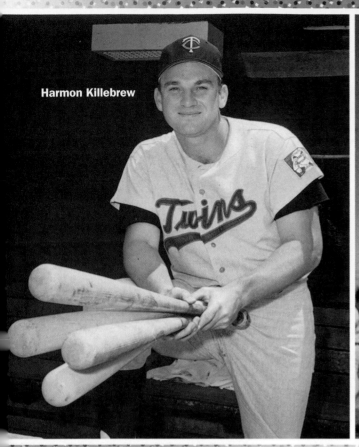

Harmon Killebrew

Orlando Cepeda and Ernie Banks

As in the post-World War II era, baseball's rising fortunes were tied closely to television. Increased sports programming was generating a tremendous infusion of dollars for hungry executives and baseball, like other sports, signed big-money contracts. Further payoff came in the form of coast-to-coast coverage of events and a national advertising base that attracted even more dollars. The success formula was simple and lucrative, and everyone clamored for more.

"More" as in franchises and cities. As baseball owners searched for the ultimate television markets, loyalties were cast aside and relocation and expansion became logical strategies. The American League added two teams (in Los Angeles and Washington) and shifted another franchise (the old Senators to Minneapolis) in 1961 and the National League added two (in New York and Houston) the following season. By the end of the decade, a major league alignment that consisted of 16 teams for 60 years would number 24.

As the baseball map grew, so did the owners' appetite for ways to satisfy a spiraling interest in the game. A natural outgrowth of expansion was the sudden need for bigger and better facilities to attract fans and replace the aging, no-frills ballparks of yesteryear. When San Francisco's beautiful new Candlestick Park opened in 1960 as home for the transplanted Giants, it introduced a ballpark-building craze that changed the face of baseball and the dynamics of the cities in which it was played.

As city populations rushed to the suburbs, so did teams that formerly had existed in the restrictive confines of the downtown areas they served. The new stadiums were bigger, fancier, cleaner and surrounded by acres of parking. Dodger Stadium opened in 1962 and Shea Stadium followed in '64. But the real breakthrough facility appeared in 1965 when Houston's Astrodome, the so-called "eighth wonder of the world," introduced the concept of indoor baseball.

The Astrodome was much more than an architectural masterpiece. It taught the world that the game could be manipulated and that comfort and luxury could be part of the

1961

The Peace Corps is established.

Alan Shepard is America's first man in space.

1962

John Glenn becomes the first U.S. astronaut to orbit the Earth.

U.S.-Soviet Union crisis ends when the Russians dismantle their missile bases in Cuba.

1963

President Kennedy is assassinated in Dallas, Texas.

Blacks' quest for social justice is symbolized by the March on Washington.

baseball experience. Unable to maintain natural grass under its massive roof, the Astrodome also introduced artificial turf. From its roots sprung the distasteful sterility of cookie-cutter baseball.

When St. Louis unveiled Busch Memorial Stadium in 1966, baseball had its first open-air multipurpose facility—round, fully enclosed and unwaveringly symmetrical. Although Busch did not have a roof, it soon converted to an AstroTurf field that would better stand up to the rigors of baseball, football and any other event the city might want to stage. Other cities followed Busch's example with lookalike facilities that encouraged a faster, more defense-oriented brand of baseball.

This unprecedented period of growth did not detract from the product on the field. The expanded form of baseball looked very much like the pre-1960 game, complete with masterful pitching performances, colorful personalities and landmark hitting accomplishments.

The 10-year stretch from 1959-68 will long be remembered for pitching exploits. Little Pittsburgh lefthander Harvey Haddix captured headlines in 1959 by pitching 12 perfect innings in a bizarre game he would eventually lose to Milwaukee, and pitchers like Detroit's Denny McLain (31 wins) and St. Louis' Bob Gibson (a 1.12 ERA) so thoroughly dominated the 1968 campaign that baseball officials changed the rules to give overmatched hitters a fighting chance. In between, Dodgers lefthander Sandy Koufax overpowered the National League like few pitchers before him and matched the

From bottom left, clockwise:
Ted Williams, Willie Mays,
Hank Aaron and Stan Musial.
Center: Mickey Mantle.

1964

The Civil Rights Act is passed.

The Beatles make their first U.S. tour. Six of their records top the U.S. charts, the first being "I Want to Hold Your Hand."

1965

Malcolm X is assassinated in New York.
Sony introduces the first commercial home videotape recorder. The cost: $995.

1966

Medicare, enacted two years earlier, goes into effect.

perfect-game efforts of Philadelphia's Jim Bunning and Oakland's Catfish Hunter.

Pittsburgh second baseman Bill Mazeroski supplied the most dramatic moment of the period when he drilled a ninth-inning home run to defeat the New York Yankees in Game 7 of the 1960 World Series, and the most dramatic seasons were turned in by New York Yankees right fielder Roger Maris and Los Angeles shortstop Maury Wills. Maris hit 61 home runs in the memorable summer of '61, finally ending Babe Ruth's long reign as baseball's single-season homer king, and Wills brought baserunning back into vogue with his record 104-steal rampage for the Dodgers in

Sandy Koufax

Denny McLain

Bob Gibson

1962—the same season those lovable expansion New York Mets were losing 120 games under former Yankees manager Casey Stengel.

Perhaps the most notable development of the 1960s was

the collapse of a Yankees dynasty that had produced 29 American League pennants and 20 World Series championships in a 44-year period from 1921-64. Six of those pennants and three of the championships came in the seven-year stretch from 1958-64, but the rest of the decade was spent in unfamiliar surroundings near the bottom of the A.L. standings.

As the 1968 season came to a close, baseball felt the ominous rumblings of unprecedented change that lurked just around the corner. As issues like postseason expansion, designated hitters and style of play dominated the thinking of baseball purists, the game's movers and shakers moved into the courtroom to debate challenges to the sport's reserve system ("baseball slavery"). The players' financial star was about to rise—dramatically.

The configuration of the Los Angeles Memorial Coliseum was geared for football, meaning improvisation was needed to turn the facility into the Dodgers' new home. One result was an inviting 40-foot-high screen in left field, 251 feet from home plate, that some critics feared would result in an assault on all major home run marks. The screen was a cozy target, all right, but the game's hallowed records remained safe.

Rhubarbs, Freakish Hits, Beanballs Recall Ebbets Field Days

Like Old Times at Dodgers' New Home

'Grand Canyon With Seats' 　 ．． 　 78,672 at Los Angeles Opener

Something old, something new ...

Dodgers owner Walter O'Malley saw dollar signs when his club moved to the mammoth Los Angeles Coliseum in 1958. Duke Snider (far right) and Gil Hodges, who starred at Brooklyn's tiny Ebbets Field (below, being razed), were now beginning to slip.

WELCOMES.F. Giants

The streets of San Francisco were abuzz over the Giants, who later won the first big-league game on the West Coast.

First Major Contest on Coast Proves Super Spectacle

San Francisco Beams as Giants Glitter in Bow

Rookies Live Up to Notices in First Game

Raised Roof at Coast's Debut in Big Time

'Say-Hey Also Puts on Show as Gomez Blanks Dodgers in Golden Gate Inaugural'

By JOE KING
SAN FRANCISCO, Calif.—

PANORAMIC VIEW of jam-packed Seals Stadium, San Francisco, for the first major league championship game in California history. A crowd of 23,448 squeezed into the former Pacific Coast League park for the Giants' opener.

'Everybody in this town is unconscious after that game. They won't come to for a while. You know, if this thing had been staged, it couldn't have come out better.'

—former major league star Lefty O'Doul, a longtime manager of the minor league San Francisco Seals and a native San Franciscan, April 23, 1958

A crash ends Campanella's career

Neck Broken, Vet Catcher Is Paralyzed

'It Could Be Two Months, Even Years, Before Roy Can Walk,' Surgeon Says

By ROSCOE McGOWEN
NEW YORK, N. Y.

There have been a lot of memorable dates in the life of Roy Campanella, many of them filled with thrills and happiness, some with pain and discomfiture.

But here is one date that will be etched on his memory as long as memory lasts — and on the memories of his family and his friends.

It was 3:34 a. m., Tuesday, January 28, 1958.

At that moment the roly-poly catcher of the Dodgers, and three-time winner of the National League Most Valuable Player Award, met the greatest disaster of his life and came within inches of instant death.

Driving a rented '57 Chevy sports sedan en route to his Glen Cove, L. I., home, and only half a mile from it, he failed to negotiate the back end of an "S" curve on the crest of a hill.

The car crashed into a telephone pole on its right, bounced away and turned over. Campanella was pinned in the car, his legs caught by a door and his body "twisted like a pretzel," according to Dr. W. S. Gurnee, a Manhattan gynecologist, who lives nearby and was first on the scene.

Nine hours later, following a four-hour operation, Campanella lay in the Glen Cove Community Hospital in serious and paralyzed from the chest [...] and paralyzed from the chest

had said "we expect recovery" from the paralysis by saying:

"It is possible he won't fully recover from the paralysis. Isn't his age a factor, too, when we add in the period needed for recovery?"

Some interpretations of the latter query assumed that the surgeon's reference to the age factor applied to Campy's playing ball because of age as well as the serious injury. Still, the statement that Roy might not "fully" recover from the paralysis certainly would mean he could never play again, regardless of his 36 years.

O'Malley already [...]

ROY CAMPANELLA . . . Improved after suffering broken neck in auto accident.

A Swerve on a Curve--Player and Car Smashed

YOUNGSTERS examine the badly damaged car in which the Dodger catcher was injured when it swerved off the road at an "S" turn near his home at Glen Glove, N. Y., and struck a tree. It required 45 minutes to extricate the injured backstop star from the wreckage.

Newcombe Considered Likely Bait in Trade to Land Catcher

NEW YORK, N. Y.—The tragic accident to Roy Campanella must mean that the Dodgers will be in the immediate market for a catcher.

It is not conceivable that a pennant-contending club, as the new Los Angeles Dodgers perforce must consider themselves, can suffer the loss of Campanella without making a replacement.

They have the dependable Rube Walker, but, no matter how much Rube is liked, nor how much his skills are respected, they are limited.

Joe Pignatano is a fine young receiver, one of the best, but hardly a [...]

had remained until 9:30, then left, returning two hours later. At about 12:30 he told one of his clerks he was going home, normally about a 45-minute drive.

He was driving a rented car because he had put his own heavier station wagon in the shop for some repairs and it wasn't ready.

Dr. Gurnee, who heard the crash, had rushed out in his pajamas and robe, telling his wife to bring his case. He administered a hypodermic to Campy, who, he said, apparently did not feel the needle, indicating the paralysis already [...]

'If it had been an inch or two higher, he would be dead.'

—Dr. Robert W. Sengstaken

WORLD SERIES 1958: On the brink of losing again to the Braves, the Yankees rallied from a three games-to-one deficit to win. New York's Bob Turley, the '58 Cy Young winner, hurled a shutout in Game 5, got the final out in relief in Game 6 and hurled 6⅔ innings of one-run ball out of the bullpen in Game 7. The Yanks' Hank Bauer ran his Series-record hitting streak to 17 games in Game 3, then was halted.

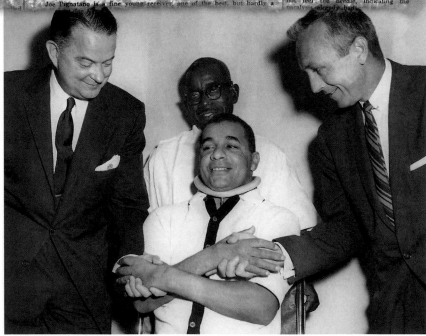

Seriously injured in a January 28, 1958, auto accident, longtime Dodgers catcher Roy Campanella later received encouragement from his doctors. Campanella was the National League's MVP in 1951, 1953 and 1955.

Musial Turns Top Seven Into Elite Eight

Ty Cobb Rated as Greatest of Game's 3,000-Hit Galaxy

Peach Played to Age of 42, Wagner to 43

Stan, 37, Has Chance to Top All But Ty and Speaker in Game's All-Time Hit List

By FREDERICK G. LIEB
ST. LOUIS, Mo.

When Stanley Frank Musial, truly "The Man" of present-day baseball, whacked out his 3,000th major league hit against the Cubs at Wrigley Field, May 13, he became the eighth man initiated into one of the National Game's most exclusive circles, the 3,000-Hit Club.

Seven master hitters of the craft preceded Stan into the club. They include the famed Georgia Peach, Ty Cobb, the hard-riding former Texas cow-puncher, Tris Speaker; the great Flying Dutchman, Hans Wagner; the graceful-fielding, hard-hitting Napoleon Lajoie; the Columbia University star, Eddie Collins; the patriarch of the last century, Adrian (Cap) Anson, and the former Pirate hitting expert, Paul Waner, last man before Musial to make the club. Paul collected his 3,000th hit during World War II, while wearing the uniform of the Boston Braves, getting it off Rip Sewell, a former Pirate teammate, 16 years ago—on May 20, 1942.

Set Three Goals

Musial sets a new record nearly every time he raises his left arm or winks at an umpire, but while in St. Petersburg during spring training last March he said he had three objectives. He wanted to get himself ready to help the Cardinals win their tenth pennant; he wanted to crash the 3,000-Hit Club as soon as possible, and he hoped to tie Wagner's record of eight National League batting championships.

With the Cardinals' slow start, the first objective already looks like a

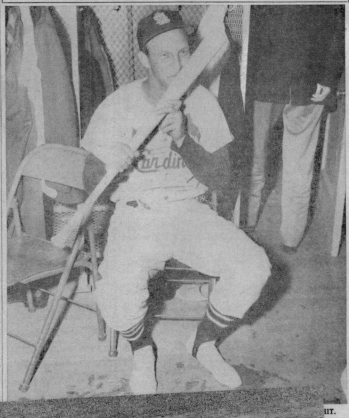

The Man Makes 'Em Move Over

ST. LOUIS AT CHICAGO (D)—Musial, making dramatic appearance as pinch-hitter in sixth inning, smashed double for 3,000th hit of his major league career to spark Cardinals to 5 to 3 victory over Cubs. The Man had not started game, being left out of lineup by Manager Hutchinson so that he might collect historic blow before homefolks at Busch Stadium. However, with Cubs leading, 3 to 1, Green doubled in sixth. After Smith grounded out, Hutchinson called on Musial and Stan responded with two-bagger off Drabowsky, Green scoring. After game had been halted to award ball to Musial, Barnes came in to run. Schofield then walked and Blasingame singled, driving in tying run. Pass to Cunningham and forceout by Noren netted leading counter and double by Moon send insurance tally across plate.

St. Louis	AB.	H.	O.	A.	Chicago	AB.	H.	O.	A.
Schofield, ss.	2	0	1	4	T. Taylor, 2b	4	1	3	5
Blas'game, 2b	5	1	1	2	Walls, rf.	3	2	2	1
Cun'gham, 1b	3	0	8	0	Banks, ss.	3	0	1	7
Noren, lf.	4	2	3	0	Moryn, lf.	4	1	1	0
Moon, cf.	4	1	3	0	Long, 1b.	4	0	11	0
Flood, cf.	1	1	2	0	S. Taylor, c.	3	2	4	0
Boyer, 3b.	4	1	1	2	Thomson, cf.	3	0	2	0
Green, rf.	5	1	1	0	Goryl, 3b.	3	1	3	1
H. Smith, c.	4	1	7	0	dTanner	1	0	0	0
Jones, p.	2	0	0	1	Drabowsky, p.	2	0	0	3
aMusial	1	1	0	0	cP. Smith	1	0	0	0
bBarnes	0	0	0	0	Phillips, p.	0	0	0	0
Muffett, p.	0	0	0	1					
Totals	35	9	27	10	Totals	31	7	27	17

St. Louis	0 0 1	0 0 4	0 0 0	—5
Chicago	1 0 1	0 1 0	0 0 0	—3

Pitchers	IP.	H.	R.	ER.	BB.	SO.
Jones (Winner 2-3)	5	5	3	3	1	5
Muffett	4	2	0	0	1	2
Drabowsky (Loser 1-3)	7	8	5	4	5	3
Phillips	2	1	0	0	2	0

aDoubled for Jones in sixth. bRan for Musial in sixth. cGrounded out for Drabowsky in seventh.

Pinch hitting against the Cubs' Moe Drabowsky at Wrigley Field on May 13, 1958, St. Louis' Stan Musial (left) reached the 3,000-hit milestone with a double and was congratulated by Cardinals manager Fred Hutchinson. Musial, 37, batted .337 that season.

Haddix: 12 perfect innings, then ...

	1	2	3	4	5	6	7	8	9	10	R	H	E
PITT	0	0	0	0	0	0	0	0	0	0		9	0
MIL	0	0	0	0	0	0	0	0		1	0	0	0

BALL   OUT 0 PLAY

STRIKE   AT BAT

'It was just another loss, but it hurt a little more'
—Harvey Haddix

There's perfection, as in 27 batters up and 27 down. And then there's what Pirates lefthander Harvey Haddix did on the night of May 26, 1959, at County Stadium in Milwaukee: 36 up, 36 down. But pitching an unprecedented 12 innings of perfect baseball was not enough for Haddix, who wound up with a loss in the 13th inning.

The Braves turned into improbable winners when Felix Mantilla reached first on an error to start the 13th, Eddie Mathews laid down a sacrifice bunt, Hank Aaron drew an intentional walk and Joe Adcock drove a Haddix pitch over the fence in right-center. (Adcock, who passed Aaron on the bases, was credited with a double. And the final score became 1-0.)

The winning pitcher: Lew Burdette, who gave up 12 hits, all singles.

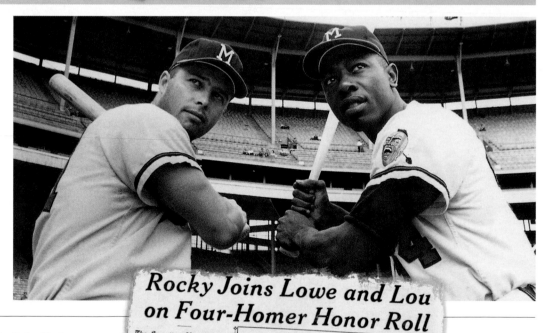

Milwaukee's Eddie Mathews and Hank Aaron posed big trouble from opposite sides of the plate. In 1959, the lefthanded-hitting Mathews led the N.L. with 46 homers; Aaron topped the league in slugging percentage (.636) and batting average (.355).

In 1959, the Indians' Rocky Colavito became only the eighth major leaguer to hit four homers in one game and just the third player to hit them in succession. The spree came at Baltimore's Memorial Stadium, where, previously, no team had hit more than three homers in one game.

Rocky Joins Lowe and Lou on Four-Homer Honor Roll

The Sporting News Feature Will Look Better, Chirps Colavito Following Feat

They Hit 'Em in Succession

By HAL LEBOVITZ
BALTIMORE, Md.
Rocky Colavito, the Indians' slugging outfielder, is a most obliging young man. The June 10 issue of THE SPORTING NEWS had featured him as the American League player most likely to emulate—and possibly surpass—Babe Ruth's record of 60 home runs in one season.

Observed the grateful Rocky, "That was a fine compliment THE SPORTING NEWS paid me. I hope my slump isn't letting the paper down."

On June 10, about an hour after he

First Inter-League Trade?

Musial to Yanks-- Berra a Redbird

'Sale' of Blaylock Seen as Forerunner of Swap

By J. G. TAYLOR SPINK
ST. LOUIS, Mo.

The first inter-league deal to be consummated n e x t November when the barriers are let down for the first time will be between the Yankees and the Cardinals, THE SPORTING NEWS has learned from a reliable authority.

Stan Musial will go from the Cardinals to the Yankees in ex-change for Yogi Berra. Other

With interleague trading to be introduced in the major leagues in the fall of 1959, The Sporting News reported that the first swap might well be a real blockbuster (left). It never happened. The initial A.L.-N.L. deal turned out to be between the Red Sox and Cubs, Boston sending first baseman Dick Gernert to Chicago for pitcher Dave Hillman and first baseman Jim Marshall.

Bosox Size Up Hillman as Big Help on Mound

Former Cub Recommended by Coach Herman; Dave Tabbed 'Real Competitor'

By HY HURWITZ
BOSTON, Mass.

As expected, the Red Sox b r o k e through the starting barrier when inter - league trading became official at 12.01 a. m., November 21.

In fact, the Red Sox and Chicago Cubs a c t u a l l y agreed to the transfer of First Baseman Dick Gernert from B o s t o n to Chicago for Righthander Dave Hillman and First Baseman Jim Marshall.

Jim Marshall

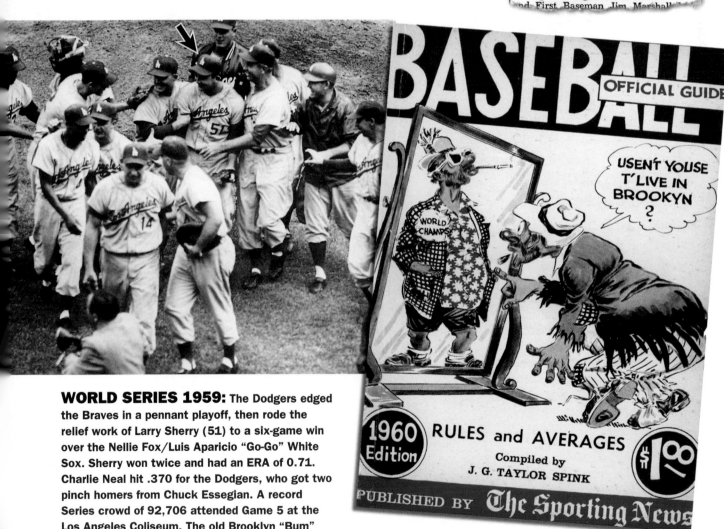

WORLD SERIES 1959: The Dodgers edged the Braves in a pennant playoff, then rode the relief work of Larry Sherry (51) to a six-game win over the Nellie Fox/Luis Aparicio "Go-Go" White Sox. Sherry won twice and had an ERA of 0.71. Charlie Neal hit .370 for the Dodgers, who got two pinch homers from Chuck Essegian. A record Series crowd of 92,706 attended Game 5 at the Los Angeles Coliseum. The old Brooklyn "Bum" (right) couldn't believe his good fortune.

Ever the innovator, White Sox owner Bill Veeck put names on the back of his players' uniforms beginning in 1960. You didn't need a program to tell who No. 22 (Dick Donovan), No. 7 (Jim Rivera) and No. 2 (Nellie Fox) were.

The Yanks' Kansas City 'farm club'

A longtime farm team of the Yankees, Kansas City still seemed to be in that feeder role after acquiring the Athletics. In many of their trades through the late '50s, the Yankees and general manager George Weiss appeared to fleece the A's, trading quantity for quality. The December 1959 deal that sent promising Roger Maris from K.C. to New York drew heavy fire from Yankees opponents, who feared Maris might blossom in pinstripes.

200

Rocky Colavito (left), an Indians favorite who tied for the '59 A.L. homer title, was traded to Detroit for batting king Harvey Kuenn just before the '60 opener.

ROGER MARIS

"

If outfielder Roger Maris, whom the Yankees acquired from Kansas City last December, plays for them for another decade, he will have a most difficult time matching the spectacular demonstration he put on in his debut for Casey Stengel in the Fenway opener. ... Leading in this showy achievement was an almost unstoppable Maris, with two homers, a double, a single and a walk. He drove in three runs and was retired only once, when Brewer threw him out in the third inning.

—April 27, 1960

"

When it was disclosed in 1960 that the majors soon would expand, it was the death knell for the Continental League, a proposed third major league that Branch Rickey and other executives originally wanted to open in 1961. The new league hoped to place teams in Houston, Atlanta, Denver, Minneapolis-St. Paul, Dallas-Fort Worth, Toronto, New York and Buffalo.

Take my manager ... please

Indians general manager Frank Lane would deal anyone—as he proved in April 1960 with the swap of popular Rocky Colavito. That August, he agreed to a trade of managers with Detroit, dealing his man, Joe Gordon, for Jimmie Dykes. It was Tigers G.M. Bill DeWitt who apparently broached this idea, though.

Ted bows out

It was September 28, 1960, and everyone knew Ted Williams was playing his last game at Fenway Park. In the eighth inning, Williams went to bat for what likely was the last time in Boston. Showing his usual flair, Williams walloped a long home run (below) off Orioles pitcher Jack Fisher. Williams was expected to play in an ensuing season-ending series at New York, but he announced after the game that he was quitting immediately. It had been quite a year for Ted, one in which he batted .316 and hit 29 homers (including the 500th of his career, which came in June).

Splinter Tips Cap to Hub Fans After Farewell Homer

Ted Socks 29th of Season in Final Game of Career; Talks at Plate Ceremony

By HY HURWITZ

BOSTON, Mass.

... the Red ... prepared ... for the ... Ted Wil-... final per-... ce couldn't ... e en more ... atic. The ... er bowed ... eptember 28, ... thunderous ... run to cap ... of the great-... history. ... ance attract-... ark on a day

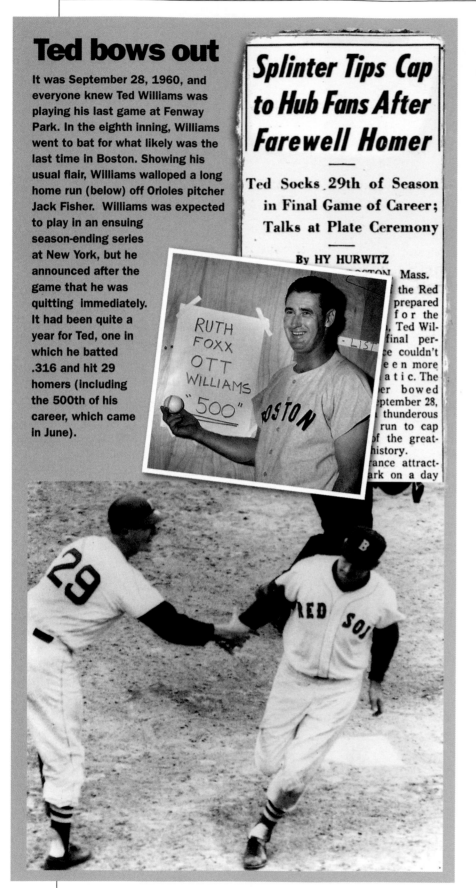

Mazeroski

WORLD SERIES 1960: It was wacky. The Yankees scored all the runs and the Pirates won all the games. A stretch, perhaps, but New York really did outscore Pittsburgh, 55-27, and the Pirates really did wind up as champions. The Pirates finessed their way to victories in Games 1, 4 and 5, winning by scores of 6-4, 3-2 and 5-2. The Yankees bludgeoned their way to 16-3, 10-0 and 12-0 triumphs in Games 2, 3 and 6. (Bobby Richardson's grand slam

levels the Yankees

and six RBIs spiced Game 3.)

Game 7 at Forbes Field was a classic, the Pirates seizing a 4-0 lead but the Yanks taking a 7-4 edge into the bottom of the eighth inning. The Pirates, aided by a bad-hop grounder that struck shortstop Tony Kubek in the throat, broke loose for five runs—the last three coming on Hal Smith's home run. The resourceful Yanks evened the game in the ninth—thanks to the alert baserunning of Mickey Mantle, whose ability to avoid a tag while diving back into first base enabled the tying run to score.

With the scoreboard reading, 9-9, in the last of the ninth, Pirates second baseman Bill Mazeroski—a player known chiefly for his fielding prowess—led off and sent Ralph Terry's second pitch over the left field wall. Remarkably, the Pirates had won the game—and, somehow, the Series. And there was bedlam on the field (above).

'The minute the ball
cleared the wall, 36,683 fans
went absolutely wild.'

—*October 19, 1960*

Say-Hey Kid's Greatest Day
Mays Boomed 4 HRs With Borrowed Bat

Willie Swung Amalfitano's Mace in Bid to End Slump

Giant Star Never Had Hit More Than Two in One Game Before Big Salvo; Shook Off Illness of Previous Night

By BOB STEVENS

CHICAGO, Ill.

Though Willie Mays would have liked a shot at a fifth home run against Milwaukee, April 30, in County Stadium, the Say-Hey Kid doesn't think he would have done it.

Mays never before had hit more than two home runs in a single game, had ripped only two this year prior to his historic afternoon in Milwaukee. Then, on April 30, he crashed one off Lew Burdette, one off Seth Morehead and the last off Don McMahon. Thus Willie became the ninth player in major league history to belt four homers in one game.

Mays was in the on-deck circle when Jimmy Davenport grounded out to end the game. The Milwaukee crowd lustily booed both Pitcher Ken Mac-Kenzie and Second Baseman Frank Bolling for conspiring to end the game and deprive Willie of a chance to go for No. 5.

"Honestly," said Mays, "I might have done a thing. I know what I did done. I heard it over the loud speakers. I had the greatest day of my career. I probably will never have another one like it again. If I'd done up again, I might have pressed too hard for the home run. And when you press, you're dead. Seldom have I ever really tried to hit a home run and got it.

Measured Spahn for Homer

"I think the last time I did, and got it, was against Warren Spahn in Milwaukee two years ago. It was the ninth inning and he was ahead by a run. We had a man on. I swung as hard as I could and it went into the bleachers. But that doesn't happen very often."

There was some interesting background music to the concert of crash played in County Stadium the day of the four home runs.

On the night of April 29, Willie and his roomie, Willie McCovey, had a

Walloper Willie

[box score statistics table]

Here's Suds In Your Eye ∴ Four Times

WILLIE MAYS, wreathed in a giant-sized grin, displays four baseballs, symbolizing the four home runs he clouted against the Braves in Milwaukee County Stadium, April 30. The 'Frisco flailer is the ninth player in major league history to hit four in one game.

The Braves' Warren Spahn and the Giants' Willie Mays gave Milwaukee fans a series to remember in 1961. Spahn tossed a no-hitter against the Giants on April 28; two days later, Mays hit four homers against the Braves. Spahn also won his 300th game in '61.

A. L. Speeds Expansion—Ten Clubs in '61

Nats Go to Minneapolis; New Teams in Capital, L. A.

Slash Player Limit to 23; 162-Tilt Sked

Group of Coast Sportsmen Led by Hank Greenberg; 12 Teams Possible in '62

By JOE KING

NEW YORK, N.Y.

SEVEN AMERICAN LEAGUE BIGWIGS who helped reshape the Junior map of the meeting in the Savoy Hilton Hotel, New York, October 26, lined up for the photographers at the conclusion of the historic session at which two new teams were added.

Magnates Who Helped Revamp ∴ Junior Circuit Map

The first modern expansion

Although the National League had beaten the American League to the punch in announcing plans to expand, saying in mid-October 1960 that it would add Houston and New York in 1962, the A.L. acted first by placing new clubs in Los Angeles and Washington, D.C., for the 1961 season and moving the old Senators to Minneapolis-St. Paul. The Los Angeles team was called the Angels, the Washington club retained the city's longtime Senators nickname and the old Senators became the Minnesota Twins.

Orlando Cepeda (right), who led the National League with 46 home runs in '61, talked it over with past and future N.L. homer kings, Ernie Banks (middle) and Willie McCovey.

Unable to find a manager to lift them from the depths, the Cubs rotated coaches as their head man in 1961 and 1962. That didn't work, either.

Wrigley Hands Himsl Job as Bruin First Head Coach

Vedie to Direct Club Two Weeks--Win, Lose or Draw; Selection Announced in Airplane Press Conference

By JERRY HOLTZMAN

CHICAGO, Ill.

To Avitus (Vedie) Himsl, one-time minor league pitcher and a major league coach since last May, went the distinction of being selected as the first head coach in all of major league history. Announcement that Himsl would be in charge of the managerless Chicago Cubs when they open the National League season was made on April 6 by Club Vice-President John Holland who emphasized that Himsl's head-coaching reign would extend for only two weeks--"even if the Cubs are unbeaten at that time."

Holland broke the news in a most unusual press conference held in the aisles of a chartered DC-6, which was carrying the club to Houston, Tex., immediately after an exhibition game with the Red Sox in San Antonio. Holland said he had received a call from Owner P. K. Wrigley during the ninth inning of the game and that Wrigley wanted Himsl's selection made known as soon as possible.

Holland stressed, ". . . . that Mr. Wrigley had chosen Himsl in recognition of his (Himsl's) seniority . . . and for his long and devoted

Vedie Himsl

Maris and Mantle: their quest for 61

Roger Maris hadn't disappointed in his first season as a Yankee, hitting 39 home runs and driving in 112 runs—and winning MVP honors in the American League. But that was 1960. This was 1961, and Maris was homer-less in his first 10 games of the season.

Mickey Mantle, a Triple Crown winner in 1956 and a three-time A.L. home run champion, was off to a great start in '61 with seven homers in 11 games.

Once Maris got hot— white-hot—with a 19-homer spree in a 3½-week period ending June 22, and Mantle continued to produce at a steady clip, baseball settled in for a spirited homer race.

The race soon turned into more than Maris vs. Mantle, though. A third party entered the picture: Babe Ruth.

Yanks Worried About Pitching, More Than Breaking Ruth Mark

Kayo Clouter

Houk's Staff Blasted for 42 Runs, 60 Hits, 32 Walks in Five-Game Nightmare

By JOE KING
NEW YORK, N. Y.

If the Yankees fail to win the pennant, the reason may prove to be their inability to wind up a trip with a flourish.

Despite their forbidding power and the wonders of their bench, the Bombers are not ... killers or fin-

Bob Turley

Switcher at Half - Way Point of Matching Babe's 714 HRs

NASHVILLE, Tenn. — Mickey Mantle was at the half-way point of matching Babe Ruth's total of 714 home runs when he hit No. 357 of his major league career against Bill Monbouquette of the Red Sox July 21.

The 29-year-old Yankee reached the milestone in his seventh season in the majors. He was 32 and in his fourteenth season when he hit No. 357 early in the 1927 campaign, when he topped his record 60. JERRY ...

... he would not risk straining ... velous, life-saving 33-year-old guy. This foresighted move cost Houk a win, when ... in the ninth ...

'Ruth Homer Mark Safe This Season,' Colavito Declares

Sees Day and Night Card as Too Tough

By WATSON SPOELSTRA

Rocky Colavito likes the chances of the Tigers to win the American League pennant, but he doesn't think Babe Ruth's swat record of 60 home runs will be broken this year.

As the Tigers ...

DETROIT, Mich.

Mantle, Maris Spark Gate Boom

By JOE KING

WASHINGTON, D. C. — With the Roger Maris-Mickey Mantle homer circus luring throngs into parks everywhere, the Yankees passed a million attendance on the road in their forty-fifth road game

in Baltimore, July 16. The Bombers toured with the hottest baseball attractions in years, one reminiscent

(CONTINUED ON PAGE 8, COL. 3)

Among those getting caught up in the Mantle-Maris race was film star Doris Day.

Mantle led Maris, 37 homers to 36, after games of July 21. But when Maris cracked four homers in a doubleheader four days later, it was an attention-getter. Was Ruth's record of 60 in jeopardy?

The exploits of both players in this expansion year—the A.L was playing a 162-game schedule, not the usual 154—already had gotten commissioner Ford Frick's attention. And Frick said that Ruth's mark of 60 couldn't be broken unless a player reached 61 within his club's first 154 games played to a decision. Reaching 61 after that would be considered the record for a 162-game schedule.

Maris and Mantle continued their assault, soaring well into the 40s and then the 50s, although Mantle fell out of the running because of a hip ailment.

Frazzled by his quest and the attendant media frenzy, Maris carried on. His total after 154 games played to a decision: 59.

Sultan's Big Shadow Starts to Toll 'Ten' Over M-and-M

Houk Proved Classy Prophet in New Park HR Prediction

TWIN CITIES, Minn.—A prediction by Ralph H...

Yank Sluggers Feeling Heat of Pressure Cooker in Drive; Homer Pace Slackens in Stars' Crazy, Mixed-Up World

Broadway Busting Buttons Over Bomber Thrill Show

Interest Balloons to Ten-Year High, Series Queries ... Sweep M and M Homer Duel

Flying Right

Mick, Rog Clout Two HRs Each in Sweep of Series

Arroyo Captures Two D...

WRITERS BACK FRICK'S HOMER DECISION

Poll Supports 154-Tilt Rule by 2-1 Margin

Dissenters Argue That Mick and Roger Should Not Be Balked by A. L. Expansion

By C. C. JOHNSON SPINK

ST. LOUIS, Mo.

Members of the Baseball Writers' Association of America gave Commissioner Ford Frick a vote of confidence in a poll conducted by THE SPORTING NEWS, sustaining his opinion that recognition for breaking Babe

Ford Frick

Ruth's home-run record must be accomplished in 154 games or less. However, the vote was by no means unanimous. There was a strong dissent. Eighteen voters disapproved of Frick's decision for a number of reasons which will be listed below.

Thirty-seven others who responded to the poll concurred with the commissioner's re...

After hitting his 60th homer of 1961 on September 26, Maris connected off Boston's Tracy Stallard on October 1 for No. 61 (left, with catcher Russ Nixon watching the flight of the ball). Regardless of the 162-game schedule or the so-called "asterisk" that accompanied his feat (the asterisk really never existed), Maris set an all-time high for homers in one season with his smash on the final day of the '61 season.

The before and after—along with the telling swing—of Roger Maris' 61st homer were shown on the pages of The Sporting News (left). Maris was greeted at home plate by Yogi Berra (8) and a Yankees batboy.

WITH ONLY FIVE INNINGS of the season remaining, Roger Maris broke his deadlock with Babe Ruth as the No. 1 home-run hitter in a major league campaign, when he connected against Tracy Stallard of the Red Sox in the fourth inning of the October 1 contest at Yankee Stadium. The Bomber belter, who clouted home run No. 60 on September 26, drove a pitch into the right field stands to give the Bombers a 1 to 0 victory. At left, Maris adjusts his batting helmet in the on-deck circle, while awaiting his turn at the plate. In center, Rog follows through on his historic clout, watching the ball sail toward the seats. Russ Nixon is the Bosox catcher. At right, the new homer king accepts congratulations from Yogi Berra as he crosses the plate.

Sal Durante, who caught Maris' 61st drive in the right field stands at Yankee Stadium, showed off the ball. Maris, meanwhile, was World Series bound. He and Mickey Mantle (right photo), who finished with 54 homers in '61, surveyed Cincinnati's Crosley Field, site of Games 3, 4 and 5.

WORLD SERIES

1961: Having replaced Casey Stengel as Yankees manager in the offseason, Ralph Houk won his first time out. Roger Maris won Game 3 against the Reds with a ninth-inning homer (right), Whitey Ford set a record by extending his Series scoreless-innings streak to 32 in Game 4 and Hector Lopez drove in five runs in the Game-5 clincher. It was a tough Series overall for Maris (.105). Ailing Mickey Mantle had only six at-bats.

Let's play two ... All-Star Games

Aimed at providing additional revenue for the players' pension fund, helping needy old-time players and boosting youth baseball, two major league All-Star Games were played from 1959 through 1962. In '59, the two games were played approximately four weeks apart; in '61 and '62, there were 20-day gaps. In 1960, the All-Star clashes were played within two days of each other.

And then there were ...

WITH NEW YORK'S N.L. CLUB HAVING SIGNED GEORGE WEISS AS BOSS MAN AND 23 SCOUTS ---ALSO HAVING JUST SELECTED NICKNAME--- THEY SHOULD SOON BE ON THEIR WAY TO DIGGING UP PLAYERS AND GROUND FOR THEIR NEW $17,500,000 STADIUM.

THE METS

AT LAST! THEY HAVE GIVEN ME A NAME

62

SIC EST SENEX TUUS.

* SO'S YOUR OLD

NEW YORK AT PHILADELPHIA (T-N) —Phillies swept twi-night double-header from Mets, 2 to 0 and 2 to 1, as Manager Stengel's new entry dropped sixteenth and seventeenth straight games in longest losing streak of any club in New York's major league history. McLish shut out Mets in opener, beating Craig, while Mahaffey edged Jackson in nightcap. Mets scored their lone run of night off Mahaffey on pass to Ashburn, stolen base and single by Neal in first inning. Jackson turned back Phillies until eighth when Taylor tied score with homer. Winning run followed in ninth on singles by Oldis, Wine and Pinch-Hitter Covington.

New York	ab	r	h	rbi		Philad'phia	ab	r	h	rbi
Chacon, ss	4	0	1	0		T. Taylor, 2b	2	1	1	0
Kanehl, 3b	4	0	2	0		Callison, rf	4	0	2	0
dMantilla	1	0	0	0		Gonzalez, cf	3	0	0	1
Neal, 2b	3	0	0	0		Covington, lf	3	0	1	1
Thomas, lf	4	0	1	0		Davis, lf	0	0	0	0
Throneb'ry, 1b	3	0	1	0		Dalrymple, c	4	0	1	0
Christopher, rf	4	0	1	0		Demeter, 3b	4	0	1	0
Hickman, rf	3	0	0	0		Torre, 1b	2	0	1	0
S. Taylor, c	1	0	0	0		Wine, ss	4	0	1	0
aMiller	0	0	0	0		McLish, p	2	1	0	0
Landrith, c	1	0	1	0						
cHook	0	0	0	0		Totals	28	2	8	2
Craig, p	3	0	0	0						
bAshburn	1	0	0	0						
Totals	32	0	7	0						

New York .... 000 000 000—0
Philadelphia .... 001 000 10x—2

Pitchers	IP.	H.	R.	ER.	BB.	SO.
Craig (L. 2-8)	8	8	2	2	2	6
McLish (W. 5-1)	9	7	0	0	6	5

aRan for S. Taylor in

> "
>
> The Mets broke all modern records in their first season (1962) by suffering 120 defeats while winning only 40 games. It was a trying year for Manager Casey Stengel after his success as a Yankee pilot. A 17-game losing streak, May 21-June 6, plunged the Mets into the dungeon for keeps. The club also lost 11 in a row in July and 13 straight in August.
> —*1963 Official Baseball Guide*
>
> "

Koufax, Wills and The Man

Dodgers lefthander Sandy Koufax pitched no-hitters in four consecutive seasons, the first coming in 1962 against the Mets (above). Koufax led the N.L. with a 2.54 ERA in '62.

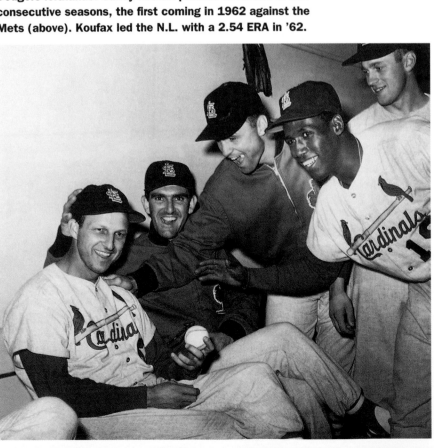

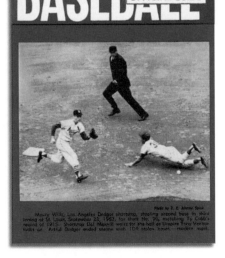

St. Louis teammates gathered around Stan Musial (left) on May 19, 1962, after he collected career hit No. 3,431 and surpassed Honus Wagner as the all-time N.L. leader. Another longtime mark fell in '62 when the Dodgers' Maury Wills (above) broke Ty Cobb's season steals mark of 96. Wills finished with 104 stolen bases.

Finley once presented Kansas City's starting lineup—which on this day included Ken Harrelson—via chauffeured limousine.

The spinning world of Charles Finley

With a subpar product on the field during his tenure as Kansas City A's owner in the 1960s, Charles Finley tried to lure fans with promotions. He introduced Harvey (left), a mechanical rabbit that delivered balls to the umpire, and the "Pennant Porch" (below, right), which mimicked the right field configuration at Yankee Stadium. Another feature was mule Charlie O. (right), the team mascot. Finley also brought sheep to Municipal Stadium—and a shepherd to tend them. And, among other Finley-isms, he brought vivid colors to uniforms—first dressing the A's in green and gold in '63.

Getting royal limousine treatment was nice, but Harrelson and other A's starters also experienced a mule-train arrival.

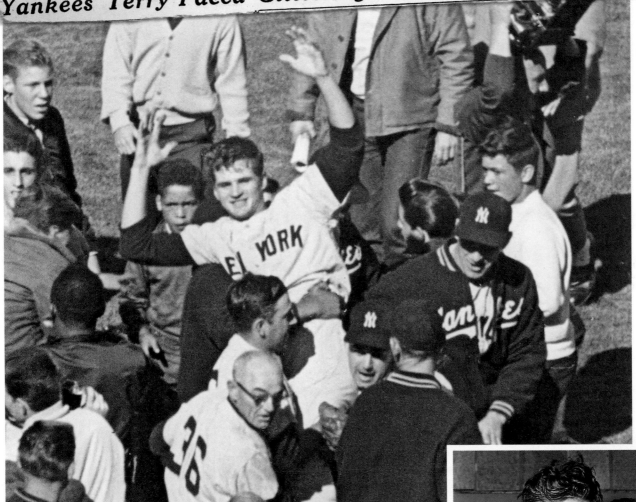

Late, Late Series Packed a Suspense Wallop
Yankees' Terry Paced Glittering Parade of Hill Heroes

WORLD SERIES 1962: In a rainout-filled Series, the Yankees beat the Giants when Ralph Terry, the Series goat in 1960, hurled a four-hit shutout in Game 7. Righthander Terry (above, and right, with Tom Tresh) protected a 1-0 lead in a sticky ninth when, with Giants on second and third and two out, he retired Willie McCovey on a heart-stopping line drive to second baseman Bobby Richardson. Before the Terry-McCovey duel, Roger Maris' ability to cut off Willie Mays' double had prevented the tying run from scoring. San Francisco had reached the Series by winning a pennant playoff against the Dodgers.

Outfielders Matty Alou and Felipe Alou (right) had a new Giants teammate late in the 1963 season—brother Jesus, also an outfielder.

The presence of first baseman Gil Hodges (left) and outfielder Duke Snider (right) gave a Brooklyn feel to Casey Stengel's early New York Mets teams. Stengel himself was a former manager and player for the Dodgers.

Youth will be served

Playing the Mets on September 27, 1963, the Houston Colt .45s started an all-rookie lineup that included Joe Morgan, Rusty Staub, Jim Wynn and Jerry Grote. Front row: pitcher Jay Dahl, catcher Grote. Middle row: third baseman Glenn Vaughan, shortstop Sonny Jackson, second baseman Morgan, first baseman Staub. Back row: Brock Davis, Aaron Pointer, Wynn.
(The Colts became the Astros in 1965.)

A baseball hero retires ...

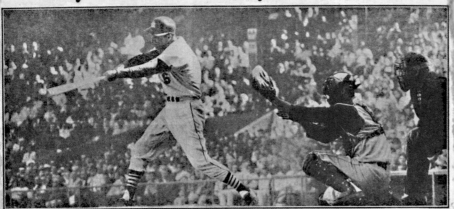

'A Day I Will Always Remember'

STORYBOOK ENDING TO A STORYBOOK CAREER ... Stan Musial Singles on His Final At-Bat. John Edwards is the Catcher, Al Barlick the Umpire.

Stan Whacks Pair of Hits in Grand Finale

By LOWELL REIDENBAUGH
ST. LOUIS, Mo.

And now, suddenly, it all was over! After 22 years of unsurpassed achievements, Stan Musial sat motionless in front of his locker in the Cardinal clubhouse, a slight slouch reflecting the tremendous pressures exerted on him during his farewell

Musial's Crouch 'Fraud, Deceit,' Mahatma Claims--and Tells Why

By JOE COPPAGE

ST. LOUIS, Mo. — From the thunder of cheers which sent Stan Musial into retirement, September 29, rose a booming voice charging "Fraud!"

The accuser was Branch Rickey, who praised The Man in typical Rickey prose, but dismissed his famous "corkscrew" batting stance as deceitful.

Rickey, now a Cardinal advisor, and other diamond notables appeared on "Stan Musial: The Man," a program prepared by KMOX-TV under the sponsorship of Brewing Corp.

view is worthy of all the commendation that is coming to him.

"There are 25,000,000 boys in this country who can look with great confidence in a study of his life. He is genuine."

Casey Stengel recalled Musial's first full season with the Cards in 1942.

"I was managing the Braves then," the veteran skipper said, "and we'd hold a meeting and I'd tell my pitchers about this young busher who used to be a pitcher and tell them to throw him some slow balls.

"But he hit them over the boulevard, and then instead ...

Stands Echo to Cheers for All-Time Star

house waiting to record his every move.

"Hey, fellows," Stan greeted the press. "I've just changed my mind, I'm not retiring."

The transition from charcoal gray into cardinal red was an unhurried process, something that was to be savored like ambrosia, that was ...

A seven-time batting champion and acknowledged as one of the game's greatest and classiest players, the Cardinals' Stan Musial closed out his career on September 29, 1963, with a two-hit game against the Reds. Musial's first hit eluded the outstretched glove of Cincinnati rookie second baseman Pete Rose. His second hit, like the first a single, gave him a career total of 3,630 and a .331 average over his 22 major league seasons.

... and a fan and friend is lost

The nation and the game were saddened on November 22, 1963, upon hearing of the assassination of President John F. Kennedy (above, with aide David Powers, middle, and Senators general manager Ed Doherty at the 1961 Washington season opener).

'The sports world has lost the best friend it ever had in the White House in the tragic death of President John F. Kennedy.'

—December 7, 1963

'WE'RE GOING TO WIN IT,' YANKS CHORUS

WORLD SERIES 1963: Manager Ralph Houk and the Yankees had confidence. Manager Walter Alston and the Dodgers had something more important—great pitching. It turned out to be a Series in which the mighty Yankees batted .171 and never held a lead. Sandy Koufax set a

Fall Classic record with 15 strikeouts in Game 1, Johnny Podres pitched 8⅓ innings of one-run ball in Game 2 and Don Drysdale hurled a three-hit shutout in Game 3 (the first Series game played at Dodger Stadium, which opened in 1962). Koufax then came back to finish off the Yankees, 2-1, in Game 4. Beating the Yankees appeared unlikely; sweeping them, well, that just couldn't be done. You could forgive Alston (right) for feeling a little smug.

COULDN'T BE DONE--BUT DODGERS DID IT

GAME 1

Sandy Spins Strikeout Tale --15 Yankees Get Message

By BOB BURNES

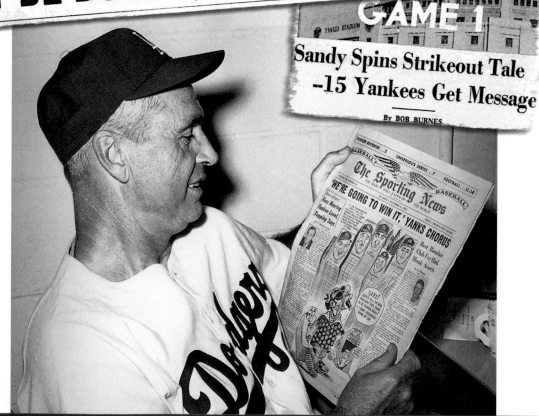

					AT BAT 49	BALL 2		STRIKE 2		OUT 2		
2	SF	2	10									
2	STL	2	7									

SF 2 10
STL 2 7

1 SS

2

AT BAT 49   BALL 2   STRIKE 2   OUT 2

49·

H-E   1 2 3 4 5 6 7 8 9 10   R   H   E   IG

PHILA.   1 1 0 0 0 4 0 0 0   6   8   0

N Y METS   0 0 0 0 0 0 0 0   0   0   0

Let's go METS!   TOP BRASS   MEDICATED HAIR DRESSING

as good to your taste   Rheingold   as it is to your thirst

Who says a good

396   371

The Phillies' Jim Bunning pitched the majors' first regular-season perfect game in 42 years in 1964, striking out Mets pinch hitter John Stephenson to end the game at new Shea Stadium. Bunning had pitched a no-hitter for the Tigers in 1958.

DOUG CLEMENS   BOBBY SHANTZ   ERNIE BROGLIO   JACK SPRING   LOU BROCK

Needing a jump-start in June 1964, the Cardinals thought that trading former 20-game winner Ernie Broglio to the Cubs in a deal that would send promising outfielder Lou Brock to St. Louis was a move worth making. The swap involved four other players.

Redbirds Label Speedy Brock Hot Asset for Present, Future

By NEAL RUSSO
ST. LOUIS, Mo.

When Bing Devine obtained Lou Brock from the Cubs in a deal involving Ernie Broglio 15 hours before the trading deadline, the Cardinals' general manager emphasized that he had the future in mind as well as the present.

"We didn't make the deal just because the club was going bad," Devine pointed out. "We had been interested in Brock for more than a year. We really talked about him a lot in the spring."

Devine, John Holland's best trading buddy in recent years, also parted with outfielder Doug Clemens and Bobby Shantz, along with

Batting Slump Grips Birds; Only 29 Runs in 14 Games

ST. LOUIS, Mo.—The Cardinals were not expected to duplicate their 1963 showing at the plate, but the Redbirds hardly figured to collapse at bat the way they did on their long June trip.

Through the first 14 games on the jaunt, the punchless Cards scored the grand total of 29 runs. In ten of those contests, they scored two or fewer runs. Over a five-game stretch, they totaled three runs and made 24 hits, yet won two of the games. The Birds had a famine of 25 straight zeroes, and three runs in 51 frames.

Even Ken Boyer was swept up in the batting depression. The captain

P. K.'s Rallying Cry Sent Cubs to Market

By EDGAR MUNZEL
CHICAGO, Ill.

action was: "Why didn't the Cardinals get more for an experienced winner like Broglio?"

The answer: The Broglio market was not as good as many persons believed.

Keane said he would use Brock against both lefthanders and righthanders until he proved he couldn't do the job against southpaws.

"We want to keep Brock's speed in the lineup," the manager said, "even against lefthanders."

Brock batted .251 for the Cubs this season. He had 54 hits, including two homers, two triples, nine doubles and 14 RBIs. In 215 official at-bats, he had struck out 20 times and walked 14 times. Brock's ten steals were five more than any Cardinal had amassed. Flood was leading with five, Javier

"If you want to hit the bull's-eye, you have to take a shot at it," said Owner P. K. Wrigley of the Cubs in one of the recent huddles with club holder.

And with that as a rallying cry, Vice-President John Holland intensified his trade negotiations that finally led to the six-player deal with the Cardinals.

"We felt that we were so close to being a topflight pennant contender one good trade might lift us into the thick of the fight," said Holland. "And we believe the deal with the Cardinals has done exactly that."

In the trade, the Cubs landed star righthanded pitcher Ernie Broglio, veteran southpaw reliever Bobby Shantz and rookie outfielder Doug Clemens in exchange for outfielder Lou Brock, righthander Paul Toth and bull-pen lefty Jack Spring.

In an accompanying separate transaction within their own farm system, the Cubs traded outfielder Billy Ott

Name	Position	Bats	Throws
Brock, Louis Clark	OF	L	L

Born-Place
El Dorado, Arkansas   Date: June 18, 1939   Married: Yes

Address 2574 Metro Boulevard
St. Louis, Missouri   Height: 5'11"   Weight: 170

Teams Played With South U. (Baton Rouge) 57-58-59-60—St. Cloud 8/22/60-for 61-rel. to Chicago NL 9/9/61-res. for 62-res. for 63-res. for 64-Traded with pitchers Jack Spring and Paul Toth for pitchers Ernie Broglio and Bobby Shantz and outfielder Doug Clemens to St. Louis 6/15/64-res. for 65-res. for 66-res. for 67-res. for 68-res. for 69-res. for 70-res. for 71-res. for 72-res. for 73-res. for 74-res. for 75-res. for 76-res. for 77-RES. FOR '78 RES. FOR '79 vol. retired list 9/1/

Koufax Leaves Fresh Hand Print on Sands of Time

WHILE MOST OF THE SPECTATORS stand in anticipation of an historic achievement, Sandy Kou- | fax blows up his th

Third No-Hitter, Vs. Phils, Labelled 'Thrill of Thrills'

By BOB HUNTER

PHILADELPHIA, Pa.

As if there ever existed any doubt, Sandy Koufax now has a name plate reserving him a place in Cooperstown as he continues to force the fabled names of baseball to move over and make room.

At the rate he's moving—one a year—the fabulous Dodger lefthander may wind up with a fist loaded with no-hitters and more cups than a coffee shop.

In his latest feat, which he labeled his "best of all," Sandy held the Phils hitless, June 4, and came within three inches of making it a perfect game.

It was his third no-hitter in three years and no man ever has managed more. Despite two 18-strikeout games against the Giants and Cubs, Koufax calls his latest no-hitter the "thrill of thrills."

In the 1880s, Lawrence Corcoran of the Chicago Nationals pitched three no-hitters; then along came Cy Young in 1897, 1904 and 1908 with three more and, finally, Bob Feller achieved th

Phils Victims of No-Hit Job a Record 13 Times

PHILADELPHIA, Pa.—When Dodger Sandy Koufax hurled his no-hitter, June 4, it added

Sandy Koufax, pitching at peak efficiency in a year in which he would win 19 games and fashion an ERA of 1.74, tossed a no-hitter against the Phillies on June 4, 1964. The Phils managed only one baserunner, Richie Allen, who walked on a 3-2 pitch in the fourth inning. Koufax had thrown no-hitters against the Mets in 1962 and the Giants in 1963.

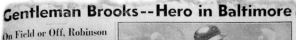

Gentleman Brooks -- Hero in Baltimore

On Field or Off, Robinson Measures Up as a Standout

By JOHN STEADMAN

BALTIMORE, Md.

BROOKS ROBINSON . . . Nice Guy Could Finish First

His defensive artistry well established, Orioles third baseman Brooks Robinson had a breakthrough offensive season in 1964—and was named the American League's Most Valuable Player. Robinson batted .317, hit 28 home runs and topped the league with 118 RBIs.

"
Tony Oliva has his Minnesota teammates talking to each other and rival catchers talking to themselves.

The 22-year-old Cuban right fielder was batting .500 during the first week of the American League season. But it was not so much his average as the way he hit different types of pitching that caused the buzzing.

Oliva hits pitches instead of pitchers. He doesn't even bother to learn the names of the hurlers.

—May 2, 1964
"

HUB'S HORTON...5   PHIL'S HARMONICA...7   FOOTBALL...39

BASEBALL SINCE 1886

The Sporting News
The Nation's Oldest and Finest Sports Paper

VOLUME 158, NUMBER 7   ST. LOUIS, SEPTEMBER 5, 1964   PRICE: TWENTY-FIVE CENTS

ROBERTO CLEMENTE
Confident Corsair
See Page 3

Pittsburgh's Roberto Clemente collected 211 hits in 1964 and captured his second batting title with a mark of .339.

Mauch Finds Hunk of Gold Among the Phillies' Rubble

By ALLEN LEWIS

PHILADELPHIA, Pa.

The Phillies expressed their confidence in Manager Gene Mauch within hours after the team lost out in its bid for the National League pennant they appeared to have wrapped up just two weeks before.

Owner Bob Carpenter and General Manager John Quinn conferred upon the team's return from Cincinnati and announced that Mauch's contract, which had one more season to run, had been torn up and a new one drawn up which would keep the peppery pilot at the helm of the Phillies through 1966.

It was a move that baseball men and most Phillies' fans applauded. This was so, even though some of the blame for the club's collapse down the stretch had to be laid at the manager's door. His handling of his pitching staff the last 17 games drew the most fire, but certainly Mauch's over-all managerial job was of the highest order.

The manager took the pennant defeat harder than anyone, but he'll undoubtedly shake off the disappointment and begin soon working for next year.

"I just wish," said Mauch after the Phillies had beaten the Reds and the Cards had downed the Mets on the final day to wrap up the race, "that I had done my job as well as the men did theirs."

Phils' Third TP of Season May Have Cost Cincy Flag

PHILADELPHIA, Pa. — The Phillies set a National League record when they executed their third triple play of the season in the course of a 4-3 victory over the Reds, October 2. It was a play that may have cost the Reds a tie for the pennant.

With the Reds ahead, 1-0, and Vada Pinson on second and Frank Robinson on first, Deron Johnson hit a long liner to...

Bob Carpenter

Any gold found in the rubble of the Phillies' 1964 season had to be fool's good. Manager Gene Mauch's team was in first place for 134 days, and it held a 6½-game lead with 12 games to play. Then the Phils lost 10 consecutive games in what ranks as the worst late-season collapse in history. The tailspin cost the Phils their lead, with first the Reds and then the Cardinals taking over first place. Entering the final day, St. Louis and Cincinnati shared the top spot, with the Phillies one game out. The Phillies crushed the Reds, 10-0, setting up the possibility of a three-way tie. But the Cards routed the Mets, 11-5, and copped the pennant despite spending only six days in first place all season. Those six days came in the final week.

After Cards take Series, Yanks take their manager

WORLD SERIES 1964: The Cardinals got two wins from Bob Gibson (below, right), a Series-squaring grand slam from Ken Boyer (below, left) in Game 4, a three-run homer in the 10th inning of Game 5 from Tim McCarver and, directed by Johnny Keane (opposite page, with Yankees manager Yogi Berra), edged the Yanks in the New Yorkers' last Series appearance for more than a decade. Gibson, establishing a reputation as a big-game pitcher, showed grit in winning Game 7 despite not having his best stuff. The Cards overcame the messiness of mid-August when general manager Bing Devine was fired.

Lou Brock (left) was a catalyst for the '64 Cards. After coming over from the Cubs, the left fielder hit .348 and stole 33 bases. Standout center fielder Curt Flood (middle) batted .311, and right fielder Mike Shannon contributed 43 RBIs in 253 at-bats.

'Lot of Little Things' Led Keane to Resign

Rumor of His Ouster Upset Card Skipper

By NEAL RUSSO
ST. LOUIS, Mo.

St. Louisans should have an easy time remembering the city's bicentennial year—1964.

They'll be able to recall it as one of the strangest years in the city's long and storied sports history, the year the Cardinal general manager was fired in mid-August for not producing a pennant in seven years. The year the club shocked fans by winning the flag with a great spurt. And the year

Yanks Couldn't Beat Keane, So They Hired Him

By HAROLD ROSENTHAL
NEW YORK, N. Y.

In a jammed mass interview made memorable by merciless grilling by the press, 99 per cent of which regard him as a class guy and friend, Johnny Keane took over the managerial reins of the Yankees on October 20.

He comes to New York under a one-year contract at a reported $45,000. This would give him $10,000 more than he was paid for leading the Cardinals to their first world championship in 18 years.

The heavy interrogation centered upon the actual date Keane had been contacted by the Yankees. Keane adhered to his story that the first time he had heard from Ralph Houk was the previous Sunday night (October 18) after Houk had already flown to Houston. Houk meanwhile denied vigorously that any member of the Yankees organization had contacted the

KEANE answers a newsman's question concerning his resignation as Cardinal manager during a press conference, October 16. In center is August of the Cardinals, and at left is G. M. Bob Howsam.

Yogi Was True to Himself--But

By LEONARD KOPPETT
Copyright 1964 by The New York Times Co.
Reprinted by Permission
NEW YORK, N. Y.

Why was Yogi Berra discharged as manager of the Yankees, even though the team won the pennant?

Because most of his players felt he was not a good manager and because the front office agreed with them.

What was wrong with the way he managed?

He was not "smart," he was not good at "handling men," and his authority was often flouted. Those, at least, were the views among most of his critics, and all of whom were necessarily objective.

Actually, Yogi was true to himself and his abilities, and handled his managerial responsibilities in exactly the fashion that those who knew him expected. Whatever shortcomings he possessed, they were certainly well known and when Dan Topping and Ralph Houk decided to

stay in shape, didn't find his own way out of a slump, was Berra's fault for not making him do it. If anything turned out right, the players believed, it was because they were good enough to overcome the handicaps put in their path.

This was almost exactly a repetition of the 1960 attitude toward Stengel.

And it was true that Berra did not possess Houk's unusual talents. The mystery was why anyone would expect him to.

Ford, Mantle Gave 100 Per Cent

Whatever anyone else did, Whitey Ford gave Berra 100 per cent support this year. Mickey Mantle was completely cooperative. Most of the others, however, let their contempt show by degrees—and the front office couldn't avoid seeing that.

Yogi, of course, had little capacity to change into the slick-thinking, pampering, father-image today's players crave

The Keane-Berra saga

The day after the Series ended, there were two stunning announcements: The Yankees fired Yogi Berra, and Johnny Keane disclosed he was leaving as Cardinals manager. Keane said the firing of general manager Bing Devine and later-season rumors that his own job was in peril led to his decision. In a strange twist, Keane then replaced Berra as Yankees manager. And St. Louis named coach Red Schoendienst (being doused, page 222) as its manager.

Berra Sought to Manage the Way He Played--But It Was Too Late

By HAROLD ROSENTHAL

NEW YORK, N. Y.

The comfort—and, some say, the sterility—of indoor baseball came to the majors in 1965 with the opening of Houston's Astrodome. The huge structure offered the ultimate in luxury—lavish suites, air conditioning and a loud, state-of-the-art scoreboard.

Everyone in Orbit Over Astrodome

LBJ, Plus 188,762, Attend Liftoff of 'Eighth Wonder'

By JOHN WILSON

Everyone agreed that the Harris County Domed Stadium, for sheer ____, was everything that had been claimed for it in advance.

HOUSTON, Tex.

An awed crowd of 47,879 was in the lavishly-colored colossus for the ____ game, April 9, between the Yankees and Astros.

President Lyndon B. Johnson and his wife, Lady Bird, ____ second inning got under way, Texan Lyndon was en route to his Johnson home, but decided to stop over and pay his respects to baseball and ____ President Roy Hofheinz, a campaign manager for Johnson in the 1940s.

That was the kind of solid success the first night was and it even turned ____ to be a cracking good ball game with Nellie Fox coming off the bench ____ driving in the winning run in the ____ ninth inning for a 2-1 Houston victory.

By the time the weekend's five games were over, a total of 188,762 ____ had paid their way through the ____ turnstiles to usher in the era of indoor baseball.

The biggest crowd was Sunday afternoon's 48,172.

Astro Bosses Praise Keane For Using Varsity Yankees

HOUSTON, Tex.—Houston baseball officials were highly complimentary of New York Manager Johnny Keane for helping make the Astrodome exhibition series a success by using his top-draw players in the games.

'INSIDE BASEBALL' at Harris County Domed Stadium was introduced ____ of Texas prepares to uncork the ceremonial ____

Leon McFadden's exhibition-game homer set off the Astrodome's animated, pistol-wielding cowboys high above the field.

Dodgers Seething Over Marichal Attack

Roseboro's Mates Blast 'Soft' Penalty

By BOB HUNTER
LOS ANGELES, Calif.

There are two established facts about the infamous and inexcusable Giant-Dodger brawl that erupted so unexpectedly in Candlestick Park in the third inning of the afternoon of August 22:

These are (a) that Juan Marichal hit John Roseboro over the head with his bat at least once and (b) that the Dodgers, from quiet Walter Alston to Roseboro, are absolutely ——— about the attack.

Team Taking A Heavy Rap, Giants Claim

By JACK McDONALD
SAN FRANCISCO, Calif.

While not condoning Juan Marichal's clubbing catcher Johnny Roseboro over the head with a bat in the final game of the Dodger series at Candlestick Park, August 22, Giant officials' reaction to their ace pitcher's nine-day suspension (eight scheduled dates) was that it penalized the club more than the individual.

"If we were going to play the Dodgers again before the suspen-

When Dodgers catcher John Roseboro came close to Juan Marichal's head while returning the ball to the mound in a 1965 game, the San Francisco pitcher took umbrage and struck Roseboro with his bat. Marichal was suspended for nine days.

Free-Agent Draft Launched Without a Hitch

Even Critics Impressed by Smooth Start

By CLIFFORD KACHLINE

An attempt to make talent acquisition more equitable, the amateur draft made its debut in 1965. Top picks: 1. Rick Monday, Arizona State, outfielder, taken by Athletics. 2. Les Rohr, high school (American Legion ball), Billings, Mont., pitcher, Mets. 3. Joe Coleman, high school, Natick, Mass., pitcher, Senators.

As expected, General Manager Hank Peters selected Robert (Rick) Monday, highly-touted 19-year-old outfielder from Arizona State University. The muscular young slugger was rated the top prospect by most organizations.

Perfect Koufax

Sandy Koufax (right, with Don Drysdale) pitched a perfect game against the Cubs in '65—a game in which Chicago's Bob Hendley tossed a one-hitter.

WORLD SERIES 1965: The Dodgers trailed the Twins, two games to none, but got a shutout from Claude Osteen in Game 3, a five-hitter from Don Drysdale in Game 4 and shutouts from Sandy Koufax in Games 5 and 7. Koufax didn't start Game 1 because it fell on Yom Kippur. He lost Game 2.

A new home for the Braves; new parks for Cards, Angels

Their glory days over in Milwaukee, the Braves saw riches in the Southeast and went to Atlanta and the city's Atlanta-Fulton County Stadium (near right, top) in '66. The Cards moved into Busch Memorial Stadium (far right) the same year, and the Angels, who had played at Los Angeles' Wrigley Field and Dodger Stadium, opened Anaheim Stadium.

46,048 Chilled Fans See Cards Win in Park Debut

By NEAL RUSSO   ST. LOUIS, Mo.

Mike Shannon and Jerry Buchek, your new park?"

play. A few innings after Shannon gunned down swift Hank Aaron try- to turn a single into a double

for the first pitch. The sphere will go to the Hall of Fame at Coopers- town.

THE 630-FOOT GATEWAY ARCH, symbolizing the great westward migration of the age and Old Man River form a backdrop for the new stadium a century ago.

Reggie Jackson

A's Ink Jackson For $85,000-- No.1 Draft Pick

By JOE McGUFF
KANSAS CITY, Mo.

Emmett Ashford: Only His Suit Is Blue

Emmett Ashford became the majors' first black umpire in 1966, moving up from the Pacific Coast League to the American League. Ashford served from 1966 through 1970.

The Sporting News

REG. U. S. PAT. OFF.

Vol. 161, No. 14   APRIL 23, 1966   Price: 35 Cents

EMMETT ASHFORD
Big Time at Last
See Page 3

JOY IN GEORGIA
... A Brave Bow
Page 5

LARRY SIEGFRIED
...Tough as Steel
Page 40

JACK NICKLAUS

Almost as significant as the Baltimore success was the crash of the New York Yankees into the cellar (in 1966). Just two years earlier they had cashed in their fifth straight American League pennant. The dip into the depths marked the first time a Yankee team finished last since 1912.

—*1967 Baseball Guide*

WORLD SERIES 1966: The Robinsons, Frank (left) and Brooks, hit home runs in the opening game as the Orioles—thanks to 6⅔ innings of stellar relief work (one hit, 11 strikeouts) by Moe Drabowsky—shut down the Dodgers, 5-2. Talk about being shut down: Los Angeles never scored again after the third inning of Game 1 as Baltimore's Jim Palmer, Wally Bunker and Dave McNally threw shutouts in the remaining games of the sweep.

The Twins were an explosive team in the mid-1960s, boasting such weapons as (left to right) Tony Oliva, Harmon Killebrew, Bob Allison and Jimmie Hall. Oliva and Killebrew were particularly menacing. Oliva hit .307 in 1966 after winning A.L. batting titles in 1964 (his rookie year) and 1965. Killebrew hit 39 home runs in '66, and he won or shared six homer titles in his career.

Mays' 512th Round-Tripper Breaks Deadlock With Ott

By BOB STEVENS
SAN FRANCISCO, Calif.

At 9:28 o'clock the evening of May 4, 1966, Willie Mays became the National League's premier home-run slugger of all time.

The incredible 35-year-old Mays slammed Dodger Claude Osteen's first pitch to him in the fifth inning high and far beyond the right field screen in Candlestick Park for a tally the Giants didn't need as they battered Los Angeles, 6-1.

But it proved home run No. 512 for the amazing Mays. It was one more than the ... Willie some da... of ... The home ...

Pilot Fran...

SANDY KOUFAX announces to newsmen his decision to retire as a Dodger pitcher because of his arthritic elbow.

One Bombshell After Another-- Dodgers Shake

By BOB HUNTER
LOS ANGELES, Calif.

As far as the Dodgers are concerned, the season of 1966 didn't reach its crest in September or October. But rather in November and...

'You'd Give Anything to Get Back a Limb,' Sandy Says

LOS ANGELES, Calif.—It was obvious Sandy Koufax, tight-faced and pale, disliked completely the stunning decision he felt he was forced to make.

"Maybe I won't earn as much outside of baseball," Koufax quietly told some 75 reporters at his astounding news conference, November 18. "But if you were going to have to go through life without the use of a limb, you...

The spectacular career of Whitey Ford (left) was winding down as the 1960s wore on. The Yankees' Ford compiled the best winning percentage, 200 or more decisions, in major league history, finishing at .690. The stylish lefthander won 236 games and lost 106, and he posted a World Series-record 10 victories. In his Cy Young Award-winning season of 1961 (often overlooked because of Roger Maris' heroics), Ford compiled a 25-4 record. Two years later, he was 24-7. At the outset of his career, he put together successive seasons of 9-1, 18-6, 16-8, 18-7 and 19-6. His career ERA: 2.74.

Fearing he could severely damage his arthritic left elbow, Sandy Koufax retired at the top—at age 30 and coming off a 1966 season in which he went 27-9 with a 1.73 ERA and won his third Cy Young Award in four years.

The '66 Pirates, sparked by (left to right) Roberto Clemente, Matty Alou, Willie Stargell and Manny Mota, got the bat on the ball. Clemente had 29 home runs and 119 RBIs; Alou batted a league-leading .342; Stargell hit 33 homers; and Mota batted .332 in 322 at-bats.

Grid Special--Official NFL Statistics...Pages 46-47

The Sporting News

REG. U S.'PAT. OFF.

Vol. 163, No. 12   APRIL 8, 1967   Price: 35 Cents

FRANK ROBINSON
A Rare Bird . . . Page 3

Hustling Dodger

BATTLER BAILEY

Page 5

Bo and Dean

FRIENDS FOREVER

Page 11

NCAA Champs

BRUIN BEAUTS

Page 39

Masters Field

LINKS LORDS

Page 41

BY MALCOLM EMMONS

Dealt by the Reds in December 1965 because, in part, he appeared to be an "old 30," Frank Robinson was a Triple Crown winner for the Orioles in 1966. In 1967, he was on The Sporting News' first four-color cover.

Boston's Carl Yastrzemski had won the American League batting title in his third major league season, 1963, but really hadn't lived up to his billing entering the 1967 season. Then he crashed through. Big time. Powering the Red Sox's rise from ninth place in 1966 to first place in 1967, Yastrzemski batted .326, smashed 44 home runs and knocked in 121 runs. It added up to a Triple Crown.

The Sporting News

REG. U. S. PAT. OFF.

Vol. 164, No. 13　　　　　OCTOBER 14, 1967　　　　　Price: 35 Cents

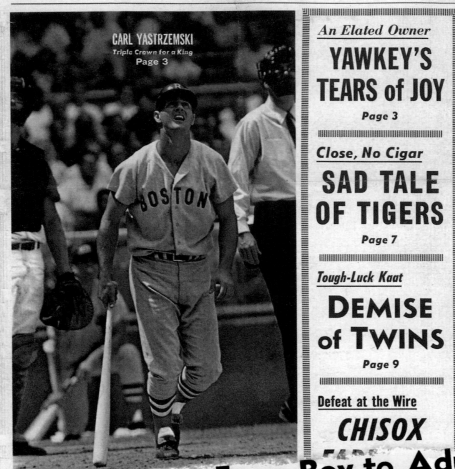

CARL YASTRZEMSKI
Triple Crown for a King
Page 3

BOSTON

An Elated Owner

YAWKEY'S TEARS of JOY

Page 3

Close, No Cigar

SAD TALE OF TIGERS

Page 7

Tough-Luck Kaat

DEMISE of TWINS

Page 9

Defeat at the Wire

CHISOX

The Year of Yaz--From Boy to Adult

Carl, a One-Time Enigma, Vowed in '66 to Be Best

By LARRY CLAFLIN　　　　　BOSTON, Mass.

The Year of Yastrzemski ended as it should have ended. It ended with Yastrzemski getting four straight hits, driving in two runs and throwing out the potential tying run at second base.

No player I have seen since I was a child watching Jimmie Foxx from the center field bleachers with my uncle at Fenway Park has dominated a pennant race as much as Yastrzemski did this year. He won the Triple Crown and he was the main reason the Red Sox won the pennant.

It has been seven years now since Yastrzemski came to spring training for the first time. You could tell even then, if you knew him and studied him, that someday he would be a great player. But, not even his devoted but stern father could have believed Carl would become what he became this Year of Yastrzemski.

When the season ended at Fenway Park in a wild melee of berserk fans on the field October 1, Yastrzemski had accomplished so many things it would be impossible to list them all. Here are a few:

1—He tied the major league lead in homers with 44, and no player except Foxx ever hit more for the Red Sox. No, not even the great Ted Williams.

2—He led the American League in hitting with a .326 average, the second time he has led it.

3—He led the major leagues in runs batted in with 121, which is 29 more than he ever drove in before.

4—He led the league in hits and runs scored.

622 Slugging Mark Topped Major

"

Down the stretch, Yastrzemski was at his best. He had four hits in the windup.
He had three hits the day before. In his last 13 times at bat,
when the pressure was toughest, Yastrzemski had 10 hits.

—*October 14, 1967*

"

'Impossible Dream' Comes True for Red Sox

By LARRY CLAFLIN

As long as baseball is discussed, the 1967 American League pennant fight will be known as "The Great Race." The Boston Red Sox, relegated to the second division by nearly-unanimous opinion of the experts in the pre-season polls, pulled one of the greatest upsets in the history of the sport by overcoming 100-to-1 odds to win the pennant in the final hour of the final day of the season.

Such was the weird drama of this pennant race that the Red Sox actually won the pennant by listening to the radio. They had defeated the Minnesota Twins at Fenway Park late Sunday afternoon, October 1. But, in Detroit, the Tigers still had a chance to tie the race and force a playoff. The Tigers lost to the California Angels and delirious Boston had its first A. L. pennant since the 1946 Fenway Park Millionaires.

Actually, four teams were in the dog fight to oppose the St. Louis Cardinals in the World Series. The Chicago White Sox joined Boston, Detroit and Minnesota in the wild scramble, and Bill Rigney's battling Angels weren't far out. The Angels, in fact, had as much to do with deciding the eventual winner as any team.

It was a season in which Boston's Carl Yastrzemski dominated his league as few players ever have done. Suddenly bursting into a mighty home-run hitter of Williamesque proportions, Yaz won the Triple Crown, the MVP and just about every honor a player can win. He finished the

After overcoming enormous odds and winning the pennant, Boston set its sights on realizing another dream—winning its first World Series crown since 1918.

The Red Sox, who won the extraordinary 1967 A.L. pennant race on the final day of the season (finishing one game ahead of the Twins and Tigers and three in front of the fourth-place White Sox), relied heavily on Carl Yastrzemski and 22-game winner Jim Lonborg (right) going into the World Series. Manager Dick Williams (middle) and the Sox had to endure the absence of outfielder Tony Conigliaro, who suffered a cheekbone fracture and career-hindering eye injury when struck by a pitch in mid-August.

Conigliaro Beaned, May Be Lost To Bosox for Rest of Campaign

BOSTON, Mass.—Tempers were short and crowds were big in Boston when the Red Sox swept a four-game series from the Angels, but lost outfielder Tony Conigliaro in the process.

Conigliaro was hit on the left side of his face August 18 by a pitch thrown by California righthander Jack Hamilton. Tony C. suffered a fractured cheek bone, among other injuries, and will be lost to the club for at least a month and possibly the remainder of the season.

More than 90,000 fans saw the four-game series which wound up with the Red Sox coming from eight runs behind to win the second game of an August 20 double-header for the sweep.

Red Sox Manager Dick Williams was ejected, a window leading to the umpires' dressing room was broken and Bosox Owner Tom Yawkey blasted an official scorer for a call.

There were no apparent hard feelings after the Conigliaro beaning. Williams said he did not believe Hamilton was throwing at Conigliaro.

GAME 7

Gibson's Third Win Brings World Crown to St. Louis

By OSCAR KAHAN

BOSTON, Mass.

If the 1967 World Series had not gone the full limit of seven games, there always would have been an unanswered and tantalizing question: What would have happened if Bob Gibson of the Cardinals and Jim Lonborg of the Red Sox, each the winner of the two games in the classic, had pitched against each other?

Well, the Series went seven games, the great confrontation took place and the question was answered. Gibson with three days of rest was a better pitcher than Lonborg with only two days to recuperate

WORLD SERIES 1967: A mid-July leg fracture sidelined St. Louis ace Bob Gibson for eight weeks. No matter. He was in top form come autumn. Gibson beat the Red Sox three times, allowing three runs. And he homered in his Game-7 clincher. Lou Brock batted .414 and stole seven bases for the Cardinals, and teammate Roger Maris, obtained after the 1966 season, hit .385 with seven RBIs. Boston's Jim Lonborg hurled a one-hitter in Game 2, and Carl Yastrzemski was 10-for-25 with three homers. The "El Birdo" Cards, led by MVP Orlando Cepeda, had breezed to the N.L. flag.

1968: year of the pitcher

How dominant were major league pitchers in 1968? Consider:

- St. Louis' Bob Gibson had an earned-run average of 1.12 and pitched 13 shutouts.
- Five A.L. starters had ERAs under 2.00.
- Detroit's Denny McLain won 31 games.
- The Dodgers' Don Drysdale pitched six consecutive shutouts.
- Five no-hitters were thrown, one a perfect game (by Oakland's Catfish Hunter, right).
- Boston's Carl Yastrzemski won the A.L. batting crown with a .301 average; runner-up Danny Cater of the A's hit .290.

Catfish Made Perfecto Look Easy

Four Balls Well Tagged, But Not One Tough Play

By RON BERGMAN

OAKLAND, Calif. — There wasn't even a tough chance in Jim (Catfish) Hunter's perfect game.

Years from now, no one will have to remember a great diving stop by an Athletics' infielder or an outfielder climbing a wall or making a running, shoestring catch to save the perfecto.

It was all Catfish on May 8, 1968. And the Catfish was king.

He threw only 107 pitches in the Oakland Coliseum game against the Twins before 6,298 fans.

The Oakland coaching staff didn't keep a record of what they were. According to John Lindblom of the San Jose Mercury-News, there were 55 strikes, 38 balls and 16 hit into outs.

Hunter struck out 11 batters. The dangerous Harmon Killebrew went down three times, twice called.

There were four hard-hit balls. In the fourth inning, Cesar Tovar lined out to rookie Joe Rudi, who was making his first start in left field after reporting from Vancouver (Pacific Coast) that day.

In the fifth, Ted Uhlaender flied fairly deep to right fielder Reggie Jackson. The next batter, Bob Allison, cracked a one-hopper to third baseman Sal Bando that took a mildly bad hop. But it went right into Bando's glove held over his left shoulder and was turned into an easy out. In the seventh, Rod Carew lined to Rudi.

3-and-0 Count on Oliva

Hunter went to a three-ball count seven times. Against Tony Oliva in the second, he went to 3-and-0. Oliva struck out swinging.

The last batter, Rich Reese, provided the real tension. The left-handed hitter fouled off four 2-and-2 pitches. The next pitch was inside. Catcher Jim Pagliaroni thought it was a strike.

Easy Does It

Minnesota	ab	r	h	rbi
Tovar, 3b	3	0	0	0
Carew, 2b	3	0	0	0
Killebrew, 1b	3	0	0	0
Oliva, rf	3	0	0	0
Uhlaender, cf	3	0	0	0
Allison, lf	3	0	0	0
Hernandez, ss	2	0	0	0
Roseboro, c	1	0	0	0
Look, c	2	0	0	0
Boswell, p	2	0	0	0
Perranoski, p	0	0	0	0
Reese, ph	1	0	0	0
Totals	27	0	0	0
Oakland	ab	r	h	rbi
Campaneris, ss	4	0	2	0
Jackson, rf	4	0	0	0
Bando, 3b	3	0	1	0
Webster, 1b	4	1	2	0
Donaldson, 2b	3	1	0	0
Pagliaroni, c	3	1	1	0
Monday, cf	3	0	0	0
Rudi, lf	3	0	0	0
Robinson, ph	0	0	0	0
Cater, ph	0	0	0	0
Hershberger, lf	0	0	0	0
Hunter, p	4	0	3	3
Totals	31	4	10	4

	IP	H	R	ER	BB	SO
Minnesota						
Boswell (L, 3-3)	7⅓	9	4	4	5	6
Perranoski	⅔	1	0	0	0	0
Oakland						
Hunter (W, 3-2)	9	0	0	0	1	11

Minnesota ..... 0 0 0 0 0 0 0 0 0—0
Oakland ..... 0 0 0 0 0 0 1 3 x—4

E—Boswell. DP—Minnesota 2. LOB—Minnesota 0, Oakland 9.

Denny Can Win Maybe 35 in '69,' Says Diz

By WATSON SPOELSTRA

DETROIT, Mich.—Denny McLain, first major league 30-game winner in more than three decades, will participate in the World Series to occupy his attention. That's the place where you really win them one at a time.

But Dizzy Dean, the last 30-game winner, isn't confined by time and space in looking ahead.

"Can Denny do it again?" muttered Dean before leaving Detroit, where he watched McLain rack up No. 30 in a nationally televised game on September 14 at Tiger Stadium.

"I know I won 28 in 1935 after I won the 30," said Dizzy. "If Denny don't get hurt, he'll win 20 for sure next year. I'd like to bet you really win them one at a time.

"If he win 20, he's capable of winning 30 again, maybe 35, because the league's gonna be in 12 clubs and all the clubs will be weaker."

McLain got a big kick out of the presence of Dean for the big day.

"Thanks, big Diz," Denny said they talked after the game.

"He's something, Denny is," observed Dean. "He's humble."

McLain had only one word for the way the Tigers rallied to push him into the $100,000 salary bracket.

A Patented Comeback

"Fantastic," gushed Denny after watching Al Kaline, Mickey Stanley, Jim Northrup and Willie Horton being rally, the kind the Tigers have become noted for this year. In fact, it was the 36th time Detroit had won by putting something together from the seventh inning

Denny had put himself at a disadvantage by giving up two home runs to Reggie Jackson. The A's had a 4-3 lead into the last half

...Kaline batted for McLain

TV Ratings Took Big Hike for McLain Game

DETROIT, Mich.—Baseball and the National Broadcasting Co. received a break when Denny McLain's turn to pitch fell on a Saturday and became NBC's "Game of the Week."

The sport not only received additional exposure, but the network's ratings took a decided hike, according to an NBC official.

It was estimated that there was a 30-40 percent increase in viewers for the Tiger hurler's successful bid for No. 30. This means that the 5-10 million Saturday average shot up to about 13 million.

"It all points up," said Carl Lindemann, vice-president of NBC sports, "that even when the pennant races are virtually decided, baseball can come up with significant interest. There are always records to be set or broken and the fans like it."

McLain is in distress and Willie won the game with a line single over the head of left fielder Jim Gosger, who was pulled in part way.

McLain and Kaline led the wild charge from the bench as Stanley ran home with the winning run.

The Tigers had 11,000 guests in the park along with a paid count of 33,688. Practically half of the crowd stayed in the park for a good 15 to 20 minutes, chanting, "We want Denny."

Some Bad Pitches

McLain made a brief appearance, waving to the fans, and then went to the clubhouse interview room which public relations director Hal Middlesworth had set...

AL KALINE (left), who scored the tying run, and Denny McLain lead the Tiger charge ... of the dugout after Willie Horton's ...

... inning hit climaxed a two-run rally and wrapped up McLain's 30th victory, a 5-4 de...

The Tigers' Denny McLain, who finished 31-6, received congratulations on his big season from the last man to win 30 games, Dizzy Dean.

Gay, Ray Play No-Hit Tit for Tat

By HARRY JUPITER

SAN FRANCISCO, Calif.—"Any pitcher could get lucky and pitch a no-hitter," said Gaylord Perry, "and let's face it—you've got to be lucky to pitch one."

Perry got lucky September 17 and pitched a no-hitter against the Cardinals at Candlestick Park.

But it wasn't his pitching that demonstrated his luck; it was the fact that Ron Hunt hit a home run off Bob Gibson for the Giants' 1-0 victory.

Perry has done a lot of fabulous pitching for San Francisco, but it's not reflected in his won-lost record. The Giants have not been especially generous to him when it comes to scoring in his behalf.

Perry's usual fate in the last two years was a sympathetic shake of the head, a pat on the back and a mumbled word of encouragement.

He's lost a ton of heartbreakers. This season, for example, despite consistently fine pitching, his record was 15-15 at last peek. Of those 15 losses, three were by 2-1 scores and three others were 2-0 jobs. It certainly wouldn't have required much luck or imagination for his record to be 21-9 instead of 15-15.

On September 21, in his first appearance after his no-hitter, life was back to normal for Gaylord Jackson Perry. The Braves beat him, 2-1.

The Realistic View

There will be more of those, and Perry knows it. He's a tremendous competitor, but he's a ... But that no-hitter against

FIRST TO HURL back-to-back no-hitters, Gaylord Perry, who beat the Cards, 1-0, September 17, and Ray Washburn, who blanked the Giants, 2-0, September 18.

By NEAL RUSSO

ST. LOUIS, Mo.—Ray Washburn had a special reception committee on his return to St. Louis September 22 after pitching a no-hitter in San Francisco four days earlier.

Washburn had achieved his biggest conquest in the West, and it was only fitting because his grandparents had been homesteaders. They traveled from Moscow, Idaho, to Heaven Horse Hills, Wash., by buckboard.

The Cardinal righthander spent considerable time working on farms in Washington, so it was no surprise that he became cowboy-minded and a country and western music devotee.

The western-garbed greeters at the St. Louis airport September 22 included the Country Aces, a group of entertainers whom Washburn knows from his visits to the Ranch Room in St. Louis. Proprietor George Edick, a longtime sportsman, planned a "Washburn Night" at his place.

When Washburn became the first Cardinal to pitch a no-hitter since Lon Warneke 27 years ago against the Reds, he had to survive the usual mobbing reception committee at the mound in Candlestick Park. Catcher John Edwards stumbled and almost spiked a few teammates who had rushed out to congratulate Ray.

Bauman a True Prophet

But there was another reception committee on the field. This was a one-man committee, trainer Bob Bauman.

"You did just what I said you would," Bauman said.

On September 17, 1968, at Candlestick Park, the Giants' Gaylord Perry (above) threw a no-hitter against the Cardinals. The next day, the Cards' Ray Washburn no-hit the Giants.

San Francisco's Juan Marichal (right), who had 25-victory seasons in 1963 and 1966, won 26 games in 1968. From 1963 through 1969, he had earned-run averages of 2.41, 2.48, 2.14, 2.23, 2.76. 2.43 and 2.10. In '63, Marichal pitched a no-hitter against Houston. His career record: 243-142 (.631 winning percentage).

Drysdale's Feat in 'Untouchable' Class

Drysdale Acclaimed N. L. Player of Month in May

CINCINNATI, O.—Don Drysdale, who pitched five of his record six straight shutouts in May, was chosen the National League Player of the Month for May by a landslide margin.

Forty-four of the 50 writers comprising the selection committee voted for Drysdale. Five voted for Rusty Staub, Astros' first baseman, and one for Braves' pitcher Ron Reed.

Drysdale's over-all performance was outstanding. The big righthander completed five of eight starts, lost only once during the month, allowed just 46 hits in 68 innings, walked 12 and struck out 45. His earned-run average for the month was 0.53.

Staub batted .368 in May with 39 hits in 106 at-bats. He hit three home runs and drove in 19 tallies.

Reed also won five of six decisions and posted an impressive 2.54 ERA. He yielded 32 hits in 46 innings, walked 11 and whiffed 18.

By BOB HUNTER

LOS ANGELES, Calif. — Big Don Drysdale added the final gem in his remarkable pitching triple crown when he blazed through history and the feats of Walter Johnson to establish an all-time consecutive 58⅔ innings scoreless skein.

After six successive shutouts, which erased the major league record posted by Guy (Doc) Harris of the White Sox back in 1904, the Dodger super star tacked on four and two-thirds more innings against the Phils, June 8, to wipe out The Big Train's mark of 56 innings, established in 1913, or 55 years ago.

The first gem in the pitching tiara was an obliteration of King Carl Hubbell's 35-year-old National League standard of 46⅓ consecutive scoreless innings.

An Historic Feat

So, in a dramatic month-long march through the pages of history, Drysdale became sole owner of the pitching ledger guarding some of the game's most coveted and difficult records.

Big D's iron man feat has to go into the books along with those of Joe DiMaggio's 56-game hitting streak and Maury Wills' 104 stolen bases as among the most untouchable in baseball.

The record-breaker against the Phils ended up as a 5-3 victory for Big D, his eighth in succession, seven of which were shutout triumphs.

In brushing aside 64 years of history, never has one pitcher created such commotion and excitement by making nothing happen.

Drysdale did not allow a hit in the seventh game of his rush to the record, until after he had passed Johnson, his last remaining goal, by getting Roberto Pena on a ground out to open the third inning.

First Run in Month

Then he struck out the next two batters and, finally, allowed his first run in almost a month in the fifth inning when Tony Taylor and Clay Dalrymple led off with singles.

Drysdale turned Pena's cap around, then struck him out and, after Howie Bedell flied to Len Gabrielson in left, Taylor scored to break the breath-taking spell.

The Big Warrior failed to finish the historic game, with Hank Aguirre coming on in the seventh to protect the lead and victory.

By allowing two earned runs, Drysdale raised his ERA ...

Drysdale, in creating both history and hysteria, pitched before a turnaway throng of 50,000 paid on Ladies Night, but to get even far enough for the showdown challenge match against Johnson's record, Big D had to survive three ninth-inning bases-loaded situations along the line.

Finally, on June 8, he completed the conquest he had started May 14 which, ironically, was the same date Johnson ended his streak in —1913.

A Tight Spot

One of the ninth-inning dilemmas occurred when the heavy-fisted Giants loaded the bases on him with none out, and Drysdale even managed to blast his way out of that one.

In these ninth-inning showdowns, Big D faced 12 batters with lifetime averages of .275, which is just about the ultimate in this age of shrinking averages, and he retired eight of them.

Two of these batters—Orlando Cepeda and Roberto Clemente—are in the exclusive .300 class.

11 Runners Die on Third

Drysdale, in his streak through the pages of time, left 11 runners on third base and ten on second.

While his 47 shutouts never will catch up with the Big Train's 113, Don can top him in another whitewash department.

If Drysdale can blank the Phils, Reds or Braves before the season ends, he will match Grover Cleveland Alexander's record for the most clubs shut out in one season—seven.

Alexander accomplished it three times, the last with the Cubs in 1919.

Now, what does Drysdale do for an encore?

Popovich Silences Critics Of Dodgers' Winter Deal

By BOB HUNTER

In 1968, the Dodgers' Don Drysdale shut out, in succession, the Cubs, Astros, Cardinals, Astros (again), Giants and Pirates. Blanking the Phillies through four innings on June 8, he ran his consecutive scoreless-innings streak to 58 and broke Walter Johnson's mark of 55⅔ innings. (Drysdale first was credited with 58⅔ innings, but that was changed when records officials decided to eliminate any fractional innings in which runs were scored at any point in that inning.)

The Sporting News

Vol. 166, No. 14   OCTOBER 19, 1968   Price: 35 Cents

SERIES REPORTS	A DASH OF O. J.	PROPHET EYES NBA
Pages 5-13	Page 29	Page 45

BOB GIBSON
King Cardinal
Page 3

WORLD SERIES 1968: With Bob Gibson setting a Series record with 17 strikeouts in Game 1, the Cardinals raced to a three games-to-one lead over Detroit. But Tigers lefthander Mickey Lolich won Game 5, 31-game winner Denny McLain coasted in Game 6 and Lolich tossed a five-hitter in Game 7, a contest that turned on St. Louis center fielder Curt Flood's misjudging of Jim Northrup's fly ball (which was ruled a triple and scored two runs). Lolich was 3-0, and Tigers outfielders Northrup and Al Kaline each had eight RBIs.

GAME 1

Gibson Message to Tigers: 17 Whiffs and 4-0 Defeat

By RALPH RAY

ST. LOUIS, Mo.—The world may be full of surprises, but it's not full of Bob Gibsons. For that, the Tigers are thankful. One Gibson was one too many for the Tigers, who turned out to be Gibson's meat in the World Series opener October 2.

After his 4-0 conquest of the American League champions, Car-

most certainly were overwhelmed. Seldom has a pitcher squelched a World Series opponent as Gibson crushed Detroit to the delight of 54,692 in Busch Memorial Stadium, the largest sports gathering ever in St. Louis. The spectators were overjoyed, but probably not much surprised because Gibson had

A standout basketball player at Creighton University, Bob Gibson found interesting offseason work (questionnaire) in his early baseball days.

The Sporting News

Baseball Questionnaire

Date Jan 13 68

Name Robert (First)   (Middle)   Gibson (Last)

Born in Omaha (City, Town or Township)   State Nebraska

on November 9 1935 (Month, Day, Year)   Height 6 1   Weight 183

Playing Position Pitch & Outfield   Bat—R or L R & L   Throw—R or L R

Date of Marriage and to Whom April 14, 1957 Miss Charline Johnson

Player's Nickname ___ How did you acquire the nickname ___

Ancestry (check): English ___; French ___; German ___; Hebrew ___; Irish ___; Italian ___; Polish ___; Slavish ___; Other Negro ___ Color of Hair Black ___ Color of Eyes Brown

Hobby or Hobbies ___ Name Pronounced ___

If a graduate of preparatory school, junior college or college, list name of institution, the years attended or when graduated and degree received 4 years Creighton University.

Address during off-season Harlem Globetrotters 127 N Dearborn (Street) Chicago, Ill. (City) (State)

Position during winter months Basketball Player

Baseball Experience (List Clubs and Years) College Semi Pro with Exterville Iowa 55 Chamberlain S.D. 56

Lower Mound, Smaller Strike Zone Next Year

SAN FRANCISCO, Calif. — Mounds will be lower next year, the strike zone will be smaller and, baseball officials hope, hitting will pick up.

The Official Playing Rules Committee decided on December 3 to reduce the legal height of the mound to ten inches. It has been 15 inches high. And major league mounds will be uniform, with the same degree of slope in each park.

The strike zone will be from the top of the knees to the armpits. It had been from the knees to the top of his shoulders, although very few National League umpires called strikes on pitches between the armpits and the top of the shoulders this year.

Fred Fleig of the National League office said there will be more attention paid to strikes being over the plate.

"There has been a lot of variance, especially on outside pitches," Fleig said. "Criticism has been more about pitches over the plate than the height of the pitches."

There was no action taken on illegal pitches, such as spitters, Vaseline balls or other doctored pitches.

Jim Gallagher of the commissioner's office said, "Illegal pitches were discussed at great length and it was decided the rule (802-A) is adequate. The rules committee recommends strict enforcement of the rule as written."

That means umpires need not warn anyone about illegal pitches. He can throw him right out of the game, zap!

A committee comprised of Bing Devine of St. Louis, Clark Griffith of Minnesota, Spec Richardson of Houston and Dick O'Connell of Boston will study synthetic playing surfaces, such as the Astroturf used in Houston's Astrodome.

Believing pitchers had truly become king of the hill, rules-makers decided to take them off their high ground, starting in the 1969 season.

OFFICIAL BASEBALL RULES

Changes made in Official Playing and Scoring Rules for 1969 are shown in bold-face, underlined type and affect Rules 1.04, 2.00, 4.12b, 7.08d, 10.09d, 10.12, 10.13f, 10.18i, 10.20.

1.04 THE PLAYING FIELD. The field shall be laid out according to the instructions below, supplemented by Diagrams No. 1 and No. 2 on adjoining pages.

The infield shall be a 90-foot square. The outfield shall be the area between two foul lines formed by extending two sides of the square, as in Diagram 1. The distance from home base to the nearest fence, stand or other obstruction on fair territory shall be 250 feet or more. A distance of 320 feet or more along the foul lines, and 400 feet or more to center field is preferable. The infield shall be graded so that the base lines and home plate are level, with a gradual slope from the baselines up to the pitcher's plate, which shall be 15 inches above the base line level. The infield and outfield, including the boundary lines, are fair territory and all other area is foul territory.

— 3 —

...ves of the Game.

...ween two teams of nine players ...ager, played on an enclosed field ...under jurisdiction of one or more

...am is to win by scoring more

...all be that team which shall ...hese rules, the greater number ...ulation game.

...field shall be laid out ac-...supplemented by Diagrams ...pages.

...square. The outfield shall ...formed by extending two ...The distance from home ...ind or other obstruction on fair ...feet or more. A distance of 320 feet or ...ong the foul lines, and 400 feet or more to center field is preferable. The infield shall be graded so that the base lines and home plate are level. **The pitcher's plate shall be ten inches above the level of home plate. The degree of slope from a point 6 inches in front of the pitcher's plate to a point 6 feet toward home plate shall be 1 inch to 1 foot, and such degree of slope shall be uniform.** The infield and outfield, including the boundary lines, are fair territory and all other area is foul territory.

— 3 —

The baseball rules for 1969 (underlined), compared with the 1968 version (highlighted), explained, officially, the attempt to reduce the push-off level of pitchers. Did hitters benefit from the lowering of the mound (and a smaller strike zone)? National League pitchers had a collective 2.99 ERA in 1968; in 1969, it rose to 3.60. American League ERA increased from 2.98 in '68 to 3.63 in '69.

Pitching at age 45 in 1968, knuckleballing reliever Hoyt Wilhelm (gripping ball) had his fifth consecutive under-2.00-ERA season. And he had time to give tips to Wilbur Wood.

THE SAVE: It's official

Because of the increased value of relief specialists, the "save" would become an official statistic in 1969—which was good news for Wilhelm (who pitched four more years) and Wood (a reliever at the time).

The Sporting News

DECEMBER 29, 1979   PRICE: $1.25

O. J.'s Farewell to Pro Football
Cage Scandal Rocks New Mexico U.
Baseball Players Ask Faster Free Agency

PETE
ROSE
Player of Decade

1969
A NEW FINANCIAL

1980

ORDER

Clockwise from top left: Pete Rose, Lou Brock, Hank Aaron,
Steve Carlton, Tom Seaver and Willie Mays.

Willie Mays

Hank Aaron

Nolan Ryan

1969

U.S. astronaut Neil Armstrong becomes the first man to walk on the moon.

The Woodstock music festival is held in New York state.

Sesame Street comes to TV.

1970

Four Kent State University (Ohio) students are killed by National Guardsmen during a protest over the U.S. incursion into Cambodia.

The first Earth Day is celebrated.

It was special, a momentous year of change, innovation, rebellion and growth. If 1969 wasn't a case of perfect timing, then it at least gave Americans the illusion of closure as well as a sense of optimism for the unpredictable future. What a way to end the traumatic 1960s ... and what a kick-off for the identity-seeking, rights-demanding society of the 1970s!

There was something for everybody in 1969—a cutting-edge new television show called *Sesame Street* for the kids, a generation-defining rock concert at Woodstock for the young adults and the enduring images of men in spacesuits taking "one giant leap for mankind." As the nation tried to move forward after the recent assassinations of Martin Luther King Jr. and Robert F. Kennedy and close the curtain on the most unpopular war in United States history, it looked forward with the inauguration of President Richard M. Nixon and significant advances in the civil rights, women's liberation and gay rights movements.

Baseball played a major role in the mystique of 1969. As man was taking his first steps on the moon, major leaguers were playing their first games outside the continental U.S. as part of a four-team expansion that included the Canada-based Montreal Expos. But such major stories as expansion, a lowered pitching mound to help hitters, a new playoff format and a new commissioner (Bowie Kuhn) became little more than backdrops

for the real story that capped off a magical season.

The nation watched in amazement as the lowly New York Mets, lovable 100-game losers in five of their first seven years, rose to unexpected prominence under manager Gil Hodges and captured the newly created National League East Division title. The Mets, featuring the Cy Young magic of Tom Seaver, then stormed past Atlanta in the inaugural National League Championship Series and dispatched the powerful Baltimore Orioles in a shocking five-game World Series. Miracle complete.

As encores go, the 1970s would never come close to matching the '60s in color and excitement. For a society trying to make sense of almost incomprehensible change, it became easy to mistrust an overstepping government that sometimes seemed to be careening out of control. For the average baseball fan, on-field accomplishments often were overshadowed by news of lawsuits, strikes, free agency and escalating player salaries.

In 1970, as Americans were mourning the deaths of four student protesters at Kent State University, former St. Louis center fielder Curt Flood was making headlines for his legal challenge of baseball's reserve clause—the restrictive rule that had kept players bound and gagged by their teams for the entire century. Flood, who termed his trade from St. Louis to Philadelphia in October

1969 a form of slavery, eventually would lose his challenge, but not before exposing owners to the frightening concept of player freedom and the prospect of having to give the players a share of ever-escalating profits.

Their fears were justified. Players, given a national celebrity by the same television cameras that had enriched the owners, discovered the power of the courtroom and organized labor unions, challenging the owners in every way imaginable. Faced with a steady barrage of lawsuits and threatened work stoppages, the owners granted labor concessions and grudgingly gave ground.

The sport's first general strike in 1972 was merely a warning shot. Baseball's first binding arbi-

Willie McCovey

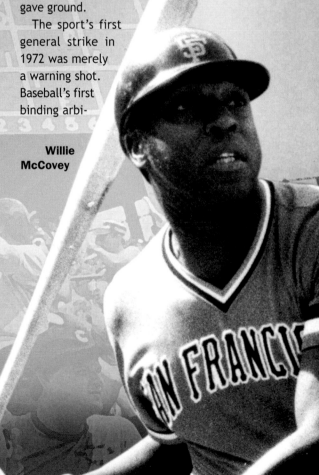

The classified Pentagon Papers, detailing U.S. strategy in Vietnam, are leaked to and published by The New York Times.

All in the Family comes to the small screen.

The voting age is lowered to 18.

Five men are arrested for breaking into the office of the Democratic National Committee at the Watergate complex in Washington, D.C.

President Nixon visits China.

The Dow Jones industrial average scores a first: It closes above 1,000.

Electronic mail is introduced.

The Vietnam War peace agreement is signed in Paris.

The Supreme Court, in Roe v. Wade, rules that states can't ban abortions in the first three months of pregnancy.

Vice President Spiro Agnew resigns.

tration hearings in 1974, a huge concession, were too little, too late.

The dawn of free agency arrived in 1975, just as the country was emerging from the shroud of the Watergate scandal, the Vietnam War and the resignation, in disgrace, of Nixon as U.S. president. Labor arbitrator Peter Seitz opened baseball's vault when he ruled that pitchers Andy Messersmith and Dave McNally had played out the option years of their contracts with the Los Angeles Dodgers and Montreal Expos and thus were unrestricted free agents, able to sell their services to the highest bidder. Soon the players

would be getting their fair share of the financial pie—and much more.

The owners, once protective of their assets and conservative in their spending habits, suddenly transformed into hungry children standing at the candy counter. As free agency became part of baseball's Basic Agreement and a free-agent re-entry draft became an annual postseason rite, owners began bidding maniacally for impact players who could lift their teams over the top. Salaries quickly shot through the ceiling. Pete Rose, who signed for $105,000 per year in 1970 with the Cincinnati Reds, was handed an $850,000-per-year free-agent payoff in 1978 by the Philadelphia Phillies. The Houston Astros made Nolan Ryan a million-dollar man a year later, and utility players began pulling in six-figure salaries. As the payoffs shot higher, player greed and solidarity naturally increased.

It didn't seem to matter. A four-year, $72 million contract with NBC in 1971 set the fiscal tone for the decade and helped feed the owners'

spending habits. And the sport continued to expand and prosper as all parties groped their way through the new economic maze.

The maze pointed the American League and National League in different directions, and most of the game-impacting change occurred on the A.L. side. Looking for additional offense to entice more fans through their turnstiles, A.L. teams implemented the controversial designated hitter rule in 1973—a strategy-affecting ploy that horrified baseball purists and spotlighted what previously had been only a subtle difference between the leagues. In 1975, Frank Robinson pioneered a change of more historical importance when he took the reins of the Cleveland Indians as baseball's first black manager, and the A.L. stepped onto Canadian soil with a two-team 1977 expansion (Toronto and Seattle) that lifted its membership to 16 teams—two more than the N.L.

The 1970s will be remembered

Reggie Jackson

Jim Palmer

Gene Tenace

The Watergate scandal forces the resignation of President Nixon. Gerald Ford succeeds him.

Initial episode of *Happy Days* is shown.

Communist forces overrun South Vietnam.

A Chorus Line opens on Broadway.

Rocky scores a knockout with movie crowds.

U.S. celebrates the 200th anniversary of its independence.

Alex Haley's *Roots* makes compelling TV drama.

Elvis Presley dies in Memphis.

socially as the decade that introduced us to *Star Wars* and *Rocky* movies, Rubik's cube, pet rocks, the smiley face, video games, VCRs, disco music and Archie Bunker, that television bigot who touched our soul as well as our conscience. In baseball, this was a decade dominated by powerful teams.

The Baltimore Orioles of Frank and Brooks Robinson swept the first three A.L. Championship Series and won a World Series. The Oakland A's of Charles O. Finley bickered and fought their way to World Series titles in 1972, '73 and '74. And Cincinnati's Big Red Machine, featuring Johnny Bench, Joe Morgan, Rose, Tony Perez and George Foster, ran roughshed over everybody in 1975 and '76. But the most shocking script was written by Catfish Hunter and Reggie Jackson, the former Oakland stars who moved to New York via free agency and helped the long-dormant Yankees dynasty return to championship prominence.

The period's award for individual honors went to Atlanta slugger Hank Aaron, who hit his 715th career home run in 1974 and became baseball's all-time homer king, passing Babe Ruth. St. Louis speedster Lou Brock also joined the milestone crusade with single-season (118) and career (938) records for stolen bases.

Other notable performances were turned in by Pittsburgh's Rennie Stennett, who made history with the game's only nine-inning 7-for-7 performance of the century; California's Ryan, who pitched four no-hitters in a little more than two years and struck out a record 383 hitters in 1973; Baltimore pitchers Jim Palmer, Mike Cuellar, McNally and Pat Dobson, all of whom reached the 20-win plateau in 1971, matching the 1920 feat of the Chicago White Sox's staff; and Rose, who thrilled the nation in 1978 with his 44-game hitting streak, the longest in the N.L. in the 20th century.

The period came to a thundering end in 1980 when Kansas City third baseman George Brett made an inspiring

run at becoming the first .400 hitter since 1941, finishing at .390. Brett led his Royals into the World Series, but not even his magic bat was enough to stop the Philadelphia Phillies from winning the first championship in the franchise's long history.

Rod Carew

Lou Brock

Catfish Hunter

The Amazin' Mets

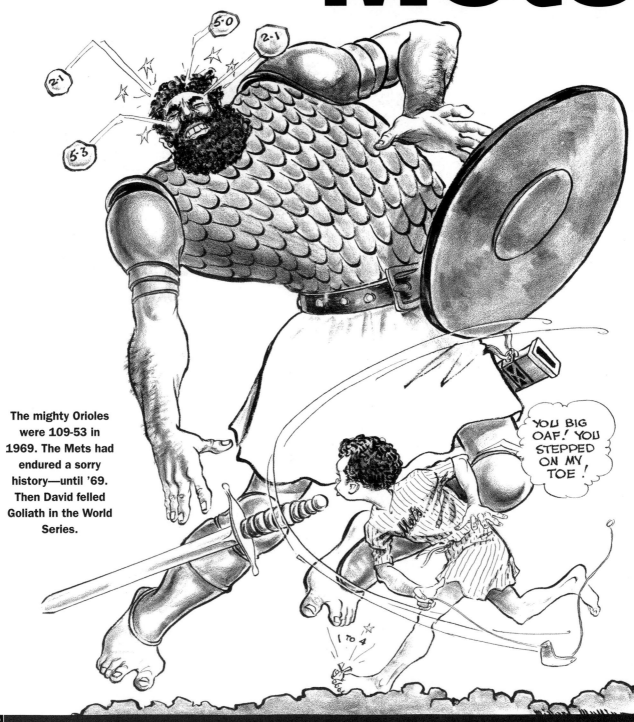

The mighty Orioles were 109-53 in 1969. The Mets had endured a sorry history—until '69. Then David felled Goliath in the World Series.

Before 1969, the New York Mets had finished no higher than ninth place since entering the National League as an expansion team in 1962. But in '69, they were downright amazing. They won 100 regular-season games and, in the first year of the majors' divisional alignment, swept Atlanta in the best-of-five N.L. Championship Series. Fielding only a so-so lineup, the Mets had exploited the strong performances of young pitchers Tom Seaver, Jerry Koosman, Gary Gentry and Tug McGraw and overcome a big Cubs lead in the N.L. East race.

Laughing Stock? Mets Wipe Grins Off Critics' Faces

'The Final Act— There Sit Mets, Atop Mount Olympus'

—November 1, 1969

Jubilation

WORLD SERIES 1969: After losing Game 1 to the juggernaut Orioles, the Mets took the next four—thanks to the pitching of Jerry Koosman (two wins), Tom Seaver and Gary Gentry, the hitting of unsung Al Weis and great catches by Tommie Agee and Ron Swoboda.

"

The New York Mets, born to be laughed at, were laughing back. And, oh, how they laughed. Symbols of five-star futility for most of their eight years, caricatured with ten thumbs and two left feet, they had suddenly, as if by divine right, been transformed into National League champions. Now it was time to celebrate.
—*October 18, 1969*

"

Mays' 600th

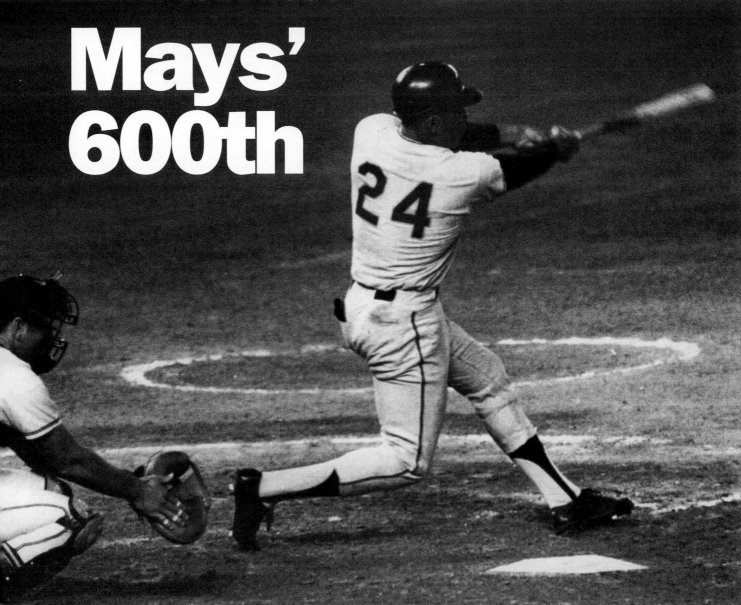

"

All manager Clyde King had to do was call on Willie Mays.

The Giants, fighting to stave off the Braves in the National League West, went into the seventh inning of their September 22 game against the Padres locked in a 2-2 tie.

King called on Mays to pinch hit for rookie outfielder George Foster, after Ron Hunt had beaten out an infield hit.

Mays smashed the first pitch by rookie righthander Mike Corkins 420 feet into the left-center stands and the Giants went on to win, 4-2.

It was the 600th homer of Mays' glittering career in the National League and the crowd, which numbered only 4,779, gave Willie a five-minute ovation. Twice he emerged from the dugout to doff his cap in appreciation.

With his historic wallop at San Diego Stadium, Mays became the second man in baseball history to hit 600 homers. Only Babe Ruth, with 714, hit more. The homer was Mays' 13th of the season.

—*October 4, 1969*

"

The National League prevailed in the 1970 All-Star Game when Cincinnati's Pete Rose (right) barreled into Indians catcher Ray Fosse in the 12th inning and scored the winning run. Rose was driven in from second base by the Cubs' Jim Hickman, who had singled to center field with two out in a 4-4 game. Fosse wound up in a heap at the plate.

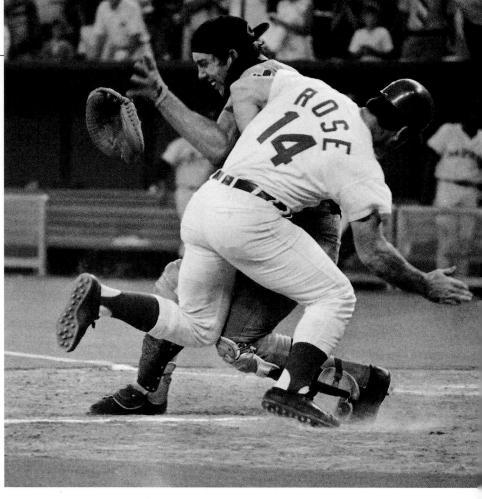

WORLD SERIES 1970: Upset in the Series a year earlier, the Orioles rebounded with a vengeance. Brooks Robinson's fielding wizardry and pitcher Dave McNally's grand slam led a trouncing of the Reds in five games.

Satch Walks in Shrine's Front Door

Having endured many indignities during a career in which he was denied entry into the majors until he was 42, legendary pitcher Satchel Paige became the first player to be inducted into the Hall of Fame by a special Negro leagues committee. He was enshrined in 1971.

A terrific trio, but ...

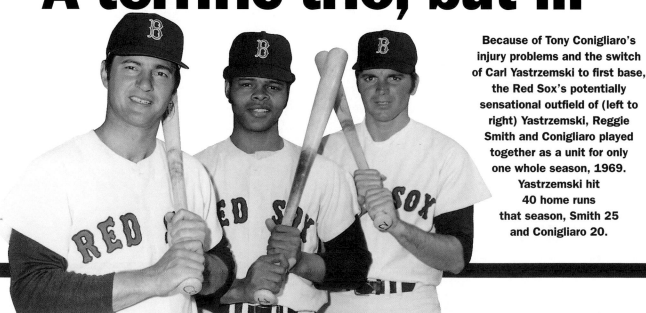

Because of Tony Conigliaro's injury problems and the switch of Carl Yastrzemski to first base, the Red Sox's potentially sensational outfield of (left to right) Yastrzemski, Reggie Smith and Conigliaro played together as a unit for only one whole season, 1969. Yastrzemski hit 40 home runs that season, Smith 25 and Conigliaro 20.

The Orioles were flying high in 1970 behind the pitching (right) of Dave McNally (24-9 record), Mike Cuellar (24-8) and Jim Palmer (20-10), and they added another meal ticket that December when they obtained Pat Dobson from the Padres in a trade. The 20-win performance was the first of eight such seasons for Palmer, who a year earlier had pitched a no-hitter against Oakland (below).

Palmer's No-No Was Bad Word Only for A's

The Orioles' four 20-game winners

Only in 1920 had four members of one big-league pitching staff reached the 20-victory plateau. The White Sox's Red Faber, Ed Cicotte, Lefty Williams and Dickie Kerr had turned the trick way back when. Fifty-one years later, it happened again when Baltimore's quartet of (left to right) Palmer, McNally, Cuellar and Dobson achieved the feat.

Powered by two-run homers off the bats of (left to right) Frank Robinson, Harmon Killebrew and Reggie Jackson in the 1971 All-Star Game at Tiger Stadium, the A.L. achieved a rarity in this era: It won the midsummer classic. Jackson's shot was a mammoth blast, crashing off a light tower on the roof in right-center. This was the only All-Star Game victory for the A.L. from 1963 through 1982.

WORLD SERIES 1971: Steve Blass (right, with catcher Manny Sanguillen) and Roberto Clemente led the Pirates past the Orioles. Blass allowed only one run in both Game 3 and Game 7; Clemente smashed a go-ahead homer in the clincher and hit .414. Game 4 was the first-ever Series night game.

In a civil suit, Flood asked that Organized Baseball and the system of rules that comprise the reserve clause be declared illegal under the federal antitrust laws; that the defendants (all 24 major league clubs, the commissioner and the major league presidents) be prevented from enforcing these rules against Flood; and that they be charged $75,000 in damages if the court grants Flood immediate free-agent status, or $3,000,00 if Flood has to wait until the case is decided.

—January 31, 1970

Curt Flood sues baseball

Traded to the Phillies in October 1969 after his 12th year with the Cardinals, Curt Flood had no intention of reporting. Instead of continuing his high-paying career, Flood chose to sue baseball over the legality of the reserve clause that controlled and limited players' movement. Although he eventually lost his case, Flood, through his challenge, led the way to freedoms (free agency) and salaries that players had never experienced.

Flood's Suit Could Cost Baseball $3 Million

By LEONARD KOPPETT

NATIONAL LEAGUE President Chub Feeney and A. L. President Joe Cronin release a joint statement in New York about their views on Curt Flood's suit against baseball.

Baseball goes on strike

Players Walk Out on April Fool's Day

By OSCAR KAHAN
Assistant Managing Editor

ST. LOUIS, Mo.—April 1, 1972, will go down as a black date in sports in the 102-year history of Organized Ball.

The strike called by the Major League Baseball Players Association forced the cancellation of a number of spring exhibition games and, for the time being, put all or part of the regular season in doubt.

However, Marvin Miller, executive director of the players' association, announced April 3 that the strikers, who are seeking an increase in pension benefits, would accept the last money offer made by the owners, but with one string attached.

The owners had offered an additional $490,000 to take care of the higher costs of the medical, hospital and dental benefits that the players receive, but had balked at extra pension contributions as being unreasonable. The players were seeking more money to compensate for the 17 percent increase in the cost of living since the last pension agreement was reached in 1969.

With the addition of the $490,000, the club owners would pay a total of $5,940,000 into the pension and benefit plan each year for the term of a new agreement. Under the players' original demands, however, the amount would have soared to $7,012,000.

Interest Money Involved

Miller made his announcement of a compromise after meeting with John Gaherin, the club owners' negotiator, for the third time since the strike was called.

"We have accepted the owners' offer of an annual $5,940,000 contribution to the players' pension fund, the same offer they made to us in Phoenix," Miller said, "provided the players' association can use the six percent interest potential the money earns."

He explained that the pension fund is set up on the premise that it will earn 4½ percent interest, when actually it was bringing in six percent and would continue to do so.

The players are proposing, Miller said, that the six percent interest be used to pay for higher pension benefits rather than be allowed to accumulate in the reserve fund.

Although the owners have said that they doubt the fund will continue to earn six percent annually, Miller said the players' association was ready "to put its money where its mouth is."

"We will put up the difference if it does not earn six percent," he asserted.

Miller Raps Owners

At that point, Miller could not resist taking a swing at the owners. He charged, "Money is not the issue. The real issue is the owners' attempt to punish the players for having the audacity not to settle and for having the audacity not to crawl."

After Miller told of the players' proposal, Gaherin said, "We are considering acceptance of this offer, but you have to understand that what they are proposing is a restructuring of the entire plan.

"It's true that this offer represents movement in the negotiations, but not necessarily the type of movement that will end this dispute. As for the opening of the season, I would have to say nothing has changed. The chances are extremely grave."

Later, Gaherin called Miller's proposal "an imprudent approach to the problem." He said he had presented the offer to the owners and they had unanimously agreed not to accept it.

The owners of the 24 major league clubs were scheduled to meet in Chicago on the evening of April 4 to review the situation further after receiving Gaherin's report.

The players also had asked for a four-year extension of the pension plan but had expressed willingness to settle for one year. The owners want to renew it for only one year so that it will expire concurrently with the present Basic Agreement between the clubs and the players' association. Their idea is that everything then could be negotiated in one package.

On the eve of the strike, the players for the first time publicly came up with a surprise gimmick to cover the higher costs of their proposal.

As explained by several player representatives, the pension fund, after catching up with all requirements, built up a reserve of $817,000 during the past year. This money, being held in escrow, accumulated from higher interest on investments, overfunding of expected retirement payments and overestimating the cost of disability benefits.

Dierker Gives Details

Larry Dierker, player representative of the Astros, explained that the pension fund needed $1,072,000 in 1972 to assure higher future pension payments.

The $817,000 in escrow, plus an additional $255,000 in club contributions at the rate of a little more than $11,000 each, would cover the bill, according to the players' calculations.

"It would bring our pension back to what it was worth in buying power three years ago," Dierker asserted.

President Mike Burke of the Yankees countered with the statement that the players' proposal for financing the 17 percent increase in pensions was not sound.

"Taking out the escrow would undermine the fund," Burke said. "Part of the strength of the fund is that reserve."

However, the whole dispute over the escrow money was set aside with the new proposal by the players.

As in the fall, winter and spring of 1968-69, pension plan negotiations between Gaherin and Miller dragged on for months. Three years ago, many of the players stayed away from the spring training camps until an agreement was reached. This year, the players went through almost all of their spring training before time ran out.

Visit to All Camps

Miller and Dick Moss, the association's attorney, visited all 24 of the camps and polled the players for strike sentiment. "We have a solid mandate," Miller said, after reporting the final vote was 663 for a strike, 10 against and two abstentions.

The final strike action was taken at a meeting of all the player representatives and alternates at Dallas March 31. The meeting lasted four hours. Miller said, "I believe every person spoke at least once and most of them two or three times. All possible developments were discussed at great length."

Presidents Joe Cronin of the American League and Chub Feeney of the National League wanted to attend the meeting, but backed off because of the conditions laid down by Miller.

"We wanted a format in which the issues could be debated, but Miller wanted some sort of limitation on the meeting and we couldn't agree to that," a spokesman for Commissioner Bowie Kuhn said.

Although a number of the player reps present expressed regret that a

(Continued on Page 6, Column 1)

It was the first general strike in the game's history. The Major League Baseball Players Association staged a walkout in the spring of 1972 that delayed the opening of the season by 10 days and forced the cancellation of 86 regular-season games. At issue were the players' demands for an across-the-board increase in retirement benefits and their insistence that owners absorb the increased premiums on their medical insurance.

When an accord was reached on April 13, many players said the various gains they achieved were secondary to establishing their rights as equals in further player/owner negotiations. Owners, on the other hand, fought what they feared would become an endless series of demands they considered out of proportion with the players' needs.

THREE VIEWS of baseball's first player strike —Cardinal Owner August A. Busch, Jr., explains management's side of the picture for Jack Buck and St. Louis radio audience from St. Petersburg, Fla. (top photo); Baltimore players collect expense money for their trip home from Miami, Fla. (middle photo), and Jeff Annas sits hopefully, but dejectedly, in the West Palm Beach stadium awaiting a game between the Texas Rangers and Montreal Expos that was cancelled because of the strike April 1.

THE SPORTING NEWS, APRIL 15, 1972

NO GAME TODAY
PLAYERS' STRIKE
CONRAC

Jackie Robinson, the first black player in the modern majors, was a fighter to the end. Honored at the 1972 World Series, he ended his brief remarks by gently criticizing baseball for its failure to name a black to a big-league managerial position. Ten days later, Jack Roosevelt Robinson was dead at age 53.

Black Pioneer Jackie Robinson Dead

IN HIS LAST public appearance, at the second game of the 1972 World Series, Jackie Robinson was honored for his work against drug addiction and then threw out the first ball at Riverfront Stadium. Commissioner Bowie Kuhn is at the right.

THE HALL OF FAMER and Branch Rickey, who brought Jackie to the major leagues in 1947 with the Dodgers.

Goodbye, Jackie

As the 1972 regular season wound down, Roberto Clemente collected his 3,000th hit—and the ball, too. The big moment spurred a headline (immediate left) that in the not-too-distant future would prove shockingly painful.

Roberto Clemente and His Prized Pirate Pellet.

Earlier in 1972, baseball was coping with the players' strike when news came of the death of Gil Hodges, who had managed the Mets to their improbable World Series championship in 1969 and was ready to begin his fifth year at the club's helm. Hodges, longtime star for the Brooklyn Dodgers, died of a heart attack on April 2 in West Palm Beach, Fla.

Gil Hodges Receives Congratulations as World Championship Manager in 1969.

The early-to-mid-1970s Athletics were a disparate group, highly volatile and downright quarrelsome. The players didn't mind taking a poke at the other guy—even if the other guy just happened to be a teammate. But play they could.

Oakland's lineup, featuring Reggie Jackson, Joe Rudi, Sal Bando and Bert Campaneris, was formidable, versatile and aggressive. But it was the pitching staff—headed by Catfish Hunter, Ken Holtzman, Vida Blue and reliever extraordinaire Rollie Fingers (right)—that carried the day.

There also was deft managing by Dick Williams and, later, Alvin Dark, and sound stewardship from owner Charles Finley, who seldom got along with his players or managers or baseball's hierarchy but managed to assemble a dynasty.

A'S World Champions '72, '73, '74

Sideshows Steal A's Series Thunder

By LOWELL REIDENBAUGH
Managing Editor

OAKLAND — Like man's allotted years upon the earth, the World Series of baseball attained "three score years and ten" in 1973.

But never in its seven decades has baseball been forced to share the spotlight with so many side issues as it did during the nine days of October 13-21.

Almost hourly bit players horned into the act. For a spell there was strong suspicion that the autumn classic was nothing more than a convenient excuse for walkers-on to muscle to center stage, elbowing the headliners into the shadows.

Not until the show hit the road a second time, shifting from New York to Oakland, did baseball emerge in its rightful role, suffused with an exciting quality.

AND ONCE IT was baseball for baseball's sake, the '73 Series assumed heroic proportions. It won't be soon forgotten.

Until order and sanity took charge, there were indications that the Mets - Athletics confrontation

Too, the fans, whose indifferent attitude led one player to snort, "They don't deserve us," suddenly appeared in capacity numbers, all wired for sound and volume turned high.

Down three games to two, Jackson and his teammates responded famously.

IN THE SIXTH game, Jackson snapped his New York lethargy, cracked two doubles and a single and led the A's to a 3-1 triumph. In the finale, it was Bert Campaneris and Jackson snapping the A's home-run drouth and spearheading a 5-2 conquest that was salted away, just as in 1972 against the Reds, by Rollie Fingers, the A's mustachioed reliever.

For the Mets, the supply of miracles ran dry at the most inopportune moment.

The club that climbed out of the National League East cellar on August 31 and won 21 of its last 29 engagements to win the division title with an 82-79 won-lost record, came within a flicker of dethroning

DRIPPING WITH champagne, Owner Charlie Finley is flanked in the victorious A's dressing room by a smiling Blue Moon Odom and a more serious Sal Bando. Could Bando be reflecting on what his unpredictable boss might do next?

When A's owner Charles Finley attempted to "fire" Mike Andrews after the second baseman's costly errors in Game 2 of the 1973 World Series (above), it was a prime example of the turmoil that often enveloped the team. Commissioner Bowie Kuhn denied Finley's attempt to deactivate Andrews. The leadership of third baseman Sal Bando (right, bare-chested) helped the A's through such crises.

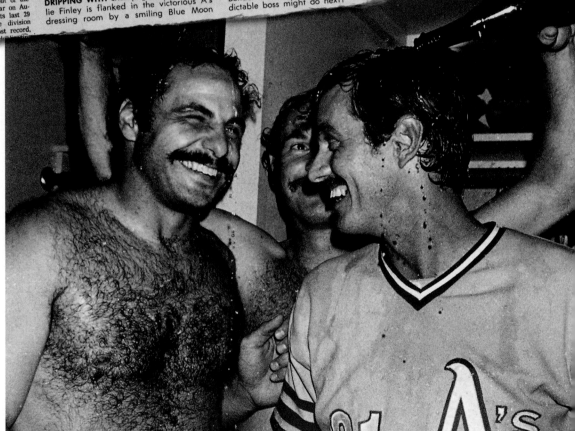

'Sometimes it was impossible to determine which act was playing in center ring.'

—November 2, 1974

WORLD SERIES 1972:
Minus injured Reggie Jackson, the A's edged the Reds for their first Series title since 1930. Oakland's Gene Tenace, who homered in his first two Series at-bats (a record), had four homers and nine RBIs.

WORLD SERIES 1973:
Despite the Andrews controversy, the A's made it two seven-game triumphs in a row under Dick Williams, this one over the Mets. Rollie Fingers and Darold Knowles allowed one earned run in 20 relief innings.

WORLD SERIES 1974:
The A's, now managed by Alvin Dark, became only the second franchise to win three consecutive Series, vanquishing the Dodgers in five games. Oakland pitchers limited Los Angeles to 10 earned runs.

1969–1980

Baseball Mourns Loss of Buc Star Clemente

On January 1, 1973, the baseball world woke up to the news that Pirates superstar Roberto Clemente had been killed the night before in a plane crash off the coast of his native Puerto Rico. Clemente, 38, was attempting to take supplies to earthquake victims in Nicaragua.

Padre Kroc Eats Humble Pie After 'Stupid' Slur

Ray Kroc . . . Good News, Followed by Some Bad, Bad, Bad News

Padres owner Ray Kroc had a few choice words to say about his bumbling team in 1974—and chose to say them over the stadium's P.A. system.

Pittsburgh's Dave Parker emerged as a force in the 1970s, hitting above .300 in five consecutive seasons and winning back-to-back National League batting titles.

Blomberg's First DH Bat Earns Cooperstown Niche

Ron Blomberg . . . Nervous on the Bench.

A boost for the offense

In modern baseball's most significant rule change, the designated hitter was introduced in 1973. Used only in the American League, it enabled teams to employ a full-time hitter in the pitcher's place in the batting order. Thinking an increase in offense would appeal to fans, the A.L. reaped immediate dividends. After hitting a collective .239 in 1972, A.L. batters finished at .259 in '73.

Just Night's Work for Nate: 5 HRs, 13 RBIs

By PHIL COLLIER

Nate Colbert . . . Home-Run Feats Made Headlines.

The National League disdained the DH, but there was no question that Nate Colbert was San Diego's designated power hitter in the early 1970s. Colbert had two 38-homer seasons, and he went on a five-homer, 13-RBI spree in a doubleheader at Atlanta in 1972.

No-hit magic

"

Ryan did his thing ... throwing the third no-hitter of his career in beating the Twins 4-0 with 15 strikeouts. Only Sandy Koufax, with four, has thrown more no-hitters in a career than the 27-year-old righthander.

—*October 12, 1974*

"

Ryan Roars Into Feller's Class With 3rd Gem

Nolan Ryan was at the top of his game in 1973 and 1974, reaching the 20-win mark the only two times in his storied career. After establishing a modern major league record for strikeouts in one season with 383 in '73 (above), he pitched the third no-hitter of his career against Minnesota in '74.

Rose:
bloomin' mad

After Pete Rose's hard slide in the 1973 N.L. playoffs, the Reds' star and Mets shortstop Bud Harrelson engaged in a shoving match that led to a pummeling session. Shea Stadium fans later threw debris at Rose, but Pete got his revenge the next day with a game-winning home run. The Mets won the series, though.

PETE ROSE of the Reds pummels Met shortstop Ken Harrelson after Rose crashed into Harrelson in the third N. L. playoff game October 8 at Shea Stadium in New York

When Willie Mays announced his retirement, effective at the end of the 1973 season, there was no doubt it was time. Though the Say Hey Kid's skills were fast eroding, his mark on the game would be long-lasting. Considered by many the greatest all-around player in baseball history, he finished his career with 660 home runs, 3,283 hits and a .302 average.

Mays Ends 'A 22-Year Love Affair'

By JACK LANG

NEW YORK—Willie Mays shed no tears at his retirement press conference, much to his own surprise.

"I thought I'd be crying by now," he said in his farewell address before some 100 members of the news media assembled in the Shea Stadium Diamond Club on the afternoon of September 20.

"But," he added, looking over to one side where all the baseball writers sat, "I see so many people here who are my friends, I can't. Maybe I'll cry tomorrow . . . or the next day."

There will be no tears shed for Willie, either. Oh, his exciting play will be missed, for sure. But in his retirement, the 42-year-old super star should be comfortably fixed. The Mets have taken care of that.

Mrs. Joan Payson and Donald Grant, principal owners, have assured Willie's future with a 10-year contract at a reported $50,000 per year. Of late, there have been rumors that they have even jacked it up to $65,000.

THE NATURE of Willie's association with the Mets for the next decade still has not been worked out. Both Mays and Grant admitted that.

But Willie wants no part of coaching or managing.

"Managing is hard work and I don't want that," he said, flashing a smile in Yogi Berra's direction.

"And I don't want to be a coach and just stand there like an Indian."

Mays said what he would prefer to do is work with young players and also have some contact with the fans and in group sales.

WILLIE SAID he announced his retirement before the end of the season to end all speculation. At the time of the announcement he was sidelined with two cracked ribs, but he hoped he could play one more time.

"I come in playing and I'd like to go out playing. Going to spring training and knowing you're not going to play anymore. I'll probably be spring training in January, but it won't be the

somewhere along the way, Willie would make an appearance.

GRANT TOLD the assembled reporters, radio and TV broadcasters, that "both Mrs. Payson and I love Willie" and they brought him back to New York with the Mets last year because they felt he should finish his career in New York.

"We feel we got paid pro quo—one thing in return for another. We feel our fans and the public of New York deserved Willie in his final days."

Mays said he quit because "when you're 42 and hitting .211, its no fun.

"Whoever heard of anyone hitting .211?" he asked.

He played this year, he said, only because he was playing in New York.

"NEW YORK fans love me. They showed that. You know New York—when they love you, they love you."

Baseball, for him, Willie said, was always fun. It ceased to be fun when he couldn't perform the way he did for his first 20 years.

"I don't think I could have finished this year in San Francisco. The people there would have run me out of town hitting .211. But the people of New York have seen me play before and they let me make up my own mind.

"I never considered myself a super star. I considered myself a complete ballplayer. I considered Mickey Mantle and Joe DiMaggio complete ballplayers. I think of the kids today, and Bobby Bonds and Cesar Cedeno are complete ballplayers."

WILLIE called his 22 years in baseball a "love affair."

"It's difficult for me to explain how much I love baseball. We've been going together for 22 years. It was a love affair."

Mays signed at the age of 19 to play for the Giants' Trenton, N. J., farm. "I was making $500 a month with the Birmingham Black Barons and I signed with Trenton for $250. It was the last cut I ever took."

Twenty-two major league seasons later, Mays left with a salary of $165,000 and a guarantee of a half million for the next 10 years. In between, he hit .302 and connected for

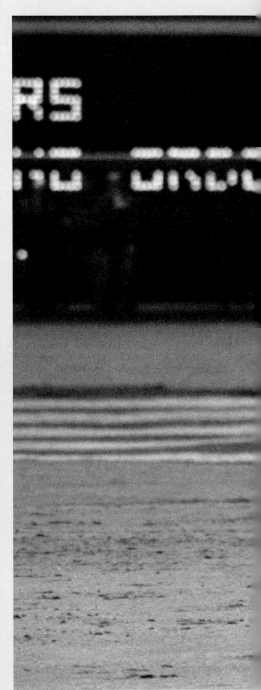

After breaking Babe Ruth's career homer record with No. 715 off the Dodgers' Al Downing on April 8, 1974, Hank Aaron was embraced by his mother (left) and an adoring public (although some fans wanted Ruth's mark to stand for purely nostalgic reasons, and some appeared to be against Aaron because of his race).

Hank Aaron, home run king

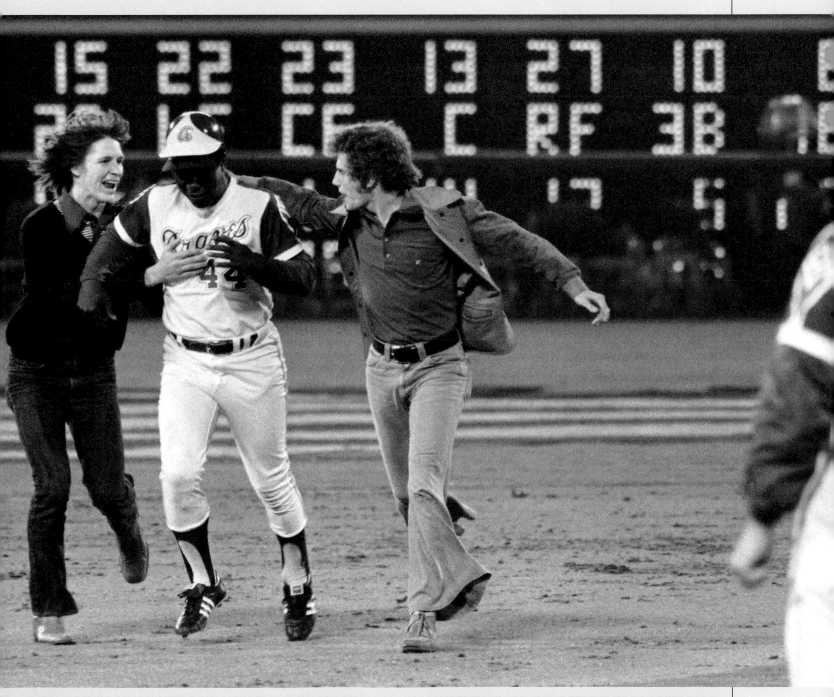

715

'At 9:07 p.m. on April 8, baseball's most sacrosanct record was pulverized.'

—April 27, 1974

Hail to the King

Mrs. Billye Aaron Shares Her Husband's Triumph

AARON (hand upraised) is mobbed by his Atlanta teammates as he crosses the plate after hitting record-breaking sma...

connected, retrieved the historic baseball and congratulates Hank.

The Hammer Hails the Big One

Mays, Jackie Robinson . . . but I can fit in there some...

By WAYNE MINSHEW

ATLANTA—It was a night marked for history, and umpire Lee Weyer was early for his assignment. He had this feeling that something big was about to happen. "I'm glad I'm here," he said, looking around at the record crowd of 53,775 still gathering in Atlanta Stadium. "History might be made tonight."

On the field, Hank Aaron was being honored. Weyer and late-arriving fans got there just in time to hear the Braves' star say, "I just hope I can get this thing over with tonight."

Al Downing of the Dodgers warmed up in the right field bullpen. If he heard Aaron's statement, it didn't show. But about an hour later, he was to become the serving end of what was to touch off the wildest spontaneous celebration sports fans here ever have seen.

IT CAME WHEN Henry Louis Aaron hit the 715th home run of his career. The date was April 8, the

DODGER CATCHER Joe Ferguson is a member of the 'welcoming committee' set to gree Henry Aaron as the new approaches the plate on his 7

The Sporting News

APRIL 20, 1974

Price: 60 Cents

715 HOME RUNS

Babe Ruth

Henry Aaron

AMADEE

Pro Football
WFL raiders mean business
PAGES 41, 42

Hockey
Hawks' White key to defense
PAGE 47

Track
Waldrop—best miler in world?
PAGE 53

Aaron had all winter to think about his date with destiny. He had finished the 1973 season with 713 homers, one shy of the Ruthian mark that once seemed untouchable. With a flair for the dramatic, Aaron tied Ruth on opening day, 1974, with a first-inning home run in Cincinnati off Jack Billingham.

Aaron wasn't a textbook slugger with bulging muscles and extraordinary power numbers. He *was* one of the finest all-around players in the game's history, one whose trademarks were slashing line drives and consistency. Aaron never hit more than 47 homers in one season, but he reached 40 eight times and twice finished at 39.

Still going strong at age 35, Cardinals outfielder Lou Brock broke Maury Wills' 12-year-old stolen-base record on September 10, 1974, with two thefts against the Phillies that raised his season total to 105. Despite troubling injuries, Brock (with Cool Papa Bell, longtime basestealing wizard for St. Louis' Negro leagues team) finished the year with 118 steals.

Larcenous Lou Brock

Brock swipes Wills' steals record

The majors' first black manager

When Frank Robinson made his debut as manager of the Cleveland Indians on April 8, 1975, he made a memorable day even more memorable by hitting a home run off the Yankees' Doc Medich in his first at-bat. Robinson, who penciled himself into the lineup as the Indians' designated hitter, was greeted by George Hendrick and ignored by New York catcher Thurman Munson. Robinson became the first black manager in the National League in 1981 when he took over the Giants.

7 at-bats, 7 hits

It was a laugher: Pirates 22, Cubs 0. And Pittsburgh second baseman Rennie Stennett had the most fun of all on September 16, 1975, becoming the first major leaguer (and, as it turned out, the only one) in the 20th century to collect seven hits in a nine-inning game. Stennett, who twice had two hits in one inning in the game at Wrigley Field, singled four times, hit two doubles and lashed a triple in seven at-bats.

Reds catcher Johnny Bench (right), a two-time National League MVP in the 1970s, destroyed the Yankees in decisive Game 4 of the 1976 World Series when he slugged two home runs and knocked in five runs. Bench and the Reds won six division titles, four pennants and two Series in the '70s.

Game Four

Bench's Bat Puts Quick End to Yank Misery

By LOWELL REIDENBAUGH
Managing Editor

JOHNNY BENCH unloads the first of his two homers, which exemplified the Reds' Series romp.

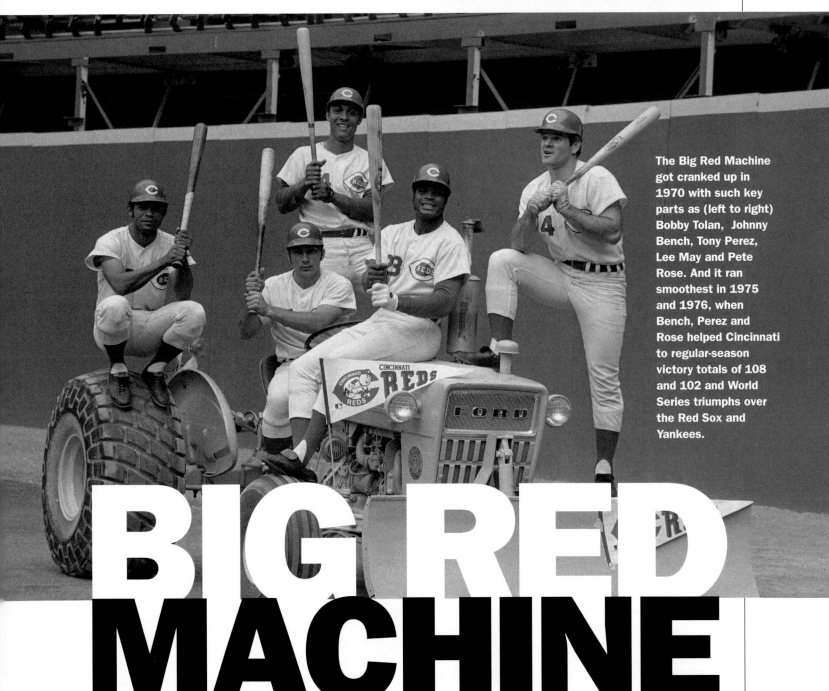

The Big Red Machine got cranked up in 1970 with such key parts as (left to right) Bobby Tolan, Johnny Bench, Tony Perez, Lee May and Pete Rose. And it ran smoothest in 1975 and 1976, when Bench, Perez and Rose helped Cincinnati to regular-season victory totals of 108 and 102 and World Series triumphs over the Red Sox and Yankees.

BIG RED MACHINE

A CLASSIC
Fall Classic goes to the REDS

WORLD SERIES 1975:
Manager Sparky Anderson and Johnny Bench were bubbly after the Reds nailed down the 1975 World Series, the winning run scoring in the ninth inning of Game 7 on a single by Joe Morgan (top, facing Jim Burton). Morgan, coming off his second straight MVP year, looped a Burton pitch into center field to break a 3-3 tie. The Reds got only one win in the Series from a starting pitcher (Don Gullett), but relievers Rawly Eastwick, Will McEnaney and Clay Carroll stood out. And Pete Rose hit .370.

Momentum seemingly had swung Boston's way in Game 6 when pinch hitter Bernie Carbo hit a tying three-run homer in the eighth, Dwight Evans made a game-saving catch in the 11th and Carlton Fisk cracked a body-English homer in the 12th that became part of baseball lore.

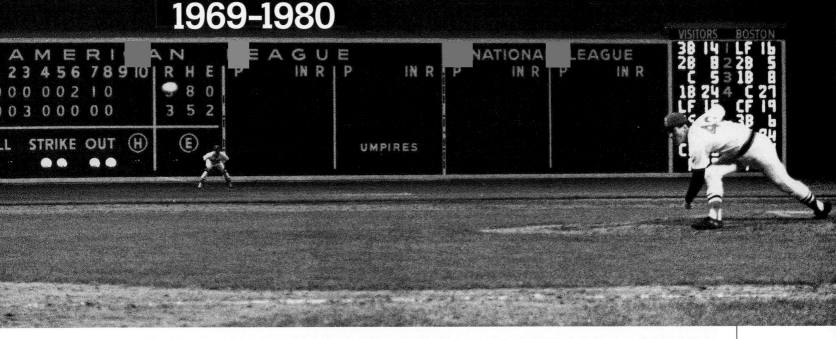

While Boston's Fisk waved his 12th-inning drive fair (below) in riveting Game 6 of the 1975 Series, Cincinnati pitcher Pat Darcy had other thoughts. Fisk's smash crashed off the left field foul pole, giving Boston a 7-6 victory and tying the Series.

Monday Earns Fans' Salute For a Flag-Rescue Mission

On April 25, 1976, at Dodger Stadium, two intruders knelt down on the outfield grass and, after spreading out an American flag, fumbled with lighter fluid. Cubs center field Rick Monday raced over, scooped up the flag and took it safely to a security guard. When Monday went to bat in the next inning, fans gave him a standing ovation.

Funny and Fantastic—That's Fidrych

By JIM HAWKINS

Mark Fidrych's antics—which included talking to the ball—made the Detroit pitcher a huge attraction. Fidrych was sensational as a rookie in 1976, going 19-9 and leading the A.L. with a 2.34 ERA. But his career burned out quickly.

WORLD SERIES 1976: The Yankees, last in the Series in '64, were back—briefly. In the first Series in which a designated hitter was used, the Reds won in four. Cincinnati DH Dan Driessen batted .357.

Chambliss connects

The Yankees hadn't won a pennant in 12 years—an eternity for them. The Kansas City Royals, a 1969 expansion team, were gunning for their first. The teams met in the 1976 A.L. Championship Series, which went to decisive Game 5 at Yankee Stadium (reopened in '76 after two years of renovation). Young George Brett tied the game for K.C. with a three-run homer in the eighth, but the Yanks won the flag in the ninth when Chris Chambliss homered off Mark Littell.

Yanks' Chambliss Makes the Right Connection

Yes, shorts

The White Sox showed a lot of leg in 1976—but not much ability. Promotion-minded Bill Veeck, back as owner of the club after an absence of 15 years, tried to stir interest with giveaways and special nights—and, from time to time, by decking out the Sox in shorts (left). Nothing obscured what happened on the field, though.
The Sox finished in last place with a 64-97 record.

'$100,000 Class Lists 33 Members'
—April 6, 1974

The dawn of free agency

Arbitrator Peter Seitz's decision in December 1975 to grant free-agent status to pitchers Andy Messersmith and Dave McNally led to free agency as we know it today. Messersmith (Dodgers) and McNally (Expos, until his retirement in June) played without contracts in '75. Seitz's ruling on the two players struck at the heart of baseball's reserve system, the renewal clause, by which a club could renew a contract into perpetuity. The decision allowed only one renewal, meaning a player no longer was bound to one club until he was released, traded or sold. The free-agent market, which originally featured a draft, was about to open for business.

The color of money

It was crazy out there, financially:

■ Arbitration came in 1974. First up: Twins pitcher Dick Woodson, who got $29,000 (the team offered $23,000).

■ Atlanta signed Andy Messersmith to a fat deal (right) in 1976. A "lifetime" contract? He went to the Yankees in '78.

■ Anticipating the loss of stars Vida Blue, Joe Rudi and Rollie Fingers to free agency, A's owner Charles Finley sold the three in June 1976 for $3.5 million. Commissioner Bowie Kuhn voided the deals, citing the game's "best interests."

A 'Lifetime Contract' Binds Andy to Braves

BY WAYNE MINSHEW

ATLANTA—The bizarre Andy Messersmith story came to a close in San Diego April 10, when the free-agent pitcher and the Braves agreed to what was called "a lifetime contract." The former Dodger can only hope the last chapter to his book will be a happy one.

Book?

"Yeah," he said. "I've been taking notes on this thing. I'm going to put it in a book. You won't believe the things that happened during all this. There's going to be some stuff to hit the fan."

MESSERSMITH did not care to go into details, but said he had bad experiences during his negotiations with the Angels and the Padres. They were among eight teams to make firm offers for the pitcher, ruled a free agent in an historic decision by arbitrator Peter Seitz.

"It's a long story," Andy said, "and I really don't care to go into it right now. I'd really rather talk about baseball."

So, leaving the mystery hanging, the 30-year-old pitcher who won 39 games the last two years with the Dodgers insists his arm is fine and that he is ready to pitch and have a good year with the Braves.

"I don't know who got that stuff (rumors of a bad arm) started," he said. "All I know is, I didn't put it out. And the players' association didn't put it out. So you can take it from there."

MEANWHILE, Braves' Owner Ted Turner said Messersmith received what amounts to a lifetime contract.

"Andy will be a Brave as long as I am," said Turner. "And I plan to be around a long, long time."

Technically, according to the pitcher's agent, Herb Osmond, the contract is a three-year deal "with renewals."

Osmond, who is based in Newport Beach, Calif., and who calls Messersmith "my best friend,"

said, "As long as he's capable and the Braves want him, he'll be pitching for them."

No money figures were disclosed, but it was learned that the former Dodger pitcher received a bonus in the neighborhood of $400,000 in cash. That and other inducements place the total package in the vicinity of $1 million for the first three years.

MESSERSMITH became a free agent after refusing to sign a 1975 contract with the Dodgers. He refused to sign because he did not receive a no-trade clause as requested.

Apparently, the Braves gave him exactly that.

Turner said, "I didn't think his request of the Dodgers was unreasonable. I'm not going to trade him. Andy Messersmith will be with the Braves as long as I am.

His contract is for forever. . . . Till death or old age do us part."

Ironically, Turner was about ready to give up on his chances of landing Messersmith after being first in line with an offer the day the pitcher officially became a free agent.

Turner received a call from an Atlanta fan by the name of Larry Foster one day and was asked, "Do you mind if I go to Los Angeles and

try to open up negotiations with Messersmith again?"

"NO, GO RIGHT ahead," said Turner.

And he did. Foster, a former New Yorker and Brooklyn Dodgers' fan, who owns a heating-cooling company in Atlanta, found his way to Osmond's office, set up further negotiations and the rest is history.

Asked the determining factor in Messersmith's choice of the Braves, Osmond said, "He's going with the finest owner in baseball. Money isn't always the essential factor. Sometimes people enter in."

Messersmith, who always has worn uniform No. 47, will not get that number with the Braves. Buzz Capra has that one. Turner said he will give the new acquisition No. 17.

"That," he explained, "is the channel at my TV station. Super 17, that's Andy."

THE RIGHTHANDED pitcher, who has 112 career victories while losing 75, will join a starting rotation which includes Carl Morton, Phil Niekro, Dick Ruthven and Roger Moret.

Most Braves polled said Messersmith means 15 or 20 more wins for their team this season.

ANDY MESSERSMITH (left) appears for the first time in a Braves uniform April 10 in San Diego. With him is Tom Paciorek, another former Dodger player.

Reggie Digs Music Made by Yankee Dollars

Yankees' $2.85 Million Land Catfish

After A's standout pitcher Jim "Catfish" Hunter was declared a free agent because his contract had been breached, teams waged a frenzied bidding war (baseball's first such free-for-all). It ended on December 31, 1974, when the Yankees signed the righthander (left), who was coming off a 25-win season. Two years later, with full-fledged free agency in effect, the Yanks reeled in another big one: Reggie Jackson.

Reggie
reigns

WORLD SERIES 1977:
Reggie Jackson's three-homer salvo against the Dodgers in Game 6 wrapped it up for the Yankees. It provided an emotional turnaround for Jackson, who had been embroiled with Billy Martin in year-long squabbles (including an ugly dugout confrontation in Boston exactly four months earlier).

"

Jackson's performance, which will serve as a gauge to measure all future World Series slugging accomplishments, climaxed a Series in which he erased a host of records. His five home runs eradicated the mark of four shared by Ruth, 1926; Lou Gehrig, Yankees, 1928; Duke Snider, Dodgers, 1952 and '55; Hank Bauer, Yankees, 1958, and Gene Tenace, Athletics, 1972. Reggie's 10 runs surpassed the nine credited to Ruth in '28 and Gehrig in '32. His 25 total bases broke by one the mark shared by Snider, '52, and Lou Brock, Cardinals, '68. As a result of having homered on his final trip to the plate in Game No. 5, Jackson attained the unique distinction of hitting for the circuit on four consecutive swings of the bat.

—November 5, 1977

"

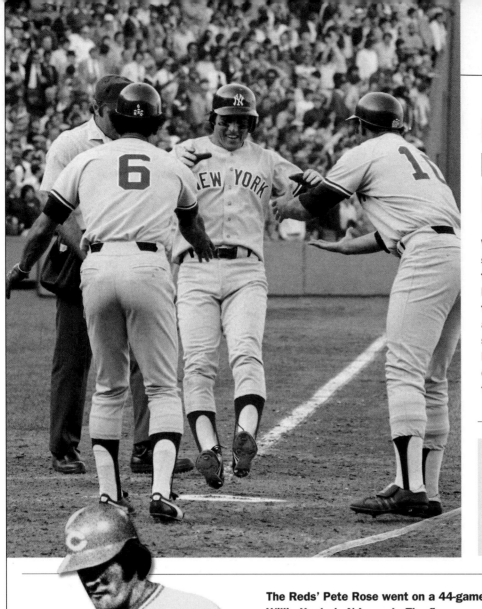

Improbable hero: Yanks' Bucky Dent

When light-hitting Bucky Dent sent a three-run home run into the netting above the Green Monster in the seventh inning of the 1978 A.L. East playoff game, a disbelieving Fenway Park crowd sat in silence. The homer off Mike Torrez overcame a 2-0 deficit, and the Yankees held on to defeat the Red Sox, 5-4.

WORLD SERIES 1978: Reggie Jackson, who fanned against Los Angeles' Bob Welch to end Game 2, still came up big (.391, eight RBIs). The Yanks won in six.

The Reds' Pete Rose went on a 44-game hitting streak in 1978, tying Willie Keeler's N.L. mark. The fierce competitor didn't take the snapping of the streak lightly (left). That fall, Rose was on the go as he checked out free-agency options (and visited with commissioner Bowie Kuhn).

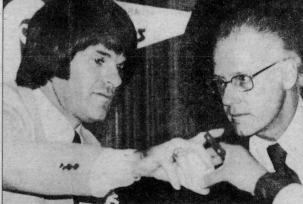

Pete Rose Arrives in Orlando, Then Sits With Commissioner Bowie Kuhn at Banquet After Signing With Phillies

Rose Rises to Challenge--and Record Falls

The Cincinnati kid no more

Pete Rose, a native of Cincinnati who had played 16 seasons for his hometown Reds, signed a free-agent contract with the Phillies in December 1978. His aggressiveness was seen as a major plus for the Phils, who had a fiery reliever in Tug McGraw (right).

The team that plays together stays together as a contender—so the Dodgers learned over almost a decade. Los Angeles' infield of (left to right) third baseman Ron Cey, shortstop Bill Russell, second baseman Davey Lopes and first baseman Steve Garvey was intact as a unit from 1973 through most of 1981, a stretch in which the club won four pennants and one World Series (and had four second-place division finishes).

Angels outfielder Lyman Bostock was shot to death in September 1978 by an assailant targeting another person. Bostock had signed a rich free-agent deal with the Angels after hitting .336 for the Twins in '77.

273

'Thurman Is Dead!' Numbed Yankees Weep

By PHIL PEPE

As the pennant races heated up in early August of 1979, stunning news came out of Ohio: Yankees catcher and captain Thurman Munson (below), at home on an off-day, had been killed when the plane he was piloting crashed and burned. Always hard-nosed and sometimes gruff, Munson, 32, was the A.L.'s MVP in 1976, Rookie of the Year in '70 and a force on two World Series title teams.

The Yankees' Ron Guidry (left) turned in one of the most dominant seasons in major league history in 1978, finishing 25-3 and recording a 1.74 ERA. He pitched nine shutouts.

Bulletin: Martin out

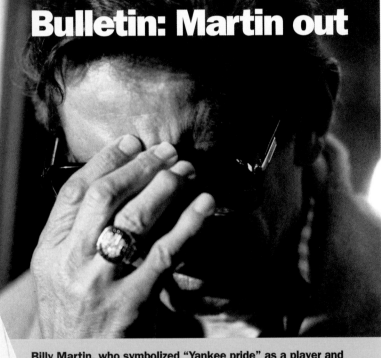

Billy Martin, who symbolized "Yankee pride" as a player and manager, was in tears when he resigned as manager of the New York club in July 1978.

Martin was having repeated run-ins with slugger Reggie Jackson, and Billy and owner George Steinbrenner weren't exactly tight. Shortly before quitting, Martin said of Jackson and Steinbrenner: " ... One's a born liar; the other's convicted." The latter referred to Steinbrenner's problems with illegal political campaign contributions.

The Yankees, 10½ games out of first place when Bob Lemon replaced Martin and 14 behind earlier, tied Boston and forced an A.L. East playoff.

The combative Martin wound up having five stints as Yankees manager.

WORLD SERIES 1979: The Orioles dethroned the Yankees as A.L. champs and led Pittsburgh, three games to one, before the Pirates roared back to win it. Willie Stargell, watching one of his drives, hit a go-ahead homer in the sixth inning of Game 7. When Kent Tekulve (far right, star-laden cap) ended the Orioles' hopes with a 1-2-3 ninth, the Pirates jumped for joy. Overall, Stargell hit three homers and drove in seven runs.

The beat did not go on at Disco Demolition Night. More than 50,000 fans showed up for the 1979 event at the White Sox's Comiskey Park, where disco records were to be burned between games of a doubleheader. But most of the 5,000 fans who raced onto the field for the torching wouldn't return to their seats, resulting in a forfeit to Detroit.

Disco Demolition Backfires; Chisox Forced to Forfeit

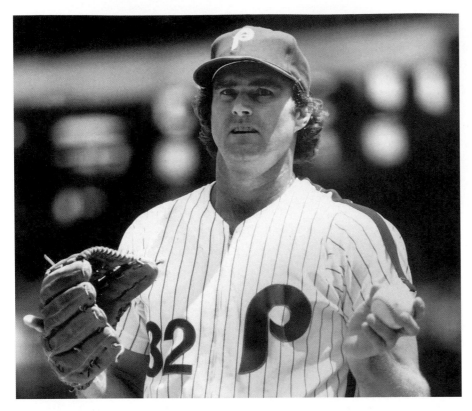

Pitching with consummate skill, Steve Carlton compiled a 24-9 record in 1980 and helped the Phillies to their first National League pennant in 30 years. The lefthander won his third of four Cy Young Awards in '80, posting a 2.34 ERA and leading the league in strikeouts with 286. It didn't take a championship cast around him for Carlton to display his brilliance, though. In 1972, he went 27-10 with a 1.98 ERA for a last-place Phillies team that won only 59 games. By career's end, Carlton had posted six 20-victory seasons and won 329 games.

.400, no, but Brett jolts Yanks

BRETT SHOW IS A BIG HIT

400 Chase Gets Hot, By George

BY MIKE DeARMOND

KANSAS CITY—Monday began for George Brett the same way Sunday had ended. Tuesday began the same way all the coming days will begin and end as he chases a .400 season.

A microphone was thrust in his face. A notebook was shoved under his nose. The eye of a television camera focused voraciously on his every move. And there was the telephone.

"To be honest with you," Brett said, "the lack of privacy bothers me. I mean, you come in my room and answer the calls at 3 o'clock in the afternoon when you're trying to take a nap. Today, I had calls from South Carolina, North Dakota, California, you name it. They always ask if I have a few minutes. I say, 'No. Come to the park and I'll give you...' "

That last line worked for a while. But then everybody took him up on the offer and did come to the park. On any particular day or on no day in particular, Brett was talking. After 20 reporters and countless more fans, Kansas City club officials finally decided to limit his availability to the press to 30 minutes before each game.

The act of completing the post-game cycle of interviews is becoming more and more arduous. That's the price you pay chasing a legend—or two.

The legend is Ted Williams, the last major leaguer to hit .400 (.406 in 1941). For a while, Brett was chasing Joe DiMaggio, who hit in 56 consecutive games in 1941. But that streak ended August 19 in Texas when Brett went 0-for-3.

George Brett fouls off a Jon Matlack pitch August 19 en route to 0-for-3 night.

The Royals' George Brett made a valiant bid in 1980 to bat .400. He fell short, finishing at .390 after being at .3995 on September 19. He didn't fall short in the ALCS. Trying to avenge playoff losses to the Yankees in 1976, 1977 and 1978, the Royals led the best-of-five series, two games to none, but trailed, 2-1, in the seventh inning of Game 3. Up stepped Brett, with two on. Goose Gossage fired. Brett swung. The ball landed in the third deck in right field. And Brett (left) and the Royals were World Series-bound.

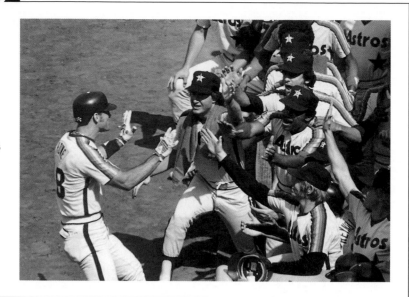

Houston's Art Howe (right, receiving congratulations) made certain his team avoided a big collapse in 1980. Entering a season-ending series in Los Angeles, the first-place Astros led the Dodgers by three games in the N.L. West. But Los Angeles swept Houston, forcing a one-game playoff for the division title. That's when Howe took over. He hit a two-run homer and a two-run single at Dodger Stadium, powering Houston to a 7-1 victory and its first division crown. Joe Niekro notched his 20th victory, pitching a six-hitter. The Astros then lost a wild NLCS to the Phillies.

PHILS PHINALLY WIN THE SERIES

WORLD SERIES 1980:
Playing their 98th season, the Phillies still were looking for their *first* Series title. Sparked by Steve Carlton, Mike Schmidt and Tug McGraw, they got it against the Royals. Cy Young Award-winning Carlton won two games, including the clincher; N.L. MVP Schmidt (right) batted .381 with seven RBIs; and McGraw ended Game 5 and decisive Game 6 with bases-full strikeouts. Phils Manager Dallas Green whoops it up (below).

278

1981
STRIKES, LOCKOUTS

1994

UNREST

It started with a devastating 50-day strike that almost wrecked the 1981 season and ended with a 234-day work stoppage that cut short an exciting 1994 campaign and forced cancellation of the World Series. In between those two forgettable breakdowns, baseball tested fans' patience with owners who raised ticket prices to support their indiscriminate spending and millionaire players who fought them for money, filed lawsuits, went on strike, jumped teams and cleansed their physical indiscretions in drug and alcohol rehabilitation centers.

This was the "Me, Me, Me Generation," both in American society and the sports arena. Status, power and monetary assets became the focus as more traditional values were shunted aside. While the business world wrestled with the realities of hard drives, hostile takeovers, leveraged buyouts and mega-mergers, baseball owners and players formed a tenuous share-the-wealth relationship that would test the loyalty of the fans they were trying to lure and entertain.

But no matter how hard they were pushed, to what emotional extreme they were subjected, the fans wouldn't let baseball mess up a good thing. They came back after the 1981 strike ... they came back after the messy 1985 Pittsburgh trials exposed widespread drug abuse ... they came despite an unending string of courtroom, arbitration and contract battles ... they came after the fall from grace by a living legend, who was declared persona non grata by baseball for gambling activities ... they came as player salaries shot skyward, with no end in sight ... and they came as players and owners postured and bickered leading up to the 1994 strike—and the first uncompleted season in modern baseball history.

This was a period of adjustment, owners to the growing power of their work force and players to the new-found wealth their talents were attracting. With the stock market rocketing to new highs, there was more money everywhere and fans with more leisure time to spend it. Despite its public relations missteps, baseball prospered to the tune of billion-dollar television deals and almost yearly attendance records.

That's because the game's on-field personality was too good to pass up. While society was embracing fast food, Cabbage Patch dolls, Nintendo, Pac Man, Calvin Klein jeans and the talk-show charms of Oprah, Phil, Sally and Geraldo, baseball was showing off its inexplicable penchant for the absurd—Fernandomania, the 1981 fan passion for a moon-faced rookie pitcher named Fernando Valenzuela; the 0-21 start by the 1988 Baltimore Orioles; a two-sport athlete named Bo Jackson; lights at Chicago's Wrigley Field; George Brett's infamous "Pine Tar homer" against the New York Yankees; a worst-to-first World Series involving Minnesota and Atlanta, teams that had finished at the bottom of their division standings the year before; and another World Series that was postponed, threatened and overshadowed by a devastating earthquake.

Fans also were entertained by the flying feet of Rickey Henderson, who stole a record 130 bases in 1982 and passed all-time steals leader Lou Brock nine years later; perfect games by Cleveland's Len Barker, California's Mike Witt, Cincinnati's Tom Browning, Montreal's Dennis Martinez and Texas' Kenny Rogers; the record 20-strikeout performance of Boston righthander Roger Clemens; the bionic arm of Nolan Ryan, who continued to pile up no-hitters and record strikeout numbers; the 59-inning scoreless streak of Dodgers righthander Orel Hershiser; and the 1985 coup de grace—Cincinnati player/manager Pete Rose's 4,192nd hit,

1981

American hostages are released in Iran shortly after the inauguration of Ronald Reagan as President.

President Reagan and Pope John Paul II survive assassination attempts.

Sandra Day O'Connor becomes the first woman appointed to the U.S. Supreme Court.

1982

The Equal Rights Amendment fails to win ratification.

U.S. unemployment reaches 10.8 percent.

Comedian John Belushi dies of a drug overdose.

1983	1984	1985	1986	1987
A bomb kills 241 U.S. servicemen in Beirut.	Geraldine Ferraro is selected as the Democratic vice-presidential candidate. President Reagan is re-elected, carrying 49 states.	The "Live Aid" concert telecast worldwide raises $70 million to fight starvation in Africa.	The space shuttle Challenger explodes shortly after liftoff, killing six astronauts and schoolteacher Christa McAuliffe.	The Dow Jones industrial average drops a record 508 points in one day.

Pan Am flight 103
explodes over
Lockerbie, Scotland;
259 die.

Hurricane Hugo devastates
the Carolinas.

The Exxon Valdez accident in
Alaska creates one of the
biggest oil spills in U.S. history.

The Simpsons proves
a hit for the fledgling
Fox TV network.

The U.S. and its allies
overwhelm Iraq in the
Persian Gulf war.

which vaulted him past Ty Cobb on the all-time list.

But the euphoria surrounding Rose's sweet victory turned into shocking disgrace four years later when commissioner A. Bartlett Giamatti, citing Rose's alleged gambling activities, handed him a lifetime ban from baseball. In a stunning sequence of events, Giamatti died of a heart attack eight days after his ruling and Rose was convicted of income tax evasion and sentenced to five months at a southern Illinois prison camp a year later.

Ten different teams won championships in the 13 seasons from 1981-93, a parity-induced byproduct of free agency. With lucrative, long-term contracts sitting at the end of the free-agent rainbow, players became more conscious of their earning power, more dedicated to training and dietary considerations that could extend their careers and more willing to jump ship if the price was right. It usually was, and owners found it difficult to keep talented lineups intact.

The Oakland Athletics, featuring the Bash Brothers tandem of Mark McGwire and Jose Canseco, managed to win three consecutive American League pennants, but the A's were upset twice in the World Series and their one victory, in the 1989 Bay Area battle against the San Francisco Giants, was overshadowed by an earthquake. The Toronto Blue Jays brought Canada its the first baseball championship in 1992 and punctuated that success a year later when Joe Carter delivered an electrifying World Series-ending home run against Philadelphia, giving the Jays distinction as the first repeat Series champions since 1978.

With prosperity comes progress, and that was manifested in another expansion and a run of new ballparks. A 1993 National League expansion introduced major league baseball to fans in Denver (the Rockies) and Miami (the Marlins) and evened the league rosters at 14 teams apiece. The new-ballparks craze began sweeping through baseball helter-skelter—a phenomenon that would carry well into the next century.

Toronto introduced the world to the mega-stadium in 1989, complete with retractable roof, built-in hotel and a mall-like collection of restaurants, arcades and shops. But the end of the multipurpose, cookie-cutter era did not officially arrive until 1992 when Baltimore opened Oriole Park at Camden Yards, an intimate, baseball-only, quirk-filled facility that sparked a run of throwback ballparks. "If you build it, they will come" became the byword as other cities scrambled to match the Camden Yards mystique.

It did not come as a great surprise in 1994 when baseball was brought to its knees by the longest strike in sports history. Players and owners had been posturing for years leading up to negotiations for a new Basic Agreement, and it was becoming increasingly apparent it would take something drastic to get the game back on course. This was the system that allowed Reggie Jackson, one of the game's original free agents in 1976, to sign a five-year, $2.9 million contract with the Yankees ... and Bobby Bonilla to sign a five-year, $29 million contract with the New York Mets 15 years later. It was all about money.

It also was about loyalty and trust, qualities baseball would not regain with baseball fans for several years after resuming play in 1995.

1992	1993	1994
Hurricane Andrew smashes south Florida and Louisiana. Johnny Carson ends a run of nearly 30 years on *The Tonight Show.*	A bomb explodes in the parking garage beneath the World Trade Center in New York. The Branch Davidian complex burns near Waco, Texas.	Richard Nixon dies. Jacqueline Kennedy dies. Former football star O.J. Simpson is charged with murdering his former wife and her friend.

A strike? Players must act fast

—March 7, 1981

There was labor unrest early in 1981, and it dated to a last-minute compromise reached in May 1980. Free-agent compensation was the major issue. Under the system in effect since free agency began in 1976, the only compensation a team losing a player to free agency received from the signing team was a choice in the June draft of high school and college players. Management insisted that compensation take the form of a professional player from the signing team. The players balked, contending such an arrangement would severely reduce the bargaining power and mobility of free agents. Terms of the 1980 agreement called for a study panel to negotiate a settlement of the compensation question. The negotiations went nowhere, and the players said they would strike if owners maintained their demands. The impasse carried into June, when the players acted (page 286).

By PHIL PEPE

NEW YORK–Don Sutton went elsewhere. So did John D'Acquisto, Dave Roberts, Rusty Staub, Claudell Washington and Geoff Zahn. But George Steinbrenner landed the big one of this year's free agent crop. He always does.

Dave Winfield didn't come cheap. Nobody thought he would, and when he put his signature on the contract, it called for the most money ever received by a baseball player—$13 million over 10 years, with a clause calling for an annual cost of living increase of up to 10 percent per year.

If Winfield collects the maximum compounded annually for the next 10 years, the worth of his contract is estimated at more than $20 million.

According to Winfield and his agent, Al Frohman, the Yankees weren't even the high bidder for Winfield.

"One club made an offer," said Frohman, "that if it was ever printed, they'd take them to Creedmore (a mental institution) here on Long Island."

That offer was said to come from the Cleveland Indians through their prospective new owners, James Nederlander and Neil Papiano. The Mets were also believed to have topped the Yankees' offer.

But the Indians could not offer Winfield the exposure he desired for his Dave Winfield Foundation for young people, and the Mets could not offer Winfield the prospect of playing in a World Series. Those were two important considerations for the 29-year-old slugger.

According to Winfield, the Yankees won out for his services because, he said, "I would enjoy contributing to a first-class organization with a winning tradition. The people of New York were influential in my coming here and

(the Yankees gave) consideration and cooperation Winfield Foundation."

Frohman cited three reasons why the Yankees "First, the tradition of the Yankees. Second, the of the players on the Yankees, such as Reggie Jac great talent they have; Dave has been yearning to a team with talent. Third, the ability of the Yan understand what the Winfield Foundation is a we're attempting to do. It's in George's hands a interested in the development of youth, and I believe

Steinbrenner said the Yankees' involvement foundation includes "no cash consideration, but a c ment to help them."

The commitment includes working with Winfield money for the foundation and a plan to provide the of New York City youngsters with health examinati diagnoses.

"I'm pleased and proud to be a part of this organ Winfield told a jam-packed press conference that in Manager Gene Michael, ex-Manager Dick Howser entire coaching staff, which had assembled in Ne for organizational meetings.

Also on hand were three of Winfield's new team Rick Cerone, Willie Randolph and Jackson.

The presence of Jackson raised the question of M plans for Winfield, who has been a right fielder mo career.

"It never came up (in negotiations)," Winfield said not worried about it. They have a fine outfielder li ready. Left field is something to look into."

Michael danced around the question by joking field "will play any place he wants." More serio

Dave Winfield and Yankees Owner George Steinbrenner put on happy faces after Winfield signed $13 million contract with New York December 15.

PERFECTO
Barker first to pitch gem since Hunter did it in '68
—May 30, 1981

Fernando mania sweeps L.A. and the nation

The Indians' Len Barker (left) pitched a perfect game against Toronto in 1981, winning 3-0 at Cleveland Stadium. The fans on hand—all 7,290 of them—saw Barker strike out 11 Blue Jays.

Fans couldn't get enough of rookie lefthander Fernando Valenzuela in 1981. For the Dodgers' opponents, it was quite a different matter. Valenzuela threw a shutout in the season opener, and by May 8 he had compiled a 7-0 record—with five shutouts. In what turned out to be an abbreviated major league season, he was 13-7 with a 2.48 ERA and eight shutouts.

'Red Wings' Ripken: The cream is rising'
—June 20, 1981

Playing for Class AAA Rochester in '81, Orioles farmhand Cal Ripken Jr. was on his way to the top. He hit 23 home runs for the Red Wings.

The Sporting News

PRICE: $1.50

Players Take a Walk

First Midseason Strike Shuts Down Baseball

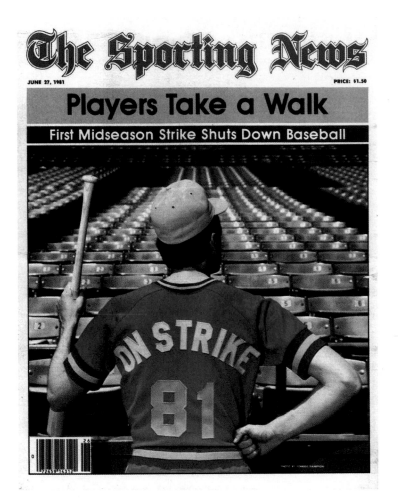

'Stakes bigger than in '72 strike.'

—June 27, 1981

'A strike against baseball is un-American.'

—July 18, 1981

'I don't care who's right or wrong. Just end the strike and PLAY BALL.'

—July 18, 1981

'If the players don't like the easy money they are making, let them go get a job in a steel mill or coal mine.'

—July 18, 1981

Now Players Must Pay the Piper

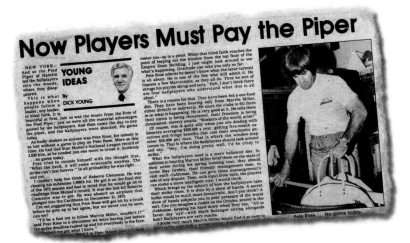

NEW YORK— And so the Pied Piper of Hamlin led the ballplayers into the woods, where they disappeared.

YOUNG IDEAS

By DICK YOUNG

This is what happens when people follow a leader, any leader, in blind faith. It is beautiful at first, just as was the music from the flute of the Pied Piper; just as were all the material advantages gained by the ballplayers. And then came the day to pay the piper, and the ballplayers were shocked. No game today.

As badly shaken as anyone was Pete Rose, for nobody is as lost without a game to play as Pete Rose. More so this time. He had tied Stan Musial's National League record of 3,630 hits, so he needed just one more to break it. Suddenly . . . no game today.

Pete tried to console himself with the thought that, "What the heck, it will come eventually anyway. The arthur can't last forever." In all probability he was right . . . and yet.

I couldn't help but think of Roberto Clemente. He was chasing his milestone 3,000th hit. He got it on the final day of the 1972 season and had in mind that he would go on to challenge Stan Musial's record. It was the last hit Roberto Clemente was to get. He was aboard an airplane that plunged into the Caribbean on December 31, 1972.

I'm not suggesting that Pete Rose will get hit by a truck before he gets up to bat again, but we never can be sure, can we?

"I'd be a fool not to follow Marvin Miller, wouldn't I?" said Pete Rose in a discussion we were having just before the strike deadline rushed up and hit everybody in the face. "Marvin got me what I have."

rooter too—up to a point. When that blind faith reaches the point of leaping out the window from the top floor of the Empire State Building, I just might look around to see what's happening. Gratitude can take you only so far.

Pete Rose admits he doesn't know what the labor turmoil is all about. He is one of the few who will admit it. He repeats a few Marvinisms, as they all do. Then he sort of shrugs his pixyish shrug and says, "Hell, I don't think there are four ballplayers who understand what this is all about."

There is a reason for that. They have been fed a one-food diet. They have been hearing only from Marvin Miller, either directly or indirectly. He tours the clubs to fill them in on what is happening. He is very good at it. He tells them their union is being threatened, their freedom is being threatened; slavery awaits. "Workers of the world, arise!"

Of course, this is quite silly when you are dealing with laborers averaging $200,000 a year, getting five-month vacations and fringe benefits that cost their employers another $50,000 per man. That is where the window-leap comes in. That is where the ballplayers should look around and say, "Hey, I'm doing pretty well. I'd be crazy to strike."

What the ballplayers need is a more balanced diet. In addition to hearing Marvin Miller brief them on the state of their union during his spring training tour, they should invite Ray Grebey, their friendly management man, to visit each clubhouse. He can give them management's side of any dispute. Then, with input from both, the players can make a more intelligent vote, I would think.

Which brings up the subject of how the ballplayers take their strike votes. It is done by a show of hands. A secret ballot would be much more democratic, don't you think? A show of hands subjects you to peer pressure of the worst sort. Can you imagine a rookie on the Orioles, seated in the clubhouse, keeping his hand down when they say, "All in favor, say 'aye'—with Mark Belanger sitting alongside him? Ballplayers are very macho.

I doubt very much Marvin Miller would find it so easy to get a strike vote with a secret ballot.

Pete Rose . . . No game today.

The Sporting News

PRICE: $1.50

Owners Say No to Mediator's Peace Plan

Early Wynn: Now There Was a Competitor

Blacks' Ranks Growing in Coaching Field

BASEBALL: THE WAITING GAME

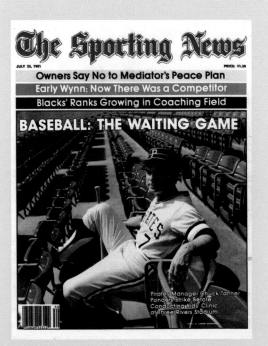

Pirates Manager Chuck Tanner Ponders Strike Before Conducting Kids' Clinic at Three Rivers Stadium

Finally, a settlement

The players' strike ended on July 31, 1981—50 days after it started. A player pool to compensate teams losing free agents, a concept at first rejected, was approved. And it was agreed that players wouldn't lose service time for the seven weeks they were away. A split-season format was adopted, with second-half division titlists to face teams that led their divisions when the strike began. The divisional playoffs created another postseason tier, with winners to meet in the League Championship Series.

urtain Falls on 33-Inning Drama

We're All in Cooperstown'

While major leaguers sat, Pawtucket and Rochester completed a 33-inning game on June 23, 1981. The game, which started April 18 and was tied after 32 innings at 4 a.m. on April 19, was won by Pawtucket. The game's third basemen: Wade Boggs and Cal Ripken.

High Five

Nolan Ryan and his Houston teammates whoop it up in the Astrodome after he fired his fifth career no-hitter September 26. Ryan blanked Los Angeles, 5-0, to surpass the record he shared with Dodger great Sandy Koufax for the most career no-hitters in major league history.

Ryan's masterpieces

Following are Nolan Ryan's five no-hit games, four of which he pitched for the Angels before notching his record fifth in 1981 with the Astros. (H) denotes home games. (A) away games.

DATE	OPPONENT	SCORE
May 15, 1973	Kansas City (A)	3-0
July 15, 1973	Detroit (A)	6-0
September 28, 1974	Minnesota (H)	4-0
June 1, 1975	Baltimore (H)	1-0
September 26, 1981	Los Angeles (H)	5-0

N.L. Stars Turn on Power

Carter, Schmidt Fuel Comeback

By Dave Nightingale
National Correspondent

CLEVELAND—They didn't change the script here August 9 for All-Star Game No. 52: The punch line still was a National League victory.

But two things made things extremely interesting for the record All-Star crowd of 72,086 and the estimated 50 million television viewers who welcomed the national pastime back to the sporting scene:

• Montreal catcher Gary Carter finally escaped from the shadow of Philadelphia third baseman Mike Schmidt for most valuable honors.

• And riverboat gambler Jim Frey of Kansas City, the American League skipper, embarrassingly managed himself into an inextricable situation by stringing with the dice one run too long.

Carter hit a pair of first-pitch solo homers (off Ken Forsch of California and Ron Davis of the New York Yankees) and Schmidt drove a two-run homer over the center field fence in the eighth inning off Rollie Fingers for the winning runs in a 5-4 National League victory.

That made it 10 straight victories and 17 in the last 18 games for the N.L. in the competition and it also marked the fourth year in succession the senior circuit had rallied in the sixth inning or later to win.

Carter, however, was awarded the Commissioner's Trophy—by Commissioner Bowie Kuhn himself—as the MVP. Gary got three votes from the five-man panel of official scorers and network broadcasting representatives. Schmidt got the other two.

Carter and Schmidt were in a dogfight for 1980 National League MVP honors, but Schmidt prevailed—partly because the Phillies beat the Expos for the East Division title. Mike then went on the capture the N.L. Championship Series and World Series MVP honors.

Gary Carter is greeted by Manny Trillo after the first of his two home runs.

Baseball chose a festive way to return in '81—by making the All-Star Game the first event on the post-strike schedule. Getting two homers from Montreal's Gary Carter (greeted by the Phillies' Manny Trillo), the N.L. won, 5-4, on August 9 before a Cleveland throng of 72,086. Regular-season play resumed the next day, and a Phillies crowd of 60,561 saw Pete Rose break Stan Musial's N.L. hits record with No. 3,631.

WORLD SERIES 1981:
The Dodgers, who reached the Fall Classic when Rick Monday hit a two-out, ninth-inning home run off Montreal's Steve Rogers in decisive Game 5 of the NLCS, exulted after finishing off the Yankees in six games. After losing the first two games, Los Angeles squeaked through with 5-4, 8-7 and 2-1 victories, the latter coming when Pedro Guerrero and Steve Yeager hit consecutive seventh-inning home runs off Ron Guidry. In Game 6, Guerrero drove in five runs in a 9-2 romp at Yankee Stadium. The Yanks' Mr. October, Reggie Jackson, missed the first three games because of a leg injury, New York reliever George Frazier was charged with three losses.

1981-1994

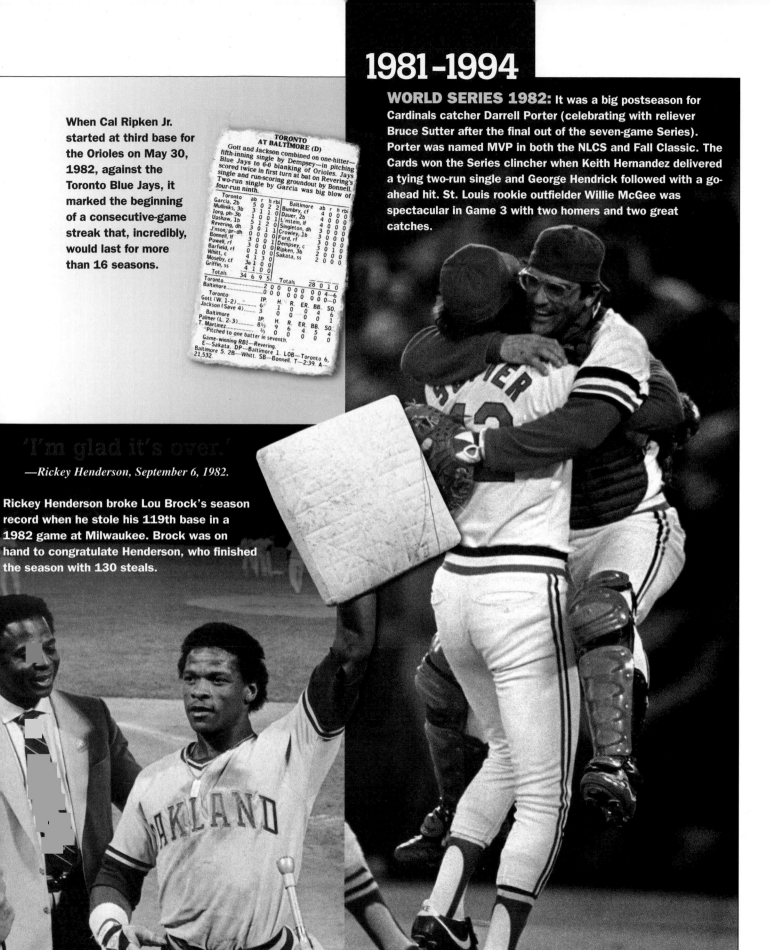

When Cal Ripken Jr. started at third base for the Orioles on May 30, 1982, against the Toronto Blue Jays, it marked the beginning of a consecutive-game streak that, incredibly, would last for more than 16 seasons.

TORONTO AT BALTIMORE (D)

Gott and Jackson combined on one-hitter—fifth-inning single by Dempsey—in pitching Blue Jays to 6-0 blanking of Orioles. Jays scored twice in first turn at bat on Revering's single and run-scoring groundout by Bonnell. Two-run single by Garcia was big blow of four-run ninth.

Toronto	ab	r	h	rbi	Baltimore	ab	r	h	rbi
Garcia, 2b	5	0	2	2	Bumbry, cf	4	0	0	0
Mulliniks, 3b	3	1	1	0	Dauer, 2b	4	0	0	0
Iorg, ph-3b	1	0	1	1	L'nstein, lf	4	0	0	0
Upshaw, 1b	5	1	2	0	Singleton, dh	4	0	0	0
Revering, dh	3	0	1	1	Crowley, 1b	3	0	0	0
J'nson, pr-dh	0	0	0	0	Ford, rf	3	0	0	0
Bonnell, lf	3	0	0	1	Dempsey, c	3	0	1	0
Powell, lf	3	0	0	0	Ripken, 3b	3	0	1	0
Barfield, rf	0	1	0	0	Sakata, ss	2	0	0	0
Whitt, c	4	1	3	0					
Moseby, cf	3	1	0	0					
Griffin, ss	4	1	0	0					
Totals	34	6	9	5	Totals	28	0	1	0

Toronto................2 0 0 0 0 0 0 0 4—6
Baltimore..............0 0 0 0 0 0 0 0 0—0

Toronto	IP.	H.	R.	ER.	BB.	SO.
Gott (W. 1-2)	6	1	0	0	4	1
Jackson (Save 4)	3	0	0	0	0	1
Baltimore						
Palmer (L. 2-3)	8⅓	9	6	4	5	4
T. Martinez	⅔	0	0	0	0	0

*Pitched to one batter in seventh.
Game-winning RBI—Revering.
E—Sakata. DP—Baltimore 1. LOB—Toronto 6, Baltimore 5. 2B—Whitt. SB—Bonnell. T—2:39. A—21,532.

'I'm glad it's over.'
—Rickey Henderson, September 6, 1982.

Rickey Henderson broke Lou Brock's season record when he stole his 119th base in a 1982 game at Milwaukee. Brock was on hand to congratulate Henderson, who finished the season with 130 steals.

WORLD SERIES 1982: It was a big postseason for Cardinals catcher Darrell Porter (celebrating with reliever Bruce Sutter after the final out of the seven-game Series). Porter was named MVP in both the NLCS and Fall Classic. The Cards won the Series clincher when Keith Hernandez delivered a tying two-run single and George Hendrick followed with a go-ahead hit. St. Louis rookie outfielder Willie McGee was spectacular in Game 3 with two homers and two great catches.

FERNANDO

'A nasty salary hassle and lost innocence ... he's still on a roll'

—July 11,1983, on the continued excellence of Dodgers pitcher Fernando Valenzuela.

"

(Fred) Lynn—his nerves intact—was able to hit the first grand slam (celebration above) in 54 games of All-Star history.
The home run climaxed a seven-run American League third inning against San Francisco pitcher Atlee Hammaker, the biggest one-inning scoring splurge in All-Star annals.

—July 18, 1983

"

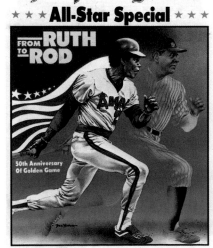

Rod Carew, who had two hits in the 1983 All-Star Game and was on base when Fred Lynn hit his bases-loaded shot, won seven batting titles—all while he was with the Twins.

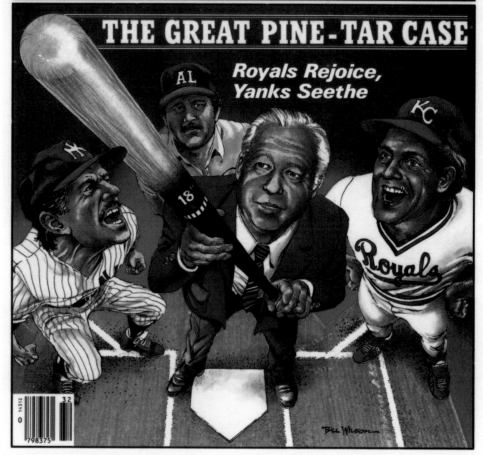

When George Brett's apparent game-winning homer in the ninth inning of a July 24, 1983, game against the Yankees was disallowed by umpires because he had pine tar too high on the bat handle, it resulted in a Royals protest and a suspension of the game.

A.L. president Lee MacPhail (middle, sketch) overruled the umpires' decision, saying the rules lacked clarity. Brett's homer stood, and the game was completed on August 18. Yankees manager Billy Martin (depicted left) was furious. Kansas City won, 5-4.

WORLD SERIES 1983: The aging '83 Phillies were the Wheeze Kids. Like the '50 Whiz Kids, they were a Series bust. The Phils won Game 1 when Garry Maddox homered in the eighth off Baltimore's Scott McGregor, who had a lengthy wait before Maddox batted because of a TV interview with President Reagan (in attendance). The Orioles then won four straight, led by Mike Boddicker's three-hitter in Game 2 and McGregor's Game-5 shutout (in which Eddie Murray hit two home runs).

Cubs second baseman Ryne Sandberg (avoiding a baserunner later in his career) won N.L. MVP honors in 1984 when he batted .314, hit 19 triples, scored 114 runs and made only six errors. Along with Rick Sutcliffe's stout pitching (16-1 record after being acquired in June), Sandberg's exploits helped the Cubs to the N.L. East title. But just when the North Side of Chicago was thinking World Series for the first time since 1945, the Cubs blew the best-of-five NLCS to the Padres after leading two games to none.

'The Cubs find a way to lose it.'

—October 15, 1984

The Sporting News

NBA Draft Preview: Who Will Take Whom?

Complete Baseball, Hockey Draft Lists

USFL QB Jim Kelly: Good Enough for NFL

ARE THE CUBS FOR REAL?

Slugger Leon Durham Helps Rekindle Hopes

The Tigers won at a furious pace in the first two months of the 1984 season, getting off to the best 40-game start in major league history. Jack Morris, who pitched a no-hitter in the first week of the season, contributed heavily to Detroit's quick getaway.

DETROIT AT CALIFORNIA (N)

Trammell's two-run homer keyed a four-run fourth as Morris improved his record to 9-1 and the Tigers upped their mark to 35-5 with a 5-1 win over Angels. Detroit's 17th consecutive road victory broke A.L. record set by Washington Senators in 1912 and tied major-league mark established by 1916 New York Giants.

Detroit	ab	r	h	rbi	California	ab	r	h	rbi
Whitaker, 2b	3	1	1	0	Pettis, cf	4	0	0	0
Trammell, ss	4	1	1	2	Carew, 1b	4	1	1	0
Gibson, rf	4	1	1	0	Lynn, rf	4	0	1	0
Parrish, c	4	2	2	1	DeCinces, 3b	4	0	1	0
Evans, dh	3	0	1	1	Downing, lf	4	0	0	0
Herndon, lf	4	0	0	0	Re. J'kson, dh	2	0	0	0
Bergman, 1b	4	0	0	0	Wilfong, 2b	2	0	1	0
Lemon, cf	4	0	0	0	Boone, c	3	0	0	0
Garbey, 3b	3	0	1	0	Picciolo, ss	2	0	0	0
Brookens, 3b	0	0	0	0	Brown, ph	1	0	0	0
					Schofield, ss	0	0	0	0
Totals	33	5	7	4	Totals	30	1	4	0

Detroit ....0 0 0 4 0 1 0 0 0—5
California ....1 0 0 0 0 0 0 0 0—1

Detroit	IP.	H.	R.	ER.	BB.	SO.
Morris (W. 9-1)	9	4	1	0	1	10

California	IP.	H.	R.	ER.	BB.	SO.
Slaton (L. 1-2)	5⅓	6	5	5	2	1
Kaufman	2⅔	1	0	0	0	1
Corbett	1	0	0	0	0	0

The Sporting News

OCTOBER 22, 1984

Sooners and Texas: Fit to Be Tied

TSN's Major League All-Star Selections

College, Pro Football Schedules, Results

Tiger - ific!

WORLD SERIES 1984: Sparky Anderson became the first manager to lead teams from both leagues to Series crowns as the Tigers dispatched San Diego in five games. Alan Trammell (above, welcomed at the plate) whacked two home runs in Game 4 in support of Jack Morris (who won for the second time). In Game 5, Kirk Gibson (right) hit two upper-deck homers that accounted for five runs.

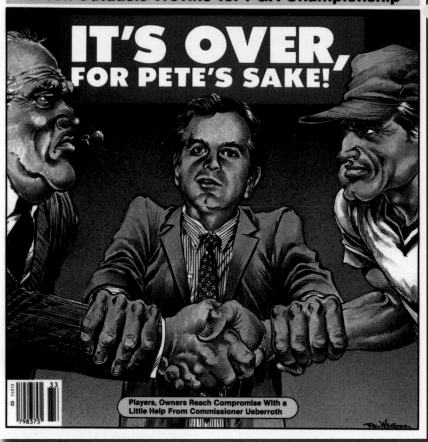

The Sporting News

AUGUST 19, 1985

PRICE: $1.95

The Best Baseball Town in the World

Green Outduels Trevino for PGA Championship

IT'S OVER, FOR PETE'S SAKE!'

Players, Owners Reach Compromise With a Little Help From Commissioner Ueberroth

When another stalemate came in negotiations on a new Basic Agreement, players walked again in 1985. This time, they were out only two days when negotiators resolved such major issues as benefit-plan contributions from a lucrative television package, revisions in free agency and tweaks in the salary-arbitration process. Commissioner Peter Ueberroth was credited with a significant role in the proceedings.

Pitching for the White Sox against the Yankees, former Mets star Tom Seaver won his 300th game in 1985. On the same day, August 4, the Angels' Rod Carew reached the 3,000-hit milestone in a game against Minnesota.

Outfielders Jim Rice (left), Dale Murphy (center) and Andre Dawson were among the game's top sluggers. The Red Sox's Rice, who had won A.L. MVP honors in 1978, exceeded 100 RBIs for the seventh time in 1985 (and did it again in '86). Atlanta's Murphy, the N.L. MVP in 1982 and 1983, led the league with 37 homers in '85. Dawson, a fixture in Montreal for a decade, moved on to the Cubs and had an MVP year (49 homers, 137 RBIs) in 1987.

Hard-throwing Dwight Gooden was a sensation at age 20, compiling a 24-4 record and a 1.53 ERA for the 1985 Mets. Pitching in his second major league season, Gooden threw eight shutouts in '85. The righthander had won 17 games in 1984 after jumping to the majors from Class A.

Pete Rose and 4,192

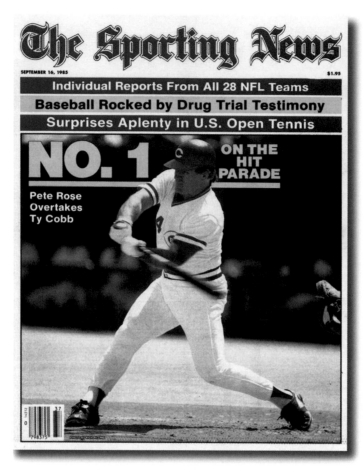

Pete Rose's quest to make a lasting mark on big-league baseball began in 1963 when he was a rookie with the Reds. Then, on September 11, 1985, Rose left a mark no one thought possible: He became the majors' all-time hits leader (right, with the Padres' Steve Garvey ready to acknowledge the moment), topping Ty Cobb's record of 4,191 with a first-inning single off San Diego's Eric Show.

In his nearly 23 seasons, Rose had captured three batting titles, collected 200 hits a record 10 times, reeled off a 44-game hitting streak, played on three World Series championship teams and won the admiration of millions with his competitive zeal and unbridled enthusiasm.

'Could anyone imagine Pete Rose ever doing anything else?'

—September 23, 1985

'Rose is not only No.1 in career hits, but in devotion to baseball.'

—September 23, 1985

COUNTDOWN TO COBB

My Diary of the
Record-Breaking
1985 Season

By
PETE ROSE
With Hal Bodley

Foreword by
Peter V. Ueberroth

Published by **The Sporting News**

Rose reflected on his season in a book published by
The Sporting News just days after his historic achievement.

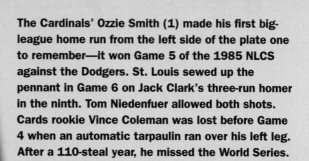

The Cardinals' Ozzie Smith (1) made his first big-league home run from the left side of the plate one to remember—it won Game 5 of the 1985 NLCS against the Dodgers. St. Louis sewed up the pennant in Game 6 on Jack Clark's three-run homer in the ninth. Tom Niedenfuer allowed both shots. Cards rookie Vince Coleman was lost before Game 4 when an automatic tarpaulin ran over his left leg. After a 110-steal year, he missed the World Series.

WORLD SERIES 1985:

St. Louis held a three games-to-two lead in the Series and a 1-0 edge in the bottom of the ninth inning of Game 6 at Kansas City when an umpire became a household name. Royals pinch hitter Jorge Orta hit a leadoff grounder to first baseman Jack Clark, whose throw to Cardinals reliever Todd Worrell, covering the bag, appeared to be in time. But umpire Don Denkinger called Orta safe, which (a) made the Cards livid (Worrell, right, was the first to vent) and (b) led to a game-winning rally capped by Dane Iorg's hit and Jim Sundberg's perfect slide home. In Game 7, the Royals routed John Tudor, who had won 20 of his last 21 regular-season decisions, and cruised, 11-0, behind ace Bret Saberhagen.

A record for the Rocket

Boston's Roger Clemens set a major league record for strikeouts in a nine-inning game on April 29, 1986, when he fanned 20 Mariners in a game at Fenway Park. Clemens (shown pitching on the road) went 24-4 in '86.

Games of Monday, August 25

OAKLAND
AT DETROIT (N)

McGwire hit his first major league homer—a 450-foot drive to center with mate aboard—and Tettleton followed with round-tripper to highlight five-run fifth inning that gave A's 8-4 triumph over Tigers.

Oakland	ab	r	h	rbi		Detroit	ab	r	h	rbi
Griffin, ss	5	0	1	0		Whitaker, 2b	3	1	0	0
Murphy, cf	4	1	1	0		Trammell, ss	4	0	0	0
Canseco, lf	4	2	2	0		Gibson, rf	4	0	0	0
Bochte, 1b	3	1	1	2		Grubb, dh	3	1	1	1
Lansford, dh	5	0	2	0		Evans, 1b	4	1	1	1
Davis, rf	5	1	1	2		Collins, lf	2	0	0	0
Hill, 2b	5	1	1	2		Coles, 3b	4	0	1	0
McGwire, 3b	3	1	1	1		Lemon, cf	4	0	1	0
Tettleton, c	3	1	1	1		Lowry, c	4	0	1	0
Totals	39	8	11	8		Totals	32	4	5	4

Oakland .... 2 0 1 0 5 0 0 0 0—8
Detroit .... 3 0 0 0 0 0 0 0 1—4

Oakland	IP.	H.	R.	ER.	BB.	SO.
Rijo (W. 6-9)	9	5	4	4	4	3

Detroit	IP.	H.	R.	ER.	BB.	SO.
Terrell (L. 11-10)	4⅔	8	7	7	3	3
Thurmond	1⅓	1	0	0	1	0
Slaton	2	2	0	0	0	1
Campbell	1	0	0	0	0	0

Game-winning RBI—Hill. E—McGwire. DP—Oakland 1. LOB—Oakland 9, Detroit 5. 2B—Griffin, Lansford, Murphy, Coles, Lemon. 3B—Canseco. HR—Evans (22), McGwire (1), Tettleton (6). SB—Whitaker. HBP—By Slaton (Canseco). T—2:50. A—20,475.

> "
>
> Fernando Arroyo was demoted to Tacoma and third baseman Mark McGwire was called up. Arroyo had walked three batters on 15 pitches in his first appearance in the majors since 1982. McGwire is the former Olympian who was the A's No. 1 draft pick in June 1984. He became the 40th player and the 10th rookie to appear on the A's roster this season.
>
> —*September 1, 1986*
>
> "

Yankees first baseman Don Mattingly, voted the American League's MVP in 1985 when he hit 35 home runs and knocked in 145 runs, batted .352 with 238 hits in 1986 and finished second to the Red Sox's Wade Boggs in the A.L. batting race. Mattingly had won the hitting crown in 1984.

Behind three games to one and one strike away from elimination in the 1986 ALCS, the Red Sox won new life when Dave Henderson (left) hit a go-ahead homer off the Angels' Donnie Moore in the ninth inning of Game 5. Boston wound up winning the game in 11 innings on Henderson's sacrifice fly, then won easily in Games 6 and 7 to advance to the World Series.

Buckner's Fatal Error Will Live in Infamy

NEW YORK—It was a great baseball season for Charles Dickens, who during the World Series was quoted more often than John McNamara or Dave Johnson.

Everybody from announcer Vin Scully to the the smallest daily newspaper seemed convinced that it was, yes, the best of times and the worst of times. In a World Series, isn't it always?

Baseball at last has disappeared into the oncoming winter, leaving us with April dreams and October memories.

The World Series of 1986 is consigned to history, to be judged, analyzed and, of course, discussed. Baseball, most of all, is a game of conversation.

The final out of a World Series is a time for celebration, players from the winning team, this year the New York Mets, leaping atop each other in a ritual not only familiar, but obligatory. Heaven help a man who doesn't express unfettered joy.

Yet the scene in the losers' clubhouse may be more appropriate for most of us. Hangdog looks and muted words reflect the feelings of an America that, for the next five months, must exist without the accompaniment of pop flies and box scores.

We get baseball's ultimate production, day after day of celebrities throwing out first balls and journalists tossing back second-guesses. And then we get nothing.

A World Series is like old age. No matter how bad it may be, it's better than the alternative—no World Series at all.

With all the long evenings—the Series set a record for average length of 3 hours, 20 minutes)—lifeless

Darryl Strawberry for home runs; the botched run-down by the Mets to avoid elimination in Game 6; the despair of the Red Sox after Game 7.

The Super Bowl is more hype than hustle, a week of buildup culminating in a game that proves a letdown. But the World Series is a moveable feast, shuttle diplomacy with bats and balls.

The Series invariably offers the tantalizing question: What if?

What if Oil Can Boyd hadn't pitched in Game 3? What if he had pitched in Game 7? What if Gary Carter hadn't singled with two out in the bottom of the 10th in Game 6? What if Calvin Schiraldi had been effective in Game 7?

The World Series of 1986 was one without the acrimony of that between the Cardinals and Royals in '85. Players on both the Mets and Red Sox proved to be sportsmen as well as athletes.

In the end, Boston realized what it nearly had, and New York understood what it finally had achieved.

Humans play these games. They are humans with special gifts, but they are humans nevertheless. Their mistakes and foibles only make us comprehend how well they perform most of the time.

What separates sport from other entertainment is its unpredictability. We know what to expect at a Beethoven concert or a Tennessee Williams play. But in sport, we never know what to expect.

It's like Schiraldi hitting Brian Downing of the Angels in the playoffs

have happened.

"Dave Henderson hits a homer to give us the lead. That shouldn't happen. Then there's a misplayed ball in the sixth game of the World Series that sends the Series to a seventh game. That shouldn't happen either. But in baseball it does happen.

And when it happens in the World Series, for better or worse, an entire country is eyewitness. A man's complete athletic career may be compressed to a few magic—or merciless—seconds.

Al Gionfriddo? He made the running catch of DiMaggio's fly in '47. Mickey Owen? He dropped the third strike that enabled the Yankees to come from behind and win in '41.

Kismet. Bill Buckner of the Red Sox will now be pigeonholed. Whatever he did before or does after will be recalled only in the context of the error in the bottom of the 10th of the sixth game.

"It's a moment that's always going to be on my mind," said Evans, Buckner's teammate.

Evans is a man of class. He was battered by the Red Sox' loss to the Mets in a Series Boston should have won. But his response to the loss was that of a gentleman.

"History?" Evans asked rhetorically. "I don't believe in it, that it had anything to do with us losing. But you do wonder. Sixty-eight years between wins in the World Series is a long time.

"This is going to be a tough winter. The only things warm in Boston this winter are going to be the logs on the fire."

Boston's Bill Buckner will be remembered more for his 10th-inning error than anything else he did in the Series.

missed it for, well, the world.

Kodacolor snapshots will forever remain in the mind's eye. Balls popping

WORLD SERIES 1986: When Red Sox reliever Bob Stanley uncorked a game-tying wild pitch in the bottom of the 10th inning of Game 6, it took Boston—which had gone ahead of the Mets, 5-3, in the top of the inning—from within one strike of the Series title to a measure of self-doubt. Mookie Wilson then finished a gripping 10-pitch at-bat by grounding a 3-2 pitch to first baseman Bill Buckner, who let the ball get through his legs. Ray Knight sprinted home (right), and the Mets made off with an unbelievable 6-5 win. Buckner's error, although egregious, didn't seal the Sox's fate in this Series. Boston could rebound in Game 7—and it led, 3-0, after five innings. But the Mets rallied for an 8-5 victory to win the crown.

Cardinals shortstop Ozzie Smith was known for his special-occasion pregame flips, but he was more noted for his acrobatic defensive play. Considered by many experts as the premier fielder in the game's history, Smith won 13 consecutive Gold Gloves. He made himself into a good offensive player, too.

Paul Molitor's 2 Streaks

For Brewers' DH, Being Healthy Was Almost As Important as Stringing All Those Hits

By TOM FLAHERTY

MILWAUKEE—Paul Molitor was the first to reach Rick Manning and slap a high-five of congratulations.

"Sorry about that," Manning said.

"Sorry?" Molitor responded, incredulous that Manning would apologize for winning a game with a pinch-hit single.

But this wasn't just any game. This was Wednesday, August 26, 1987, the night Molitor didn't get a hit for the first time in six weeks.

Hitless in four previous at-bats against Cleveland Indians rookie John Farrell, Molitor was in the on-deck circle when Manning's 10th-inning single off Doug Jones gave the Milwaukee Brewers a 1-0 victory. Thus, Molitor's hitting streak ended at 39 games.

For just a few moments after Mike Felder scored the winning run, there was a strange blanket of silence at Milwaukee County Stadium. Finally, a few in the crowd of 11,246 applauded. Some groaned. Many even booed.

To them, Manning wasn't a hero for winning the game; he was a bum for depriving Molitor of another at-bat, one final swing at continuing to pursue Joe DiMaggio's immortality.

Finally, there was a great cheer.

As Molitor headed to the dugout, the fans rose to their feet for a thunderous ovation. Moments later, he popped out of the dugout waving his cap as the applause crescendoed.

"That was probably the most emotional moment of the entire streak," Molitor said.

DiMaggio's record 56-game hitting streak had withstood the assault of another challenger. But Molitor had become a member of an elite group. Only six other players in baseball history hit in more consecutive games—DiMaggio (1941), Pete Rose (44 in 1978), Willie Keeler (44 in 1897), Bill Dahlen (42 in 1894), George Sisler (41 in 1922) and Ty Cobb (40 in 1911).

Molitor's streak began on July 16, the first game after the All-Star break. It was his first day back in the lineup after coming off the disabled list for the second time this season.

Nobody really noticed the streak until Molitor eclipsed the team record of 34 straight games, set by Davey May in 1973. As it grew, baseball fans watched and counted as Molitor climbed a ladder occupied by some of the best players ever to play the game.

Molitor's ascent finally was halted by Farrell, who was pitching only his third major league game. Coincidentally, Molitor was the

first batter Farrell had faced in his debut August 18. Molitor had promptly singled to extend his streak in 33 games.

In their second meeting, Molitor failed to hit the ball out of the infield. He struck out in the first inning, grounded into a double play in the third, grounded out in the sixth and reached base on an error in the eighth when first baseman Pat Tabler bobbled a throw.

"I give John the credit tonight because of the way he pitched," Molitor said. "It was meant to be 39 and not 40. . . . If I had to say what was the reason the streak ended, I would have to give the credit to him."

The following day, Farrell asked Molitor to autograph a baseball. Molitor wrote: "To John, Wishing you a great career. My best always, Paul Molitor."

Molitor stood up to the challenge of other pitchers for 39 games. Only three times had he extended the streak in his final at-bat. Only once did he bunt for a hit.

During the streak, he batted .405 (48 for 104), hit seven homers, drove in 33 runs and scored 43. He also helped the Brewers improve their record from 42-43 to 67-58.

Molitor learned a lot about himself during the streak, and he learned a lot about DiMaggio and Rose, too.

"It's hard to imagine hitting in that many games at this level," Molitor said. "It's a tough daily grind, and it wears on you mentally. It helps me appreciate these

Monitoring Molitor

Date	Opp.	AB	R	H	RBI	Type of Hits

Milwaukee's Paul Molitor went on the seventh-longest batting streak in major league history in 1987, hitting safely in 39 consecutive games. Those with longer streaks: Joe DiMaggio (56), Willie Keeler (44), Pete Rose (44), Bill Dahlen (42), George Sisler (41) and Ty Cobb (40).

WORLD SERIES 1987: The home team won every game in the first Series featuring indoor play. Minnesota got a first-game grand slam from Dan Gladden (above, right) at the Metrodome and a Game-6 slam from Kent Hrbek at the cozy, noisy ballpark. That the Twins dropped all three games in St. Louis was no surprise: Their regular-season road record was 29-52. Frank Viola won Games 1 and 7 for Minnesota. Cards power hitter Jack Clark sat out the Series with an ankle injury.

Cubs escape the dark ages

Red Sox third baseman Wade Boggs won his fourth consecutive American League batting title in 1988. It was his fifth crown in six seasons.

Night baseball came to Wrigley Field on August 8, 1988, and Mother Nature didn't seem to approve. The Cubs and Phillies played into the fourth inning that evening before lightning and heavy rain forced the game to be called off. As a result of the rainout, the August 9 Cubs-Mets game became the first official night game in Wrigley history.

Billy Martin's on-again, off-again job as Yankees manager was off for good when he was let go 68 games into the 1988 season.

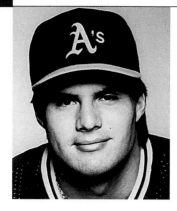

O's: Worst Month on Record

CHICAGO—By the time the Baltimore Orioles recorded their first victory of 1988, they had already broken two records. But they didn't get the big one.

After 21 consecutive losses, most ever by a major league team at the start of the season and the longest losing streak in American League history, the Orioles finally won, defeating the Chicago White Sox, 9-0, on April 29. The Orioles thus escaped going 0 for April, but a 4-1 loss the following night left them 1-22 for April, an .043 percentage that set a major league record for the worst month ever. The 1916 Phil-

Though there was obvious relief at the end of the dreadful journey, the Orioles did not stage a wild celebration when the losing streak came to an end. "It's a relief, but I'll keep it in perspective. This isn't the seventh game of the World Series," said winning pitcher Mark Williamson, who pitched six shutout innings.

The victory also was the first for Frank Robinson as the Orioles' manager. He had succeeded Cal Ripken Sr. six games into the season and had to wait 2½ weeks before winning.

When Dave Schmidt relieved Williamson in the seventh inning

opportunity of the year for the Orioles, who had not previously had a lead after the seventh.

"It (the streak) was a tremendous burden," said Schmidt. "Everyone in this clubhouse has pride. To lose this many in a row to have to answer the same questions every day and read all those bad things about us, it's just great to win."

After the Orioles finally won a game, catcher Terry Kennedy talked of winning 20 series in a row and reaching .500. But the O's lost the last two games to the White Sox and headed for home with a 1-23 record.

Until 1988, no team had lost more than 13 consecutive games at the start of a big-league season. The '88 Orioles reached a new high (or low) in season-opening futility, going 0-21 before notching a win. After Baltimore started 0-6, Cal Ripken Sr. was replaced as manager by Frank Robinson.

"
He said he would do it, and now he has. Oakland's Jose Canseco has become the first player in history to hit 40 home runs and steal 40 bases in the same season.

—*October 3, 1988*
"

'The A's ... as in artillery'
—*May 16, 1988*

The 1988 Oakland A's had a terrific 1-2 punch in Jose Canseco and Mark McGwire (left). Canseco hit 42 home runs and drove in 124 runs. McGwire had 32 homers and 99 RBIs.

The Dodgers' Orel Hershiser pitched 59 consecutive scoreless innings in 1988—and he did it down the stretch. The feat broke Don Drysdale's record of 58, which had been deemed "untouchable."

WORLD SERIES 1988: Never before had a Series game ended on a come-from-behind home run in the last inning. That changed in oh-so-dramatic fashion in Game 1 when injured Dodgers outfielder Kirk Gibson, swinging almost one-handed as a pinch hitter, hit a 3-2 pitch from Oakland's Dennis Eckersley into the seats in the ninth inning. The two-run shot (celebrated below) gave Los Angeles a 5-4 win. The underdog Dodgers won in five as Orel Hershiser dominated Games 2 and 5. A's stars Jose Canseco and Mark McGwire were a combined 2-for-36.

THE

Sporting News

OCTOBER 31, 1988

DESTINY'S DODGERS

Orel Hershiser and an unlikely supporting cast stun the A's in the World Series

See page 10

The Story of Seattle's Surprising Kelly Stouffer

Is There a New Dynasty Looming in the NBA?

The A's got a lot of hype in April 1989—and by season's end, they had earned it. Manager Tony La Russa (middle) boasted a nucleus of (left to right) pitcher Dave Stewart, outfielder Jose Canseco, first baseman Mark McGwire and closer Dennis Eckersley.

Rose Summoned, You Bet

PLANT CITY, Fla.—Although Cincinnati Reds Manager Pete Rose would not say whether gambling was discussed in his meeting February 20 with Commissioner Peter Ueberroth in New York, a source in Ueberroth's office confirmed that Rose's alleged betting was the topic.

"But the commissioner was satisfied with all of Pete's answers," the source said. "It's closed."

Rose and Ueberroth both said that Rose was summoned to New York to "give his opinion on a couple of things."

A Cincinnati television station reported recently that Rose was rumored to have been a betting partner in a $265,669.20 Pik Six payoff on January 25 at Turfway Park in Florence, Ky., across the Ohio River from Cincinnati. Rose denied any involvement.

The New York Times reported that Arnold Metz, a friend of Rose, had signed for two Pik Six tickets worth $132,834.60 each. The Reds' manager was quoted by the Times as saying, "You can read anything into it, but I don't see anything bad."

Baseball personnel are prohibited from betting on baseball games, but betting on other sporting events is permissible.

Rose asked, "How can baseball frown on horse racing? Some of the game's biggest names are (or were) involved in horse racing—George Steinbrenner, John Galbreath . . .

"When I was a free agent, Galbreath offered me race horses to sign with the Pirates, and when I played with the Phillies, they presented me with a race horse at home plate. I can't believe people think the commissioner called me in because of horse racing."

HAL M...

In early 1989, The Sporting News reported that Reds manager Pete Rose had been called to New York by commissioner Peter Ueberroth—apparently to discuss Rose's alleged betting.

Bill White became the first black to serve as a league president when he took over as head of the National League on April 1, 1989. White was a former player, having spent 13 seasons in the major leagues.

The cloud over Cincinnati

After disclosures and rumors about Pete Rose's alleged betting had circulated for months, commissioner Bart Giamatti announced in a statement on August 24, 1989, that he was handing Rose a lifetime suspension for engaging "in a variety of acts which have stained the game, and he must now live with the consequences of those acts." Later, while fielding questions, Giamatti said that "in the absence of a hearing and therefore in the absence of any evidence to the contrary, I am confronted by the factual record of the Dowd report, and on the basis of that, yes, I have concluded that he (Rose) bet on baseball." Rose asserted that—Giamatti's post-statement remarks to the contrary—he did not wager on baseball, and the game's all-time hits leader emphasized that the official wording of the ban never said he did.

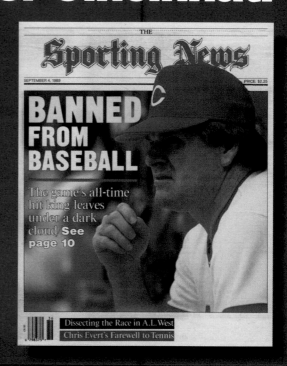

A. Bartlett "Bart" Giamatti had held the commissioner's job less than five months before making one of the most momentous decisions in the history of the office—the Pete Rose suspension. Giamatti, a former Yale University president who served as president of the National League from December 11, 1986, through March 31, 1989, succeeded Peter Ueberroth as commissioner on April 1, 1989.

Shockingly, eight days after suspending Rose, Giamatti died of a heart attack at his vacation home in Massachusetts. He was 51.

Dave Dravecky says he'll pitch again.

Dravecky's Comeback Halted by Broken Arm

SAN FRANCISCO—San Francisco Giants lefthander Dave Dravecky thought he was shot by a sniper when he crashed to the ground at Montreal's Olympic Stadium August 15 after throwing a sixth-inning pitch.

Teammates rushed to Dravecky, who was writhing in pain and gripping his left arm. It was later determined that Dravecky had suffered a stress fracture of the humerus, the largest bone between the elbow and shoulder.

The injury halted Dravecky's remarkable comeback from surgery for the removal of a cancerous tumor from his left arm last October. Because the tumor was attached to the humerus, a freezing agent was applied to the bone during surgery, leaving it susceptible to such a fracture.

"Dave and I discussed it, and we had opened up the possibility for him to have a fracture," said Dr. George Muschler, who performed the surgery. "The possibility of a fracture was there for up to two years after the surgery."

Doctors said the prognosis for

3 victory against Cincinnati August 10 at Candlestick Park.

He was nearly as effective against the Expos, carrying a three-hit shutout into the sixth. While Dravecky was pitching to Tim Raines, however, the bone in his arm snapped.

"It sounded like a firecracker," Expos outfielder Hubie Brooks said.

Manager Roger Craig and teammates fought back tears as they discussed the injury.

"It's unfair," Craig said. "It's like it was an act of God, but it was an act of God just for him to be out there.

"The last thing he told (pitching coach) Norm Sherry before he went to the hospital was, 'Win the game.'"

The Giants did win, 3-2, and Dravecky ended his short season with a 2-0 record. The next morning, Dravecky met with reporters before returning to San Francisco.

"There was absolutely no indication prior to that pitch that anything was wrong," Dravecky said.

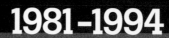

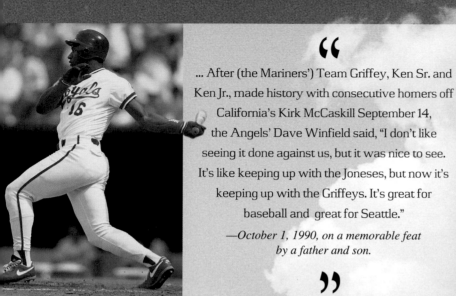

"

... After (the Mariners') Team Griffey, Ken Sr. and Ken Jr., made history with consecutive homers off California's Kirk McCaskill September 14, the Angels' Dave Winfield said, "I don't like seeing it done against us, but it was nice to see. It's like keeping up with the Joneses, but now it's keeping up with the Griffeys. It's great for baseball and great for Seattle."

—*October 1, 1990, on a memorable feat by a father and son.*

"

The opening of Toronto's glitzy SkyDome in June 1989 ushered in a new technological— and even sociological—era in baseball. The stadium was the game's first facility with a fully retractable roof, one that could be closed during a game if necessary. SkyDome also was a "city within a city," its vast structure housing a hotel, restaurants, shops and theaters.

SKYDOME
595-1131

WORLD SERIES 1989: The baseball wasn't particularly memorable—except for Oakland's domination of the Giants. But the '89 Series remains vivid in most fans' minds. A strong earthquake prior to Game 3 resulted in evacuation of Candlestick Park (below), with news of death and destruction in the Bay Area soon coming in. Amid a somber mood, the Series resumed after a 12-day gap in games—and the A's went on to a sweep. Dave Stewart and Mike Moore each won twice.

A no-hit weekend

On Friday, June 29, 1990, Oakland's Dave Stewart (left) pitched a no-hitter against the Blue Jays in Toronto. The same night, the Dodgers' Fernando Valenzuela threw a no-hit game against St. Louis in Los Angeles. Then, on Sunday, July 1, Andy Hawkins pitched no-hit ball while working all eight innings for the visiting Yankees in a loss at Chicago.

A day when crass gave way to class

Their paths had crossed on big days before, these two future Hall of Famers. On August 22, 1989, the day Nolan Ryan registered his 5,000th strikeout, Rickey Henderson was there. In fact, Henderson was victim No. 5,000.

And last June 11, when Ryan pitched his sixth career no-hitter, Oakland's Henderson made the final out. The next day, against Ryan's Texas team, Henderson reached a milestone of his own with his 900th stolen base.

This time, they were some 1,700 miles apart when baseball's spotlight shined on one and then, several hours later, the other. Henderson was the first to make history last Wednesday.

In the fourth inning, on a 1-and-0 pitch from Tim Leary of the Yankees to Athletics designated hitter Harold Baines, Henderson did what he does best. He bolted off second base and slid headfirst into third, beating the throw from catcher Matt Nokes. It was stolen base No. 939, a major league record, surpassing the mark set by Lou Brock.

Let's go to the videotape.

Henderson jumps to his feet, yanks the base out of the ground and holds it high above his head. He pumps his fist and waves to the crowd. The game comes to a halt...

On May 1, 1991, playing 1,700 miles apart, Oakland's Rickey Henderson got his record 939th career steal and Texas' Nolan Ryan (above) pitched his seventh no-hitter. TSN praised Ryan's humility but found fault with Henderson's braggadocio.

Reds punch out A's

A sweep: 'They crushed us twice and beat us at our game'

—*October 29, 1990*

WORLD SERIES 1990:

The A's had won three consecutive pennants and swept the 1989 Series. They had power (Jose Canseco, Mark McGwire), speed (Rickey Henderson) and great pitching (Dave Stewart, Bob Welch, closer Dennis Eckersley). The N.L. champions Reds had no chance. It was over in four games, all right. Only thing is, Cincinnati won. Starter Jose Rijo was 2-0, Reds relievers yielded no runs in 13 innings, Billy Hatcher hit .750 and Chris Sabo batted .563.

WORLD SERIES 1991: Last-place finishers in 1990, the Twins and Braves reached baseball's showcase event—and put on a rousing show. Game 7, a 10-inning 1-0 thriller won by the Twins, was decided on a single by Gene Larkin (above, right, hugging Kirby Puckett) and featured a route-going performance by Jack Morris. Also prominent in the finale: a baserunning gaffe by Atlanta's Lonnie Smith (top, opposite page), who hesitated rounding second base on Terry Pendleton's eighth-inning double and failed to score a "cinch" run. Puckett (above) was ecstatic after hitting a game-winning home run in the 11th inning of Game 6, a contest in which he also made a spectacular catch.

'Skates' lets chance slip away

Outfielder Lonnie Smith is officially under contract to the Atlanta Braves in 1992 at a salary of $2 million, a deal that kicked into place because Smith managed to get to bat 400 times during the '91 season after Otis Nixon's drug-abuse suspension.

But don't bet that Smith — the man they call "Skates" because of his slip-sliding approach to running — will play his first inning for the Braves next season.

After what happened last Sunday, there's a pretty good chance they will have to eat that contract and just get rid of him.

What happened last Sunday, in the seventh game of the World Series in Minneapolis, was that Smith pulled a baserunning error that should put him right up there with Fred Merkle in baseball's bonehead department.

And without that mistake, the Braves could be world champions today.

Smith led off the eighth inning of a scoreless Series Game 7 with a broken-bat single to right field. Terry Pendleton followed with a long drive up the gap in left center that bounced off the wall. But Smith still was not able to score — and never did get beyond third as Sid Bream eventually grounded into an inning-ending double play.

What happened? Why did Smith round ___se, then come to a complete stop

and start looking for the ball, or something, rather than look toward his third base coach, Jimy Williams, for guidance?

"If I saw (Pendleton's) ball off the bat, there's a good chance I could have scored," one report quoted Smith as saying. "But I didn't look in. That was my mistake."

That's about all anyone got out of Smith.

"All I know is that when there is a ball hit to the wall, a fast runner on first has to score," Braves General Manager John Schuerholz said.

"But when he (Smith) got 20 feet or so beyond second base, he just stopped. Why? Who knows? Somebody said that (Twins second baseman Chuck) Knoblauch decoyed him. But that doesn't make any sense to me because Lonnie was just standing there and looking down at the base."

Manager Bobby Cox, who was equally anguished and confused, said: "There wasn't any decoy by the infielders. I don't know who thought there was, but there wasn't. He didn't run. He held up. Why? I don't know."

Schuerholz continued: "Smith wasn't looking at Knoblauch. He wasn't looking at his coach. He wasn't looking at anything except second base, just looking at that damned base.

"I thought after Saturday's game we'd

Doubled up: *After his baserunning error, Smith was forced at home, then Harper completed the double play.*

used up all of our bad luck. I thought that we had some luck coming to us in the last game.

"Boy, I sure as hell was wrong about that, wasn't I?"

— DAVE NIGHTINGALE

'A swinging celebration: Pinch hitter Larkin's first-pitch drive to left-center sent a joyful Gladden home with the winning run and set off the dancing in the streets of Minneapolis.'

—November 4, 1991

"

(The Mets smashed) the salary ceiling by signing free agent Bobby Bonilla to a five-year, $29 million contract and, at the same time, (took) him away from the division champion Pittsburgh Pirates.

—December 16, 1991

"

big number: The Mets' Harazin (left), Bonilla and Torborg display the jersey Bonilla will wear in 1992 after Bonilla got a record contract.

Shea-ZAM!

Harazin's rapid-fire acquisitions of Torborg, Murray and Bonilla empty vault but make Mets favorites

■ Targeting Jeff Torborg, and only Jeff Torborg, as the manager to replace Bud Harrelson, then hiring him away from the Chicago White Sox.

■ Signing free-agent first baseman Eddie Murray, a switch-hitter who is still respected, even at the age of 36, to a two-year, $7.5 million contract.

■ Smashing the salary ceiling by signing free agent Bobby Bonilla to a five-year, $29 million contract and, at the same time, taking him away from the division champion Pittsburgh Pirates.

A New York baseball team is flexing its

share of mistakes, but if we keep ___ we're doing, we are heade___ destruction."

Pirates Manager Jim Leyla___ baseball's competitiveness is h___ ened by the big-money deals.

"This is not just the Mets. V___ me is that there are four or five ___ division who can afford to do th___ said Leyland, who has led the P___ consecutive National Leagu___ "You work your tail off to de___ then all of a sudden the guys___ have a bad year, and the___

Ballpark redux

Proving that the cookie-cutter era of multipurpose stadiums was absolutely, positively over, Baltimore opened intimate, quaint, baseball-only Oriole Park at Camden Yards in 1992. With yesterday's look suddenly considered fashionable, other "retro" ballparks soon followed in the majors.

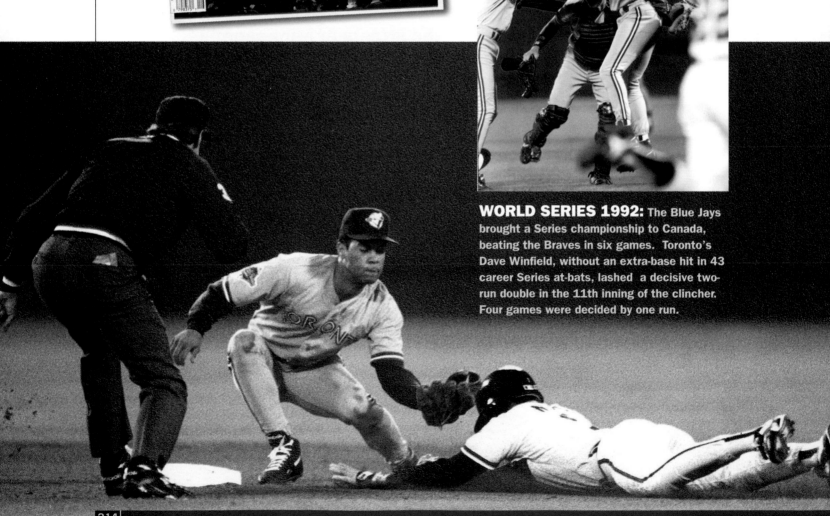

WORLD SERIES 1992: The Blue Jays brought a Series championship to Canada, beating the Braves in six games. Toronto's Dave Winfield, without an extra-base hit in 43 career Series at-bats, lashed a decisive two-run double in the 11th inning of the clincher. Four games were decided by one run.

1981-1994

Standing on the wire of life

Dave Kindred

The homemade wooden pier goes far ... Little Lake Nellie because the little ... fills a soft and gentle valley. The ... goes almost 200 feet out into the ... because even there the water is ... three feet deep. The dock goes al- ... 200 feet until it finds enough ... to carry a little lake's fishing boat. ... almost a toy lake, a tub full of water. ... Lake Nellie touches folks' back- ... s and makes them neighbors.

... you see the lake and you see the ... pier and you imagine neighbors ... ing out to the end of the pier, their ... eps making a hollow sound, there ... t a spell. They might watch sunlight ... e on the water or at night they ... t pick out the brightest stars. The ... is a soft and gentle place where ... ren laugh and grown-ups stop in ... hurryings.

... ow many such places might there ... millions of such places we've never ... d of? But now we know about Little ... Nellie and we know that on a black ... t, not a star in the sky, a fishing ... t moved through the dark toward the ... made pier reaching out from a

Saying goodbye: *Ojeda, the lone survivor, weeps during a moment alone before the funeral for Crews.*

> THEY DID ALL THAT BECAUSE
> THEY WERE FATHERS AND
> HUSBANDS AND PITCHERS AND
> YOUNG MEN FULL OF
> THEMSELVES.

wire-walker Karl Wallenda. "The r... waiting." He died, almost 80 years ... falling from the wire that gave his l... majesty.

But to put your life at risk in a fis... boat on a little lake in the dark of a ... spring night, to die during a family ... nic, is to confirm a madness afoot. ... for even a second would anyone pu... boat at speed on a little lake in the st... less dark? Why dare the devil?

I've done it and lived to wonder ... The first time came in an Oldsmobi... 98, a friend's fancy car, so fancy we ... wondered if, indeed, it would go 98 ... miles per hour. On Route 66, halfwa... between Chicago and St. Louis, we ... found out the Olds 98 would do 98. A... about 80 mph, I wanted out of the ca... but I said nothing, possibly because it... hard to talk while holding your breath. ... was 15 years old. Twenty-seven years ... later, I last rode a motorcycle 85 mph ... down a country road.

How slow we are to get smart, to ... learn how fine the thread is. Just last ... summer, young and strong, the Detroi... Lions lineman Eric Andolsek worked in ... his yard. A truck came off the road and ... killed him. A son alive, a second later ... dead, not of his foolishness but of this ... time's.

In this time, when Magic Johnson is ... HIV-positive, three New York Mets a... named in an alleged rape. In this time... Magic talking about AIDS, six Portlan... Trail Blazers are accused of statutory ... rape. It's enough to persuade us that in ... this time no one learns anything exc... by his own experience.

There was grim news out of spring training in March 1993: Indians pitchers Steve Olin and Tim Crews had been killed in a Florida boating accident, a crash that seriously injured teammate Bob Ojeda.

The Phillies' John Kruk provided levity in the 1993 All-Star Game when the lefthanded hitter kept his distance—and swung feebly on strike three— while facing hard-throwing Seattle lefty Randy Johnson, who had sailed a pitch over his head.

Baseball's newest teams, the Florida Marlins and Colorado Rockies, couldn't wait to get going in 1993. The expansion clubs went nowhere, though. The Rockies finished 67-95 in '93; the Marlins were 64-98.

Playing at Cincinnati on September 7, 1993, St. Louis' Mark Whiten tied three records with four homers and 12 RBIs in one game and 13 RBIs in a doubleheader.

Frank Thomas' first of two straight MVP years helped power the White Sox to the A.L. West crown in 1993. Emerging as one of the game's leading players, Thomas hit 41 homers and drove in 128 runs for a Chicago team that finished eight games ahead of Texas. The Sox lost to Toronto in the League Championship Series, though.

'Frank Thomas and the White Sox finally earn some respect'

—September 20, 1993

Relax, realignment will not hurt baseball

Peter Pascarelli

Baseball Report

Home by Christmas: Bud Selig's reign as acting commissioner is coming to an end.

WORLD SERIES 1993:
Trying to protect a 6-5 Phillies lead in the ninth inning of Game 6 and nail down a Series-squaring victory over Toronto, reliever Mitch "Wild Thing" Williams quickly got himself into a two-on, one-out mess. Joe Carter (right) tidied up in dramatic fashion, rocketing a Series-winning homer to left. Paul Molitor (below) hit .500 for the Blue Jays.

"

... Yes, the Republic will remain standing after this latest break with tradition.

—September 20, 1993, on baseball's plan for three divisions in each league in 1994 and inclusion of postseason wild-card teams.

"

Player	Avg.	G	TPA	AB	R	H	TB	2B	3B	HR	RBI	SH	SF	HP	BB	IntBB	SO	SB	CS	GIDP	Sig.	OBP
Jordan, Michael	202	127	497	436	46	88	116	17	1	3	51	3	3	4	51	0	114	30	18	4	.266	.289

Having walked away from a sport in which he was considered the best ever, Michael Jordan turned to baseball in 1994. It was more than a mere change of sports. Jordan went from the glory of the NBA to the obscurity of *minor league* baseball. Of course, he was hardly inconspicuous in the Class AA Southern League.

Playing for the White Sox's Birmingham farm club, Jordan was the object of everyone's attention. He also was the object of pitchers' attention, as his offensive line (above) shows. Still, despite only 21 extra-base hits, he drove in 51 runs. And he was a competent outfielder. Before long, though, Michael Jordan was back playing that other game.

Dare Jordan

Bullish on baseball? *Jordan took some cuts in 1990 (above) and again this winter is fueling speculation of a baseball career.*

"If Willie Mays had played only basketball from the time he was 8 years old, he'd have been Michael Jordan. And if Michael Jordan had played only baseball, he'd have been Willie Mays."

—Bulls General Manager Jerry Krause

'Joe Carter ended the Blue Jays' second consecutive title run with a bang, and it's not too early to ask if Toronto can do it again.'

—*November 1, 1993*

FEHR and RAVITCH
on the campaign trail

The immediate fate of baseball's 1994 season, the future of a $1.8-billion industry, is in the hands of two attorneys, Donald Fehr, representing the players' union, and Richard Ravitch, representing the 28 clubs.

Their collective-bargaining sessions have turned into debate over conflicting economic philosophies, Fehr arguing that clubs should be allowed to pay players as much as little as they choose, Ravitch arguing that clubs and players should agree to limit the amount paid to players. Here's an idea of what goes on when Fehr and Ravitch get together:

Baseball's main players this summer aren't on the field but on opposite sides of the negotiating table—a fact that Joe Fan simply can't ignore. By Steve Marantz

The owners and players were back at it in 1994, unable to reach an accord on a new collective bargaining agreement. The owners, led by chief negotiator Richard Ravitch, said baseball was in a financial crisis and sought a salary cap to control operating costs. Donald Fehr, head of the players' union, said players would not accept any system that failed to compensate them at the "market rate."

STEEEEE

Unable to resolve their labor differences, players and owners broke off talks on August 10, 1994. Players then went on strike at the conclusion of August 11 games, and the impasse continued with no foreseeable breakthrough. On September 14, owners announced they were canceling the remainder of the regular season (668 games) and all postseason play.

WORLD SERIES 1994: Canceled.

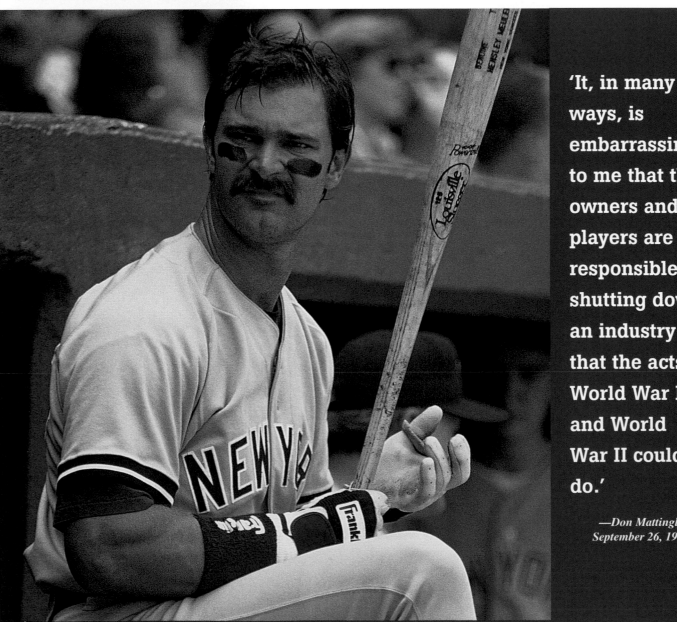

'It, in many ways, is embarrassing to me that the owners and players are responsible for shutting down an industry that the acts of World War I and World War II couldn't do.'

—*Don Mattingly,*
September 26, 1994

EE-RIIIIIIKE!

The Sporting News

SEPTEMBER 26, 1994 / $2.50 ($2.95 Can.)

"...THE PEOPLE OF AMERICA CARE ABOUT BASEBALL,
NOT ABOUT YOUR SQUALID LITTLE SQUABBLES.
REASSUME YOUR DIGNITY AND REMEMBER THAT YOU ARE
THE TEMPORARY CUSTODIANS OF AN ENDURING PUBLIC TRUST."

—*Bart Giamatti*

39 >

35665

0 798375 7

The Sporting News

SEPTEMBER 11, 1995 / $2.50 ($2.95 Can.)

'It is doubtful if any future performer will attempt to go

320

1995

CAL, BIG MAC AN

–2000

REBIRTH

Mark McGwire hits No. 62 on September 8, 1998.

A s millennium celebrations go, the one staged in 2000 was grand theater, the largest, most anticipated, all-
encompassing, exhilarating party in the history of the world. And why not? In the 20th century alone, mankind
had advanced from horse-and-buggy innocence to space-travel sophistication with promises of even newer and
more spectacular technological advancements just around the corner.

The celebration was a culmination of ideas that had been shaped and nurtured, obstacles that had been
overcome, breakthroughs that had changed the course of history and dreams that still were being fulfilled.
What once was about the struggle to survive now was about quality of life, complete with portfolios and
special effects.

For baseball purists, quality was in the eye of the beholder. The game, too, had reason to celebrate after overcoming a long,
bitter 1994 work stoppage that had wrecked a season and forced cancellation of a World Series. But the prosperity that
returned in the form of record attendance, mind-boggling player contracts, new ballpark construction, huge television deals and
pervasive corporate sponsorships was accompanied by mistrust and suspicion.

Such feelings would not be easily overcome. Much like Babe Ruth rescued baseball after
the 1919 Black Sox scandal, the game needed a savior. It got three—one who delivered a
heartwarming message on a magical September night in 1995 and two others who
brought a new glow to the game during a dramatic and magical summer three
years later.

1995

The Murrah federal office building in
Oklahoma City is bombed; 168 die.

O.J. Simpson is acquitted of
murder charges.

1996

TWA flight 800, bound to Paris from New York, crashes into the
Atlantic; 230 die.

A bomb explodes at an Atlanta park where Olympic Games revelers
are gathered.

Nobody did more to close the wounds than Cal Ripken, who brought his pursuit of Lou Gehrig's iron-man record to a successful conclusion in 1995 with the ultimate spirit-raising party that charmed a national television audience and a capacity crowd at Baltimore's Camden Yards. Ripken, the consummate blue-collar professional who was playing in his 2,131st consecutive game, celebrated his special moment in the middle of the fifth inning with a long, slow, hand-slapping victory lap around the stadium's perimeter—an emotional pull at the country's heartstrings and a symbolic reaching out to the wavering fans.

The Summer of '98 was more about drama, excitement—and power, the kind generated by the swing of a Sammy Sosa or Mark McGwire bat. In a riveting home run race that captured the imagination of the nation, McGwire beat his Cubs rival to Roger Maris' 37-year-old home run record when he hit No. 62 on September 8 in St. Louis, and then he slugged his way to the phenomenal total of 70, with Sosa not far behind at 66.

Big Mac and Sammy were not home run pioneers, merely leading men in a drama that had been building for years. They were the epitome of power baseball, the poster boys for an offensive explosion that was changing the look of the game and attracting the young, action-craving fan. Year after year, home runs were sailing out of ballparks in record numbers, fueled by bigger, stronger players—and rumors of a lively ball.

Fascination for the home run and offensive baseball was not surprising in a society that craved the spectacular headline and fast-paced news story. This was the period that gave us the O.J. Simpson murder trial, a destructive Oklahoma City bombing, the shocking death of a princess, the Columbine school shootings and a series of scandals that almost brought down a President. While Tom Clancy captivated readers with his techno-thrillers, Bill Gates continued to wow us with his techno-wonders.

Cable television and the World Wide Web brought the world and its most intricate secrets to our fingertips. The electronic age taught us new ways to communicate (e-mail), do business (e-commerce) and spend our

1997

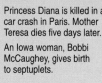

Princess Diana is killed in a car crash in Paris. Mother Teresa dies five days later.

An Iowa woman, Bobbi McCaughey, gives birth to septuplets.

1998

President Clinton acknowledges an improper relationship with a White House intern.

The hit television show *Seinfeld* airs its last episode.

Michael Jordan leads the Bulls to their third consecutive NBA championship.

Former Alabama governor George Wallace dies.

money. And it changed our sports-viewing habits, both in terms of information-gathering and access to our favorite teams.

With the increased revenues produced by cable television and corporate affiliations came the $100-million-plus contracts (even $200 million) and more outraged cries from the fans who paid for player greed at the turnstiles. To make those turnstiles more attractive, owners continued a ballpark-building frenzy that combined nostalgia, technological frills and mall-like distractions aimed at the "new-age fan."

Nothing could discourage expansion, which brought the century's team roster to 30 and further watered down an already depleted pitching pool. In additional attempts to generate dollars and increase excitement for the fans, owners defiled almost 100 years of tradition by instituting interleague play, moved from two to three divisions, set up a third tier of playoffs that rewarded wild-card qualifiers and took steps toward division realignment that would make geographic, if not traditional, sense.

Once you got past the body-piercing and tattoos, the ballpark video arcades and Beanie Babies giveaways, and the cool, businesslike relationship between players, fans and teams, the game still retained its simple charms and unpredictability. Many of the baseball pleasures fans experienced in 1901 still could be felt almost a century later.

New York returned to its championship throne with the re-emergence of the Yankees, who won three consecutive World Series and four in a five-year span (1996-2000). Not only did the Yankees win in 1998, they mauled their way through opponents for an American League-record 114 regular-season wins—125 victories, including postseason play. Not only did the 2000 Yankees claim the franchise's 37th pennant, they completed their title march with an emphatic five-game victory over the crosstown Mets in the first Subway Series in 44 years. It was

1998

Two law-enforcement officers are killed by a gunman at the Capitol in Washington, D.C.

John Glenn, now 77, returns to space aboard the shuttle Discovery.

President Clinton is impeached.

1999

President Clinton is acquitted of impeachment charges.

Two youths fatally shoot 12 students and a teacher at a Colorado high school.

their 26th World Series crown.

The Yankees' success was extraordinary in this free-agent era, a tribute to George Steinbrenner's willingness to finance a $100-million-plus payroll that kept his key players in place. Likewise Ted Turner, who paid dearly to finance an Atlanta Braves machine that rolled to nine consecutive division titles, eight straight NLCS appearances, five World Series berths and one Series championship from 1991-2000.

There was no dearth of outstanding performances—and not just the McGwire-Sosa variety. Braves righthander Greg Maddux claimed his record fourth straight Cy Young Award in 1995 and Roger Clemens won his record fifth overall three years later for Toronto. Clemens, who already owned the single-game, nine-inning record for strikeouts with 20, matched that feat in 1996 and then watched Cubs rookie Kerry Wood join his exclusive club two years later. Yankees David Wells and David Cone joined exclusive company in 1998 and '99 when they threw perfect games—the first at Yankee Stadium since Don Larsen's perfecto in the 1956 World Series.

Veterans Tony Gwynn and Wade Boggs contributed to the highlight reels with their 3,000th career hits, and Eddie Murray joined both the 3,000-hit and 500-home run clubs. But St. Louis third baseman Fernando Tatis might have raised the most eyebrows when he hit an unprecedented two grand slams in the same inning of a game against the Los Angeles Dodgers.

By the end of 2000, it was clear that the game, 100 seasons old in its National League/American League configuration, was still vibrant and entertaining, if not always judicious in its decision-making and spending habits. Whether it is equipped to handle the inevitable financial battles that lie just around the corner or deal with its continued evolution in the entertainment industry remains to be seen. But one thing seems certain: Baseball's resiliency and ability to mirror the society into which it is intricately entwined bodes well for the next hundred years.

2000

Federal agents seize Cuban boy Elián González from the home of his Miami relatives and reunite the boat-wreck survivor with his father.

In an election so close that it precipitates five weeks of ballot disputes and legal wrangling, George W. Bush wins the Presidency over Al Gore.

It might be
It could be
IT IS

The real thing is back and fans can only
hope it is here to stay   By STEVE MARANTZ

It's back to the ol' ball yard

Baseball was still idle early in 1995, and owners were threatening to use replacement players—minor leaguers and fringe major leaguers—to fill the void and get the game back on the field. Owners also were attempting to operate the game under rules they had imposed unilaterally in December 1994 after declaring that the collective-bargaining process was at a dead end. At issue was whether the players should be willing to accept a salary cap or a payroll tax, restrictions on free agency and an end to salary arbitration. At the players' urging, the National Labor Relations Board in March acted on a claim of unfair labor practices and sought an injunction against the owners' imposition of new rules. (Players voted to end their strike if the injunction were granted.) A District Court judge issued an injunction on March 31, ending the strike and restoring terms of the expired Basic Agreement. After a late spring training, which resulted in the adoption of a 144-game regular-season schedule, it was time to ... play ball! (And it was time, below, to buy tickets in anticipation of Cal Ripken's march toward Lou Gehrig's consecutive-games record.)

Record business: *Gary Rowe (above) typified the renewed enthusiasm of fans all around the majors*

'(Mickey) Mantle lived on many levels and swung through many moods, but I think you begin with a poor boy, the lead miner's son, who ran with the hounds of poverty at his winged heels.'

—*author Roger Kahn, reflecting on the death of Mickey Mantle, August 1995.*

For a generation of fans, the one-word cover headline said it all. Mickey Charles Mantle was the Mick—forever flashing his boyish grin, running like the wind and bashing a baseball to distant places. Mantle died on August 13, 1995, at age 63.

Overtaking
the Iron Horse

It was the ultimate feel-good story—just what baseball needed after seemingly endless labor strife had cast a pall over the game and disconnected it from a fan base that seemed to shrink whenever anyone mentioned "work stoppage" or "lockout."

The story was the culmination of Cal Ripken's dogged, inspirational pursuit of a record long thought unbreakable: The consecutive-game streak of 2,130, set by Lou Gehrig, the game's Iron Horse.

After a players strike ended the 1994 season in August and forced a 144-game schedule in 1995, fans were in a resentful and distrusting mood. Then Ripken and his American-as-apple-pie work ethic got them back—in large measure, anyway.

In a euphoric atmosphere on September 6, 1995, at Baltimore's Camden Yards, the Orioles' thoroughbred played in his 2,131st consecutive game and set off a festive, nationally televised celebration—one that seemed to reaffirm the game's appeal when Ripken took a spine-tingling victory lap around the ballpark (right).

'I know that if Lou Gehrig is looking down ... he isn't concerned about someone playing one more consecutive game than he did. ... He's viewing tonight as another example of what is good and right about the great American game.'

—Cal Ripken, on the night he played in his 2,131st consecutive game.

Cal Ripken acknowledged the fans' midgame salute (left) after breaking Lou Gehrig's consecutive-games record. The next day, baseball's new iron man received another tribute—a parade in downtown Baltimore.

'At minimum, the Braves are a dynasty-in-waiting.'
—*November 6, 1995*

WORLD SERIES 1995:

Winners of eight division titles and five pennants in the 1990s, the Braves won their only Series title of the decade when they defeated Cleveland in six games. Tom Glavine pitched eight innings of one-hit ball in the clincher, a 1-0 Atlanta victory decided on Dave Justice's sixth-inning home run. Glavine won twice, and Greg Maddux tossed a two-hitter in the opener for the Braves.

Greg Maddux (below) was phenomenal for the Braves in '95, going 19-2 with a 1.63 ERA and winning his fourth consecutive Cy Young Award. Maddux had captured his first Cy Young as a member of the Cubs before signing a free-agent contract with Atlanta in December 1992.

The Sporting News got together with two of baseball's "naturals," San Diego's Tony Gwynn and former St. Louis star Stan Musial, to talk about the fine art of hitting. They spoke with consummate authority. Musial won seven National League batting crowns and Gwynn notched his eighth N.L. title in 1997.

The Americanational League

When owners accepted a plan in 1996 to introduce interleague play the next year, it evoked one writer's boyhood memories of watching Pirates superstar Roberto Clemente (immediate right) but not having the chance to see another great right fielder, Detroit's Al Kaline. Stars from both leagues would be on the field for more than 200 interleague games in '97.

Let's pl

JOHNSON 15   ANDERSON 9   ALOMAR 12

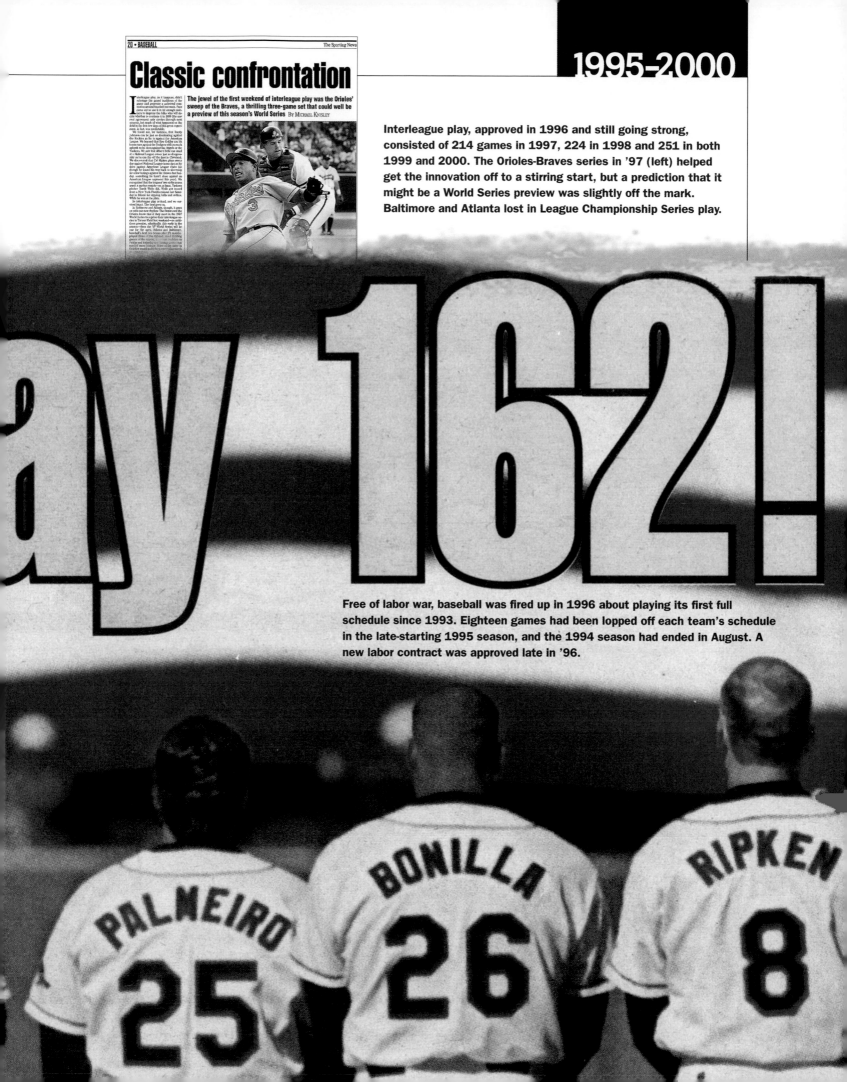

Classic confrontation

The jewel of the first weekend of interleague play was the Orioles' sweep of the Braves, a thrilling three-game set that could well be a preview of this season's World Series By Michael Knisley

1995-2000

Interleague play, approved in 1996 and still going strong, consisted of 214 games in 1997, 224 in 1998 and 251 in both 1999 and 2000. The Orioles-Braves series in '97 (left) helped get the innovation off to a stirring start, but a prediction that it might be a World Series preview was slightly off the mark. Baltimore and Atlanta lost in League Championship Series play.

Free of labor war, baseball was fired up in 1996 about playing its first full schedule since 1993. Eighteen games had been lopped off each team's schedule in the late-starting 1995 season, and the 1994 season had ended in August. A new labor contract was approved late in '96.

Roger Clemens' second 20-strikeout performance of his career—against Detroit at Tiger Stadium on September 18, 1996—came in his last victory as a member of the Red Sox. A three-time Cy Young Award winner at the time, Clemens signed a free-agent contract with Toronto that December.

Tony Tarasco's hopes of catching Derek Jeter's drive in Game 1 of the 1996 Orioles-Yankees ALCS ended when a boy reached over the wall and interfered with the ball. The ruling: a home run.

WORLD SERIES 1996:
John Wetteland (four saves in the Series) was right—the Yankees were No. 1, winning their first Fall Classic since '78. Atlanta won Games 1 and 2, but New York took the next four. The big hit: Jim Leyritz's three-run, eighth-inning homer that tied Game 4, which the Yanks won, 8-6. The big play: Right fielder Paul O'Neill's over-the-shoulder catch that wrapped up the Yanks' 1-0 win in Game 5.

When Baltimore's Roberto Alomar spit on umpire John Hirschbeck in the final week of the 1996 regular season—and was allowed to play in the postseason—there was outrage and a sense that the game had lost its self-respect. Alomar was suspended for five days of the 1997 regular season.

BratBall leads to SpitBall

Dave **KINDRED**

A wonderful thing happened before the Braves and Dodgers played the third game of their playoff series in Atlanta.

When the game's six umpires walked through a right-field gate and into sight, 50,000 people began to applaud. As the umpires moved toward home plate, the applauding fans rose to their feet. They rose all around the stadium, from owner Ted Turner's box to the highest seats in center field. Warm and sustained, the applause came to the men in blue.

On first hearing the applause and not sure what to make of it, crew chief Harry Wendelstedt allowed himself a small smile. In 31 seasons as an umpire, Wendelstedt had heard nothing like it. In 100 seasons of baseball, no one heard anything like it.

In an essay on Ted Williams' last game, author John Updike spoke of the great hitter's refusal to tip his cap to Fenway Park fans. "Gods don't answer letters," Updike wrote.

Maybe not, but now the next best thing has happened. Because the applause followed his crew the 200 feet they walked to home plate, Wendelstedt at last believed what he heard. So he looked around the ballpark. And he tipped his cap.

We should name the umpires: Wendelstedt, Dana DeMuth, Frank Pulli, Greg Bonin, Jim Quick and Gerry Davis. And we would write down the date, October 5, 1996. If you're lucky, the date

Second chance: Alomar made the most of his reprieve, eliminating the Indians with a game-tying single and extra-inning homer in Game 4.

It will be a long time before anyone who understands respect and compassion can look upon Roberto Alomar and see the sweetheart we thought was there. Now we know he can be a snarling cur who would spit in our face, all because a ball was called a strike.

compassion can look upon Roberto Alomar and see the sweetheart we thought was there. Now we know he can be a snarling cur who would spit in our face and explain the act by speaking of our dead children, all because a ball was called a strike.

He should have been suspended immediately for 60 days with his docked salary—$1.5 million—going to a trust fund for umpire John Hirschbeck's surviving child.

But the only suspension was for five days in 1997. That's because the fools who run baseball distrust each other so profoundly that they have created a thicket of legalities that call for meetings, hearings and appeals before anything can be done. As dispiriting as such paralysis is, it is a consequence of decades in which owners arbitrarily punished players.

Even so, and though no one so much as suggested it, there yet existed a simple way to do the right thing with Alomar. The Orioles had the power to make a common-sense decision. They could have benched the brat's butt.

Instead, Alomar's home runs moved the Orioles into the playoffs and then into the ALCS. Those will always be tainted victories. They will stand as proof, certain of the moral and ethical black hole at baseball's center.

It's sad for anyone who grew up believing baseball is beautiful. Some of us who long since have grown weary of millionaire jerks yet believe the game itself is beautiful. We counted Alomar among the players who confirmed that beauty.

But now his presence in the Orioles' lineup is so distressing it is as if the game itself has been disfigured. It is as if Alomar's spit had been spit thrown at

336

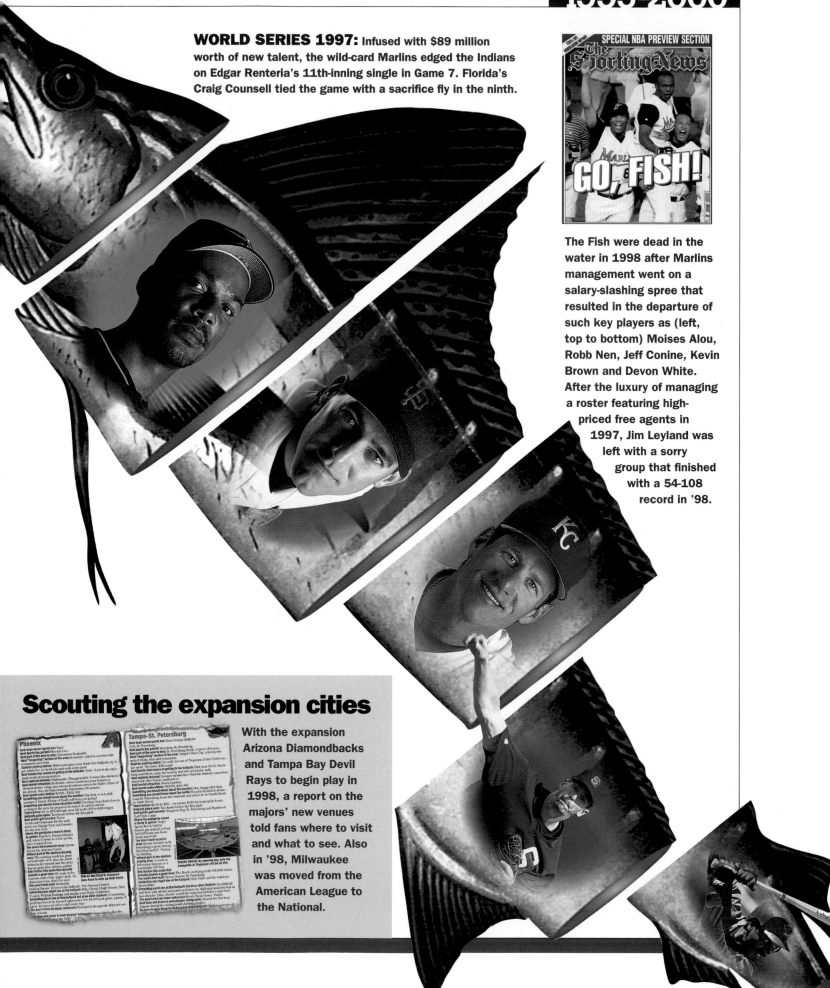

WORLD SERIES 1997: Infused with $89 million worth of new talent, the wild-card Marlins edged the Indians on Edgar Renteria's 11th-inning single in Game 7. Florida's Craig Counsell tied the game with a sacrifice fly in the ninth.

SPECIAL NBA PREVIEW SECTION

The Sporting News

GO, FISH!

The Fish were dead in the water in 1998 after Marlins management went on a salary-slashing spree that resulted in the departure of such key players as (left, top to bottom) Moises Alou, Robb Nen, Jeff Conine, Kevin Brown and Devon White. After the luxury of managing a roster featuring high-priced free agents in 1997, Jim Leyland was left with a sorry group that finished with a 54-108 record in '98.

Scouting the expansion cities

With the expansion Arizona Diamondbacks and Tampa Bay Devil Rays to begin play in 1998, a report on the majors' new venues told fans where to visit and what to see. Also in '98, Milwaukee was moved from the American League to the National.

Kerry Wood's Texas-tall feat is, fittingly, the stuff of Clemens and Ryan
By Steve Marantz

20 at 20

erry Wood is showing me how to grip a curveball. He takes my $8 souvenir Cubs baseball, wraps his index finger along one seam and touches his thumb to another. Three other fingers go to precise positions. His fingers are curiously autonomous, as if each has a mind of its own. Pianists have similar dexterity. If Wood were not going to be the next Nolan Ryan or Roger Clemens, he might be the next Vladimir Horowitz or Jerry Lee Lewis.

"Make a horseshoe shape on the right side there," Wood says.

"If I show this to my son, will he throw a curve..."

Making his fifth major league start on May 6, 1998, the Cubs' Kerry Wood turned in a spectacular—and record—performance. Wood, 20, struck out 20 Astros and permitted only one hit in a 2-0 victory at Wrigley Field. The strikeout total set a National League record, and it tied the major league mark for a nine-inning game.

The Yankees' David Wells received a victory ride after pitching a perfect game against the Twins at Yankee Stadium on May 17, 1998. Fourteen months later, the Yanks' David Cone hurled a perfect game against the Expos, also at Yankee Stadium.

'LET ME HEAR YA': Harry Caray, who broadcast big-league games for 53 seasons, died in 1998. A longtime voice of the Cardinals, he gained icon status with the Cubs, with whom he spent his last 16 seasons and made seventh-inning sing-alongs a fun part of games. Lovable yet critical, Caray never hid his emotions and was known to take erring players to task.

Cal Ripken was a late scratch from the Orioles' lineup on September 20, 1998, ending his record consecutive-game streak at 2,632. Ripken took himself out of the lineup, simply saying the time had come. Rookie Ryan Minor started in his place at third base.

The Big Mac and Sammy show

Sammy Sosa had only nine homers in the Cubs' first 49 games in '98, but an incredible four-week spree of 21 home runs in 22 games made everyone take notice.

McGwire no savior, just 'piece of the pie'

Expectations for newly acquired first baseman Mark McGwire are high, but McGwire says they should be tempered. "One guy does not control the game of baseball," he says. "It's not like basketball where Michael Jordan can take the ball and control the game. I hope (people) don't look at it that way. I hope they look at it like I'm a piece of the pie." There is no telling yet whether McGwire will want to stay in St. Louis or if the Cardinals will be able to afford him. But former Oakland teammate Dennis Eckersley can appreciate the magnitude of the acquisition. "It's not easy to get one of the best home-run hitters ever," Eckersley says. "He's got a chance to hit 500

When the Cardinals acquired Mark McGwire from the A's in a July 31, 1997, trade, St. Louis expected big things from Big Mac. McGwire tried to downplay those expectations. "One guy does not control the game of baseball," he said. Control it, no. Dominate it, yes. In the 51 games he played for the Cardinals in '97, McGwire gave a preview of coming attractions by hitting 24 home runs and bringing his season total to 58. Roger Maris' homer mark of 61 had survived. This time, anyway.

McGwire then set the tone for what would captivate America—the Great Home Run Race—with a grand slam on opening day, 1998, and four homers in his first four games. He hit No. 20 in the Cards' 43rd game, his 30th by their 64th. By the All-Star break, he had 37 home runs—and a man hot on his heels.

'McGwire is turning fans of all ages into gawking kids with his Bunyanesque feats—and the eye-popping begins long before game time.'

WHY THE DOLPHINS ARE ON THE RUN

The Sporting News

See a Different Game

McGWIRE mania

An inside look at the Great Home Run Chase of '98

NFL: | THE TOP 100 PLAYERS | WEEK 1 LOWDOWN

DISPLAY UNTIL SEPT. 16, 1998

The Sporting News

See a Different Game

WOW!

SPECIAL COLLECTORS ISSUE

McGWIRE POSTER INSIDE

The Sporting News

See a Different Game

DISPLAY UNTIL SEPT. 23, 1998

MARK McGWIRE has smashed the home run record, energized baseball and captivated America— and he's not finished yet

HERO

McGwire got his challenge from Sammy Sosa, who had surged to 33 homers at the break. McGwire led Sosa, 45-42, on August 1, but they were tied at 55 entering September. Big Mac's four-homer salvo in two games at Florida and his 60th on September 5 against the Reds left him two up on Sosa—and one from Maris—when the Cubs visited St. Louis for two games. On September 7, McGwire hit No. 61 off Mike Morgan. Then, facing Steve Trachsel on September 8, McGwire laced a low liner to left field. The ball cleared the wall. Barely. No. 62. There was a new home run king.

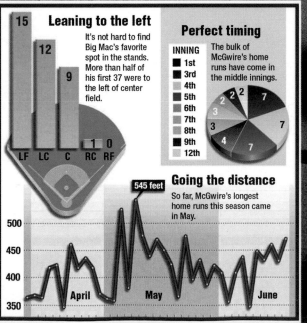

Leaning to the left

15 12 9 1 0

LF LC C RC RF

It's not hard to find Big Mac's favorite spot in the stands. More than half of his first 37 were to the left of center field.

Perfect timing

INNING
- 1st
- 3rd
- 4th
- 5th
- 6th
- 7th
- 8th
- 9th
- 12th

The bulk of McGwire's home runs have come in the middle innings.

2 2 7 3 3 4 7 7

Going the distance

545 feet

So far, McGwire's longest home runs this season came in May.

500
450
400
350

April   May   June

After the flashbulb explosion (left) that greeted No. 62 (Sosa was still at 58), McGwire cooled off. Entering the final weekend, Big Mac and Sosa were tied at 65—and Sammy momentarily took the lead when he hit No. 66 at the Astrodome. But before Houston fans hardly had time to settle back into their seats, news came that McGwire had homered against Montreal at Busch Stadium. McGwire then hit two homers on both Saturday and Sunday, and the exhilarating Great Home Run Race was over. Mark McGwire *70*, Sammy Sosa 66.

McGwire-Sosa, the encore

Mark McGwire and Sammy Sosa did their best to reprise their '98 performances in 1999—and they came amazingly close. If the drama wasn't quite there, the monstrous home runs and batting-practice crowds still were. McGwire finished with 65 homers, and Sosa hit 63.

NFL: In the trenches with the O-line   NHL: Bowman's back

The Sporting News
NOVEMBER 2, 1998
See a Different Game

YANKS!

They dominated the Series like they dominated the season

Now, TSN tells you where they rank in baseball history

WORLD SERIES 1998:
Down two games to none to the Yankees, the Padres had a chance to rebound in Game 3. But San Diego's 3-2 eighth-inning lead disappeared when ace reliever Trevor Hoffman yielded a three-run homer to Scott Brosius (left, on TSN cover, and right, congratulated by Paul O'Neill). Brosius also homered in the seventh inning. New York held on, 5-4. Padres ace Kevin Brown, hit by a line drive in the Series opener, showed pluck in Game 4 but lost, 3-0, as the Yanks swept the Series.

'98 Yankees were great, but not the greatest ever

The 1998 Yankees were the winningest team in major league history. They won 125 times.

If not fielding, man for man, the best team ever to play the game, the '98 Yankees arguably completed the best season on record: 114 American League victories (a league mark), followed by sweeps in the Division Series and World Series (and a six-game ALCS triumph).

But talent-wise, were these Yankees even close to, say, the '27 Yanks? The Sporting News put it this way in November 1998: "This club ranks among the finest in baseball history because of its uncommon—perhaps unprecedented—ability to play well in nearly every aspect of the game. But without immortals, it won't truly be immortalized."

The passing of time has shown that at least two of the '98 Yanks—Derek Jeter and Mariano Rivera—likely are headed for "immortal" status. Still, the judgment stands—as determined by a poll of TSN editors in '98—that this New York team was a bit down the list of the greatest teams. (Poll findings: 1. 1927 Yankees. 2. 1976 Reds. 3. 1929 Athletics, shown above. 4. 1961 Yankees. 5. 1998 Yankees.)

Most impressive, really, was the sustained success of the Yankees under the deft leadership of manager Joe Torre (top, center). Beginning in 1996, they captured four World Series titles in five years. They won in '96, when Torre reached the Series for the first time in his career—an emotional scenario in itself, but made more so by his brother's health problems (there were happy endings all around). They won in '98, playing with remarkable precision. They won in '99, falling short of their '98 achievements but still winning the franchise's 25th Series title (easily making the Yankees—from the days of Babe Ruth to those of Jeter—the "Team of the Century").

And they won in 2000, for the 26th time, when a lot of experts thought their run was surely over. Those experts should have known better than to doubt the *New York Yankees*.

WORLD SERIES 1999: It was another Yankees sweep, this one against the powerful Braves. Orlando "El Duque" Hernandez and David Cone each allowed only one hit over seven innings in Games 1 and 2, and journeyman outfielder Chad Curtis hit two home runs in Game 3, the second a game-winner in the 10th inning. In Game 4, Roger Clemens went 7⅔ innings for the first Series triumph of his career. Mariano Rivera had two saves for the Yankees, whose pitching staff limited Atlanta to one home run and a team batting average of .200.

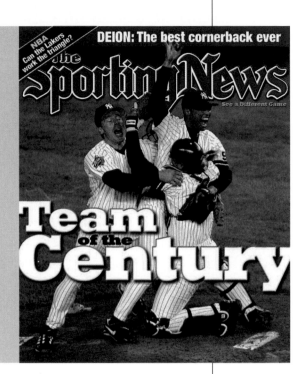

It seemed the Yankees always had the resources to obtain a player they coveted. It dated to the Babe Ruth deal. Still, the trade in early 1999 that sent Roger Clemens to the Bronx resulted in more groans than usual from Yankee opponents and Yankee haters (sometimes one and the same). Clemens, the longtime Red Sox star who was coming off two Cy Young Award-winning seasons with Toronto, had made the rich even richer. For the Yankee-phobes in Boston, the vision of Clemens wearing a uniform with "NEW YORK" on the front was particularly galling.

By giving up David Wells in the Clemens deal, the Yankees were messing with their chemistry. But the team retained its cohesiveness, Clemens contributed intensity and a total of 27 wins in 1999 and 2000, and the Yanks rolled on.

History has shown that by hook or by crook the Yankees find a way to create dynasties. And whether you want to admit it, obtaining makes them even tougher to beat.

Joe DiMaggio, whose skill and grace on the field and enduring celebrity status off it helped make him an American icon, died in March 1999. The Yankee Clipper's 56-game batting streak in 1941 remains one of baseball's landmark achievements.

NEVER FORGOTTEN: In '98, DiMaggio received a standing ovation during Old-Timers Day at Yankee Stadium.

would draw
shipers, eac
"You look g
"Someday
line of the 1
"there would
But Red didn
couldn't have
again would
possible to sa
the great D
honeymoon
Poor Ma
stood fame o
to her hus
pearance b
Korea. Sh
never heard
said, "Yes, N

Dave Kind
writer for TH

When baseball mattered the most, no one mattered as much as

Joe DiMaggio

The future is now

Baseball didn't lack for star power as it moved into a new millennium. Clutch-hitting, sure-fielding Derek Jeter (left) was the acknowledged leader of the Yankees, and in 2000 he helped the club to its fourth World Series title in his five full seasons with the club. The shortstop scored an MVP double in 2000, winning that honor in the All-Star Game and in the Yanks' Series triumph over the Mets. Jeter batted a career-high .349 in the 1999 season. Boston shortstop Nomar Garciaparra (left, below) became the first righthanded hitter since Joe DiMaggio in 1939-1940 to lead the American League in batting in back-to-back seasons, finishing at .357 in 1999 and .372 in 2000. Hard-hitting Texas catcher Ivan "Pudge" Rodriguez (right) won his ninth consecutive Gold Glove in 2000, and Atlanta third baseman Chipper Jones was the '99 National League MVP.

500 ... 3,000 ... 3,000

In 1999, Mark McGwire got three consecutive nights of milestone achievements off to a rousing start. On August 5, he cracked his 500th and 501st career home runs off San Diego's Andy Ashby. On August 6, the Padres' Tony Gwynn singled off Montreal's Dan Smith for his 3,000th hit. And on August 7, the Devil Rays' Wade

Boggs collected his 3,000th hit with a home run off Cleveland's Chris Haney. Boggs became the first player ever to reach the hits milestone with a homer.

In the 1990s, Barry Bonds had eight 100-RBI seasons, won eight Gold Gloves and was a three-time MVP. He moved from Pittsburgh to the Giants in December 1992.

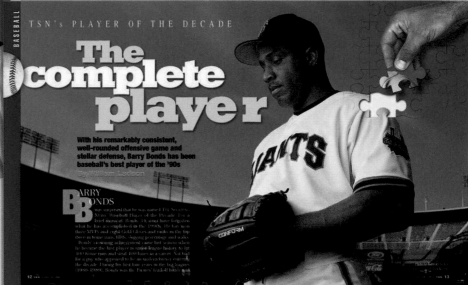

Build it and they will come. And they did in 2000. Fans flocked to the majors' three newest ballparks— Detroit's Comerica Park (left, top), San Francisco's Pacific Bell Park (left, middle) and Houston's Enron Field.

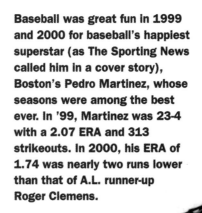

Baseball was great fun in 1999 and 2000 for baseball's happiest superstar (as The Sporting News called him in a cover story), Boston's Pedro Martinez, whose seasons were among the best ever. In '99, Martinez was 23-4 with a 2.07 ERA and 313 strikeouts. In 2000, his ERA of 1.74 was nearly two runs lower than that of A.L. runner-up Roger Clemens.

A Cardinals player made home run history last week—and it wasn't Mark McGwire.

Last Friday, Fernando Tatis, a 6-1, 175-pound third baseman, became the first player in major league history to hit two grand slams in one inning, smashing two against Dodgers pitcher Chan Ho

SLAM DANCE

Park in an 11-run third on the way to a 12-5 Cardinals victory.

In so doing, Tatis became a celebrity across late-night America and reached near-deity status in his native Dominican Republic. All night and into the day, Tatis fielded calls from family, friends and media back home. "Almost everybody," he says. "They were watching the game, and they were having a party."

Tatis had a little help making history from Cardinals third base coach Rene Lachemann. Lachemann held Darren Bragg at third on McGwire's check-swing single before the first grand slam and stopped slow-footed pitcher Jose Jimenez twice—once on Edgar Renteria's single that loaded the bases and the other time on McGwire's fly to medium right—before the second slam.

Tatis' two grand slams also helped him set a major league record with eight RBIs during the inning—one more than his manager Tony La Russa had in his big-league career. The feat marked only the second time a

He did what? On April 23, 1999, at Los Angeles, St. Louis' Fernando Tatis achieved a feat that left fans disbelieving—he hit two bases-loaded homers in one inning (the third). Both grand slams came off Chan Ho Park.

SPRING TRAINING PREVIEW The buzz on all six divisions
Your team's to-do list

The Sporting News

See a Different Game

ANATOMY OF A BLOCKBUSTER

How the Reds lowballed the Mariners and lived to sign hometown kid Ken Griffey Jr.

Cincinnati fans could hardly contain themselves in early 2000 when the Reds traded for superstar Ken Griffey Jr., a local kid and son of a Big Red Machine standout. Griffey twice had 56-homer years for Seattle.

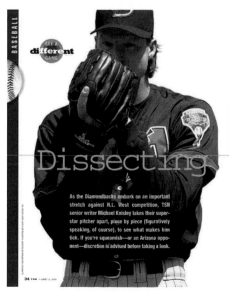

In June 2000, The Sporting News gave readers the inside story on how towering Diamondbacks pitcher Randy Johnson dominated hitters. The lefthander, a former Cy Young Award winner in the American League, was on the way to a 347-strikeout season and his second consecutive Cy Young honor in the National League.

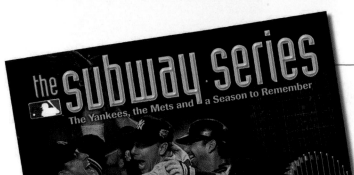

WORLD SERIES 2000: In the first all-New York Series since 1956, the Yankees won their third title in a row by beating the Mets in five games. The Yanks' Derek Jeter had three hits in Game 2, hit a home run to lead off Game 4 and belted a tying homer in the finale, which Luis Sojo won with a ninth-inning single that scored Jorge Posada (right, top). The Yankees' Roger Clemens was great—and controversial—in Game 2. Clemens allowed only two hits in eight innings, but he stunned everyone by throwing a jagged piece of Mike Piazza's bat toward Piazza (right) after the Mets slugger shattered the bat on a foul roller.

Yankees pitcher Roger Clemens (middle photo) and Mets catcher Mike Piazza had a history—Clemens had beaned Piazza in July. So Piazza didn't take it kindly when Clemens sent a piece of broken bat in his direction. Clemens, later fined, said there was no intent. Piazza just glared.

Getting leverage from a buyout

Rangers owner Tom Hicks saw it as an investment, not a cost. By refusing to scrape nickels off the table, he landed Alex Rodriguez, the most prized free agent inbaseball history. *By Sean Deveney*

When the Rangers signed shortstop Alex Rodriguez to a 10-year, $252 million contract in December 2000, it left the game's salary structure in ruins. *Again.* If Kevin Brown's signing with the Dodgers in late 1998 had given baseball a $105 million headache (which it did, according to a headline in The Sporting News), then the contract handed Rodriguez, the former Seattle star, gave the game a full-blown migraine. Said Mariners G.M. Pat Gillick: "I don't know if the sports can withstand this sort of thing." Sandy Alderson, Major League Baseball's executive vice president of operations, weighed in, too: "The perception is that there is no competition (to sign players). And that perception is accurate. This is not healthy. It's time we realize we have a crisis." Rangers owner Tom Hicks offered another view: "I know there is a problem in baseball. But I cannot fix it myself. Something needs to be changed, but until it is changed, I have to do what is best for the Texas Rangers. ..."

All photographs come from
The Sporting News' archives with the
following exceptions: